W9-CQY-839

The
Short
Prose
Reader

The Short Prose Reader

Gilbert H. Muller

Harvey S. Wiener

LaGuardia Community College

McGraw-Hill Book Company

New York   St. Louis   San Francisco   Auckland
Bogotá   Düsseldorf   Johannesburg   London   Madrid
Mexico   Montreal   New Delhi   Panama   Paris
São Paulo   Singapore   Sydney   Tokyo   Toronto

This book was set in Century Schoolbook
by Monotype Composition Company, Inc.
The editors were William A. Talkington and David Dunham;
the designer was Robin Hessel;
the production supervisor was Dominick Petrellese.
The Murray Printing Company was printer and binder.

The Short Prose Reader

2 3 4 5 6 7 8 9 0   MUMU   7 8 3 2 1 0 9

See Acknowledgments on pages 386–389.
Copyrights included on this page by reference.

Library of Congress Cataloging in Publication Data

Main entry under title:

The Short prose reader.

   Includes index.
   1. College readers. I. Muller, Gilbert H.,
date   II. Wiener, Harvey S.
PE1417.S446   808'.042   78-13284
ISBN 0-07-043991-5

Contents

Preface

The Short Prose Reader is a text for college composition courses. Its ten chapters cover all important patterns of writing, offering students concise and lively prose models for analysis, discussion, and imitation. Designed as a practical text, it addresses the challenge that faces today's college students in reading and writing short prose compositions.

The organization of *The Short Prose Reader* is one of its major strengths. Each of the first nine chapters contains four short essays that illustrate clearly a specific pattern or technique—description, narration, illustration, comparison and contrast, definition, classification, process analysis, causal analysis, or argumentation. We start with the forms of prose mastered most readily by college students, and move carefully to more difficult types of analytical and argumentative writing; students learn to build upon earlier techniques and patterns as they progress through the book. The last chapter, consisting of ten essays, offers students the opportunity to read and discuss short prose pieces that reflect the various rhetorical strategies.

Teachers and students will discover that the essays have been selected carefully to appeal to a broad audience. Readers will be excited by Jade Snow Wong's "Uncle Kwok," Langston Hughes' "Salvation," Alex Haley's "Roots," Ray Bradbury's "Tricks! Treats! Gangway!" Judy Syfer's "I Want a Wife," and the many other timely or controversial pieces included in the text. This is a *readable* text, and one that has ample representation by many different types of writers. Moreover, the essays, which range typically between 300 and 1,200 words, achieve their goals succinctly and clearly and are easy to read and understand. The essays will alert students both to the *types* of college writing expected of them and to the *length* of essay required frequently by teachers.

Finally, the exercises we have included for each essay are comprehensive and integrated—designed to develop and reinforce the key skills required in college writing. We have included two vocabulary exercises for each selection; the Words to Watch exercise alerts students to words they will read in context, and the Building Vocabulary exercise uses other effective methods (prefix/suffix, context clues, synonym/antonym, abstract/concrete) of teaching vocabulary. A section called Understanding the Writer's Ideas reinforces reading comprehension. Sections entitled Understanding the Writer's Techniques and Exploring the Writer's Ideas provide an excellent basis for class discussion and independent reading and analysis. The last exercise for each essay involves a dynamic approach to writing projects. Guided writing activities—a novel feature of *The Short Prose Reader*—tie the writing projects to the reading selections. Instead of simply being told to write an essay on a certain topic, students through Guided Writing will be able to move from step to step in the process of composition.

The Short Prose Reader can be used flexibly and effectively by students and teachers alike. The text is simple yet sophisticated, presenting essays and exercises that are easy to follow but never condescending. Weighing the needs and expectations of today's college freshmen, we have designed a rhetoric-reader that can serve as the major text for the composition course.

We wish to thank our colleagues for support and are especially grateful to those who read the manuscript and offered helpful suggestions: Professors Harry Crosby, Boston University; Robert Esch, University of Texas, El Paso; Roland Holmes, University of Illinois, Champaign-Urbana; Sharon Katz, Iona College; and Robert Reising, Pembroke State University.

Gilbert H. Muller
Harvey S. Wiener

one

Description

Since a writer's main purpose is to explain things clearly, description is an important aid. To add liveliness to an essay, descriptive details are necessary to create a clear, unified impression of an object or a scene. As a technique in writing, description matches the sorts of details we see in vivid and effective photographs. Good descriptive writers help the reader to "see" objects, scenes, and even moods by means of language.

The essays in this section reflect key qualities in all good descriptive writing. First, description relies on a basic talent that we all have—the ability to see, touch, taste, hear, or smell various elements in the world. Talented descriptive writers refine the power of their five senses in order to recreate people, places, things, emotions, and ideas. Second, in descriptive writing, the author must select details carefully. There might be thousands of details in any given scene, but clearly a writer cannot present all of them. Instead, the writer must choose only those details most useful in painting a picture for the reader. Third, writers must organize their descriptions carefully. With description, the writer must decide on a perspective (for instance, top to bottom, left to right, front to back) and then move carefully from detail to detail. The descriptive writer has a "camera eye" that ranges over its subject in a careful, consistent way. Fourth, descriptive writing creates a "dominant impression" of its subject. This main impression arises from the author's focus on a single subject, and from the feelings that the writer brings to that subject. Finally, descriptive writing offers a thesis or main idea concerning its subject, as does all sound writing. In short, description makes a point.

Writing good descriptive papers is a challenge, because we (like the authors in this section) have to look at our world anew, to remember, to search for meaningful details, to recreate the images around us. As we write descriptive paragraphs and essays, we should keep a basic goal in mind—to permit the reader to see the world that we describe in a fresh, vivid, and concrete way. As descriptive writers, we have to be willing to look at the world, perhaps for the first time, close up.

Jade Snow Wong

UNCLE KWOK

In this selection from *Fifth Chinese Daughter,* an autobiography of her childhood in San Francisco's Chinatown,
Jade Snow Wong creates a unique portrait of her Uncle
Kwok. As you read this short essay, try to picture Uncle
Kwok—his dress, features, and behavior. How does the
description the author provides show that, from the moment that he enters the Wong Factory (which also serves
as the family's home), Uncle Kwok is a decidedly unusual
man?

Words to Watch

ambled (par. 1): walked in a leisurely manner
satchel (par. 1): a small bag for carrying clothes, books, or articles
deviation (par. 3): a turning aside from a normal pattern of
   behavior
sauntered (par. 4): walked carelessly or idly
meticulousness (par. 4): extreme care about details
fastidious (par. 5): not easy to please; excessively refined

Among the workers in Daddy's factory, Uncle Kwok 1
was one of the strangest—a large-framed, awkward, unshaven man whose worn clothes hung on him as if they did

not belong to him. Each afternoon around three-thirty, as some of the workers were about to go home to prepare their early dinners, Uncle Kwok slowly and deliberately ambled in through the Wong front door, dragging his feet heavily, and gripping in one hand the small black satchel from which he was never separated.

Going to his own place at the sewing machine, he 2 took off his battered hat and ragged coat, hung both up carefully, and then sat down. At first Jade Snow was rather afraid of this extraordinary person, and unseen, watched his actions from a safe distance. After Uncle Kwok was settled in his chair, he took off his black, slipperlike shoes. Then, taking a piece of stout cardboard from a miscellaneous pile which he kept in a box near his sewing machine, he traced the outline of his shoes on the cardboard. Having closely examined the blades of his scissors and tested their sharpness, he would cut out a pair of cardboard soles, squinting critically through his inaccurate glasses. Next he removed from both shoes the cardboard soles he had made the day before and inserted the new pair. Satisfied with his inspection of his renewed footwear, he got up, went to the waste can some seventy-five feet away, disposed of the old soles, and returned to his machine. He had not yet said a word to anyone.

Daily this process was repeated without deviation. 3

The next thing Uncle Kwok always did was to put 4 on his own special apron, homemade from double thicknesses of heavy burlap and fastened at the waist by strong denim ties. This long apron covered his thin, patched trousers and protected him from dirt and draft. After a half hour had been consumed by these chores, Uncle Kwok was ready to wash his hands. He sauntered into the Wong kitchen, stationed himself at the one sink which served both family and factory, and with characteristic meticulousness, now proceeded to clean his hands and fingernails.

It was Mama's custom to begin cooking the evening 5 meal at this hour so that the children could have their dinner before they went to the Chinese school, but every day she had to delay her preparations at the sink until slow-moving Uncle Kwok's last clean fingernail passed his fastidious inspection. One day, however, the inconvenience tried her patience to its final limit.

Trying to sound pleasantly persuasive, she said, 6 "Uncle Kwok, please don't be so slow and awkward. Why don't you wash your hands at a different time, or else wash them faster?"

Uncle Kwok loudly protested the injustice of her 7 comment. "Mama, I am not awkward. The only awkward thing about my life is that it has not yet prospered!" And he strode off, too hurt even to dry his hands finger by finger, as was his custom.

BUILDING VOCABULARY

1. You can sometimes determine what words mean if you look at smaller words which make them up. What are definitions for the words below? First write down words within them, or based on them, that you may be able to recognize; then write your definition.

    a. deliberately (par. 1)
    b. ragged (par. 2)
    c. inaccurate (par. 2)
    d. thicknesses (par. 4)
    e. characteristic (par. 4)

2. In several of her sentences, Jade Snow Wong uses two or three descriptive words in a series. For example, in the first sentence she describes Uncle Kwok as a "large-framed, awkward, unshaven man." Write similar sentences, using a series of descriptive words for the following subjects.

    a. woman
    b. factory
    c. subway
    d. storm
    e. highway

UNDERSTANDING THE WRITER'S IDEAS

1.   What is the main point that Jade Snow Wong wants to make about Uncle Kwok? In which sentence in the selection is the point clearly established?

2.   Describe in your own words the specific details we learn about Uncle Kwok.

3.   Describe Uncle Kwok's daily routine.

4.   What do we learn about Jade Snow Wong's attitude toward Uncle Kwok and about her mother's attitude toward him?

UNDERSTANDING THE WRITER'S TECHNIQUES

1.   Descriptive writing relies on words which create pictures (images) that the reader can see. These words create images because they appeal to our sense of sight (through color and action), sound, smell, touch, and taste. In this essay, the writer concentrates on the sense of sight because she wants to create a visual impression of her uncle. What are some details about Uncle Kwok's features and his clothing? How do these descriptive details help to create a dominant impression of him?

2.   We also see Uncle Kwok in motion. Describe the way he moves. Find five words in the essay that capture the quality of his motion.

3.   Writers often provide a *thesis sentence* to express the main idea of a composition. The thesis sentence establishes the subject, limits it, expresses the writer's attitude toward it, and when well expressed, captures the reader's interest. Is there a thesis sentence in this essay? Which one is it?

4.   Why does the thesis sentence appear in the place that it does? Which functions of a good thesis sentence does it reflect? Does it capture your interest?

5.   Wong arranges details carefully; the essay progresses from one stage in the description to another until we have a sound impression of Uncle Kwok. At what point do we meet Uncle Kwok? What are the stages in his

activities? How do these stages correspond to the paragraphs in the essay? How do the individual paragraphs help us understand the pattern of Uncle Kwok's activity?

6. What is the purpose in selecting a short one-sentence paragraph (par. 4)?

EXPLORING THE WRITER'S IDEAS

1. The author suggests that people (like Jade Snow's mother) become upset by those who follow set routines. Do you agree? Describe someone you know who annoys you because he or she follows set patterns.

2. Why do we fall back on set routines or repeat the same pattern of behavior from day to day?

3. What makes an individual "strange"? Is the word ever misleading? Should we fear "strange" individuals?

4. What does Uncle Kwok's statement in paragraph 7 explain about his behavior?

IDEAS FOR WRITING

Guided Writing

Write an extended paragraph or a short essay describing someone you found strange, frightening, delightful, amusing, or eccentric when you were a child.

1. Establish a strong thesis sentence and place it near the start of your composition.

2. Concentrate on images of sight (color, outline, appearance, and action) to describe the individual.

3. Try to use a series of descriptive terms in several sentences. See paragraph 4 in Wong's essay, for example.

4. Fill in the details of your character in a carefully organized manner. Place the character in a particular setting at a given point in time. Try to use a "camera eye" movement that follows the character from detail to detail in the description.

5. Try to create a "dominant impression" of the character, one that conforms with the main idea expressed in your thesis sentence.

More Writing Projects

     1. Write a vivid description of one of your teachers or of someone in your class.

     2. Cut out a photograph of someone from a newspaper or magazine and then write a clear description of that individual.

     3. Describe one of your favorite television or movie personalities.

Patricia Cayo Sexton

BACKDROP OF POVERTY

In this selection from *Spanish Harlem,* Patricia Cayo Sexton uses description selectively in order to support her analysis of the subject. Her commentary never becomes dull or lengthy, because it is balanced by the clarity of her description. Sexton has long been involved in social causes, and the thesis that she offers in this selection reflects her concerns.

Words to Watch

silk-stocking (par. 1): upper class
bustle (par. 1): to be active and noisy
affluent (par. 4): rich
kibitz (par. 5): to gossip
disdain (par. 6): to consider unworthy; to scorn
estranged (par. 6): alienated; cut off

At 6:30 A.M., while silk-stocking Manhattan is 1 asleep, East Harlem is starting to bustle. The poor are early risers. They have the jobs others don't want: the early-hour jobs, the late-hour jobs. Many rise early because it is a rural habit.

Along about 7:30 the streets are filled with fast- 2 moving people: men, women, and swarms of children of all sizes. The parochial school children can be seen in clusters, with their togetherness identity tag—a school hat, a blouse, a uniform.

You may be able to buy a *New York Times* at the 3 corner newsstand in the morning, but you probably will not be able to buy a cup of coffee. The poor drink their coffee and eat their breakfasts, such as they are, at home. Few eat out.

Some will stand at the bus stops, but most will crowd 4 into the downtown subways that speed them to jobs in commercial or silk-stocking areas: to serve the affluent, or work in their stores or small industrial shops. Many of the Negro women will go to domestic service; and the Puerto Rican women, to their sewing machines in the garment shops.

Later in the day, if it is warm, the men who have 5 no jobs will come out and stand on the sidewalks and talk together. They will watch the street and the passers-by and kibitz with one another. The old people, and from time to time the housewives, will sit at the window and join the watchers. And those with leisure may call them idle. Later, when the children return from school, the sidewalks and streets will jump with activity. Clusters of men, sitting on orange crates on the sidewalks, will play checkers or cards. The women will sit on the stoop, arms folded, and watch the young at play; and the young men, flexing their muscles, will look for some adventure. Vendors, ringing their bells, will hawk hot dogs, orange drinks, ice cream; and the caressing but often jarring noise of honking horns, music, children's games, and casual quarrels, whistles, singing, will go on late into the night. When you are in it you don't notice the noise, but when you stand away and listen to a taped conversation, the sound suddenly appears as a background roar. This loud stimulation of the senses may produce some of the emotionalism of the poor.

East Harlem is a busy place, night and day, filled 6 with the joyous and troubled lives of residents—rather than the heavy commercial traffic of mid-Manhattan. New York's street life is unique. So much action, so much togetherness. The critics who lament its passing have a point. The middle class who disdain life conducted so openly in the streets might compare its satisfactions to the sometimes parched and estranged quality of their own backyards.

BUILDING VOCABULARY

1. In her attempt to capture the noise and rhythms of life in East Harlem, Patricia Cayo Sexton employs many words that suggest action. For instance, in the first sentence of the essay she writes that at an early hour East Harlem "is starting to bustle." Find five action words in the essay, and explain why you think the writer chose them and whether you think they are effective.

2. Write original sentences in which you use the five action words you selected above.

UNDERSTANDING THE WRITER'S IDEAS

1. What is the tone of this essay? (*Tone* means the writer's attitude toward her materials). In other words, what is Sexton's attitude toward the people of East Harlem? Is she critical, supportive, angry, humorous, impartial? Give examples to support your idea.

2. Why are the poor "early risers"? What are some other traits of the poor that Sexton mentions?

3. What contrasts are established between the poor and the rich, between upper and lower Manhattan, between the city and the suburbs?

4. Describe the activities that take place on the streets of East Harlem.

5. Clarify Sexton's statement in paragraph 5 that "those with leisure will call them idle."

UNDERSTANDING THE WRITER'S TECHNIQUES

1. Is there a thesis sentence in this essay? If not, why not?

2. In what sense does *time* serve as an important structuring principle for this selection? How much time passes in the essay? Does Sexton concentrate on particular times of the day? Which words in paragraph 5 indicate the passing of time?

3. The first four paragraphs in this essay are short. Are they effective? Why? Could they have been combined into one longer paragraph without hurting the impact of the message?

4. The fifth paragraph has the most description in it. What is the quality of this description? What senses are appealed to by the description? What is the dominant impression that emerges from the paragraph? What single sentence in this paragraph ties all of the thoughts together?

5. Of what value is Sexton's use of the future tense in many of the paragraphs in this selection (for example, "Some will stand at the bus stops")?

6. Which two paragraphs have the least amount of description? Why?

7. How effective is the conclusion of the essay? How does Sexton suggest a contrast between the poor and the middle class in paragraph 6?

8. What do the words "So much action, so much togetherness" mean? This is not a complete sentence; it is a fragment. Do you think it effective or ineffective in the conclusion? Why?

EXPLORING THE WRITER'S IDEAS

1. Judging from what you have seen or read, why might you agree or disagree with Sexton's thesis that middle-class life is not necessarily more satisfying than the lives of the poor?

2. Why do many people have misconceptions about poverty and about poor people in America?

3. Do you agree or disagree with the assertion that the poor frequently "serve the affluent"? Why do they?

IDEAS FOR WRITING

Guided Writing

Select a neighborhood (either your own or one that you know well), and write a description of a typical street, its residents and their activities.

    1. Establish an early morning scene that incorporates description and commentary. Name the street.

    2. Identify clearly whether you are describing a poor, rich, middle-class, or possibly mixed neighborhood.

    3. Try to capture the various rhythms and activities of the people. Use colors, sounds, smells, actions to make the scene alive.

    4. If possible, compare and contrast this street with other sections of the town, city, or region.

    5. Be certain that your own attitude toward the neighborhood and its people is clear.

More Writing Projects

    1. Using both description and commentary, analyze the people you observed in one of the following situations:

    a. a bus during rush hour
    b. breakfast at a diner
    c. a highway during a storm
    d. a park at dusk
    e. a concert or a game on a summer evening

    2. Bring to class photographs from newspapers or magazines that capture the lives of people in a particular surrounding. Be prepared to analyze the descriptive details in these photographs.

N. Scott Momaday

THE WAY TO RAINY MOUNTAIN

In this selection, N. Scott Momaday, a Kiowa Indian who teaches at Stanford University, remembers his grandmother after her death. Momaday, who won the Pulitzer Prize in 1969 for his novel, *House Made of Dawn*, combines description of both person and place to give a rich impression of his grandmother's life. In this description, you will notice also the skill with which Momaday uses narration (we will study *narration* in the next unit) in order to tell the story of his grandmother, his people, and his relation to the Kiowa heritage.

Words to Watch

inherently (par. 1): naturally; inseparably; inborn
sentinels (par. 2): guards
opaque (par. 2): dull; not permitting light to pass through
domain (par. 2): territory
abide (par. 3): endure; put up with
enmities (par. 3): hatreds; hostilities
compensation (par. 3): reward; that which is received as an equivalent for services rendered; anything given to make up for a loss or damage done
servitude (par. 3): bondage; submission
purled (par. 5): murmured
scissortail (par. 6): a bird found in Mexico and the southwestern part of the United States
hied (par. 6): hastened; moved quickly

Now that I can have her only in memory, I see my grandmother in the several postures that were peculiar to her: standing at the wood stove on a winter morning and turning meat in a great iron skillet; sitting at the south window, bent above her beadwork, and afterwards, when her vision failed, looking down for a long time into the fold of her hands; going out upon a cane, very slowly as she did when the weight of age came upon her; praying. I remember her most often at prayer. She made long, rambling prayers out of suffering and hope, having seen many things. I was never sure that I had the right to hear, so exclusive were they of all mere custom and company. The last time I saw her she prayed standing by the side of her bed at night, naked to the waist, the light of a kerosene lamp moving upon her dark skin. Her long, black hair, always drawn and braided in the day, lay upon her shoulders and against her breasts like a shawl. I do not speak Kiowa, and I never understood her prayers, but there was something inherently sad in the sound, some merest hesitation upon the syllables of sorrow. She began in a high and descending pitch, exhausting her breath to silence; then again and again—and always the same intensity of effort, of something that is, and is not, like urgency in the human voice. Transported so in the dancing light among the shadows of her room, she seemed beyond the reach of time. But that was illusion; I think I knew then that I should not see her again.

Houses are like sentinels in the plain, old keepers of the weather watch. There, in a very little while, wood takes on the appearance of great age. All colors wear soon away in the wind and rain, and then the wood is burned gray and the grain appears and the nails turn red with rust. The windowpanes are black and opaque; you imagine there is nothing within, and indeed there are many ghosts, bones given up to the land. They stand here and there against the sky, and you approach them for a longer time than you expect. They belong in the distance; it is their domain.

Once there was a lot of sound in my grandmother's house, a lot of coming and going, feasting and talk. The summers there were full of excitement and reunion. The

Kiowas are a summer people; they abide the cold and keep to themselves, but when the season turns and the land becomes warm and vital they cannot hold still; an old love of going returns upon them. The aged visitors who came to my grandmother's house when I was a child were made of lean and leather, and they bore themselves upright. They wore great black hats and bright ample shirts that shook in the wind. They rubbed fat upon their hair and wound their braids with strips of colored cloth. Some of them painted their faces and carried the scars of old and cherished enmities. They were an old council of warlords, come to remind and be reminded of who they were. Their wives and daughters served them well. The women might indulge themselves; gossip was at once the mark and compensation of their servitude. They made loud and elaborate talk among themselves, full of jest and gesture, fright and false alarm. They went abroad in fringed and flowered shawls, bright beadwork and German silver. They were at home in the kitchen, and they prepared meals that were banquets.

There were frequent prayer meetings, and great 4 nocturnal feasts. When I was a child I played with my cousins outside, where the lamplight fell upon the ground and the singing of the old people rose up around us and carried away into the darkness. There were a lot of good things to eat, a lot of laughter and surprise. And afterwards, when the quiet returned, I lay down with my grandmother and could hear the frogs away by the river and feel the motion of the air.

Now there is a funeral silence in the rooms, the 5 endless wake of some final word. The walls have closed in upon my grandmother's house. When I returned to it in mourning, I saw for the first time in my life how small it was. It was late at night, and there was a white moon, nearly full. I sat for a long time on the stone steps by the kitchen door. From there I could see out across the land; I could see the long row of trees by the creek, the low light upon the rolling plains, and the stars of the Big Dipper. Once I looked at the moon and caught sight of a strange thing. A cricket had perched upon the handrail, only a few inches away from me. My line of vision was such that the creature filled the moon like a fossil. It had gone there, I thought, to live and die, for there, of all places, was its small definition made whole and eternal. A warm wind rose up and purled like the longing within me.

The next morning I awoke at dawn and went out on 6 the dirt road to Rainy Mountain. It was already hot, and the grasshoppers began to fill the air. Still, it was early in the morning, and the birds sang out of the shadows. The long yellow grass on the mountain shone in the bright light, and a scissortail hied above the land. There, where it ought to be, at the end of a long and legendary way, was my grandmother's grave. Here and there on the dark stones were ancestral names. Looking back once, I saw the mountain and came away.

BUILDING VOCABULARY

1. Descriptive writing tends to be *concrete* in the sense that it deals with specific people, places, objects, and things that can be seen and touched. Concrete language relies heavily on sensory details. Locate five sentences in the essay that rely heavily on concrete language. What is the effect of this language in the description?

2. There are many other words that are *abstract* because they deal with ideas, concepts, and conditions. Using a dictionary write definitions for the following abstract words from Momaday's essay.

   a. memory (par. 1)
   b. hope (par. 1)
   c. illusion (par. 1)
   d. eternal (par. 5)
   e. legendary (par. 6)

3. Use any five words from the Words to Watch section in complete sentences of your own.

UNDERSTANDING THE WRITER'S IDEAS

1. What is Momaday's attitude toward his grandmother? toward the Kiowas? toward the land? toward rituals, such as prayer?

2. Explain more fully the following sentences from Momaday's essay.

a. "I was never sure that I had the right to hear, so exclusive were they [his grandmother's prayers] of mere custom and company." (par. 1)

b. "Houses are like sentinels in the plain, old keepers of the weather watch." (par. 2)

c. "Now there is a funeral silence in the rooms, the endless wake of some final word." (par. 5)

3. Why does Momaday return to his grandmother's house and grave? Does he ever state the reason precisely? What clues does he provide the reader?

4. Explain in your own words what Momaday tells the reader about Kiowa culture.

UNDERSTANDING THE WRITER'S TECHNIQUES

1. How does Momaday arrange details within the first paragraph? Other paragraphs?

2. How has Momaday arranged the details from paragraph to paragraph in this essay? In other words, what is the subject of the description in the first paragraph, the second paragraph, and so forth?

3. Momaday's *selection* of descriptive details is as interesting as his arrangement of them. Explain why you think he has used the following details to focus parts of his essay.

a. the grandmother praying (par. 1)
b. the house (pars. 1–5)
c. the "aged visitors" (par. 3)
d. the cricket (par. 5)

EXPLORING THE WRITER'S IDEAS

1. Momaday writes that the Kiowas are a "summer" people. What does he mean? How do seasons, climate, and geography influence the life of a people?

2. What is the value of memory—a word that Momaday stresses in the first sentence of this selection? Can you actually recapture the past through memory? If so, how?

3. How does the role of women in Kiowa culture compare with the role of women in American society? How does the role of "old people" in Kiowa culture compare with the role of the aged in America today?

IDEAS FOR WRITING

Guided Writing

Write a paragraph or essay in which you describe someone who was special to you but who left you or is now dead.

1. Begin with a sentence similar to Momaday's first sentence in which he describes a key action of his grandmother.

2. Place your subject in a specific *setting* (a landscape) the way that Momaday does.

3. If possible, surround your subject with other individuals, and describe their behavior. You might want to use some exact spoken words of the individuals.

4. Include in your paragraph a description of the person the last time you saw him or her as Momaday does in paragraph 1.

5. Describe what a particular place you associate strongly with the person looks like now that the person no longer is there. See paragraph 5.

More Writing Projects

1. Describe a place (your neighborhood, a favorite vacation site, a store) that you remember vividly from your childhood. Try to recapture the sights, sounds, and smells of the place.

2. Select some object or creature from nature and describe it in detail. If you want, try to suggest (as Momaday did in his essay) what it tells us about the human condition.

Alfred Kazin

THE KITCHEN

In this selection from *A Walker in the City* (1951), Kazin describes a particular room in his childhood apartment in Brownsville, a section of East Brooklyn settled by Jewish immigrants earlier in this century. Kazin relies on highly visual descriptions to evoke people, places, and things, and to recapture what he calls "the aliveness of the moment." This is a longer selection than the other essays in this chapter. As you read it, look for the many techniques used to unify the piece.

Words to Watch

annexed (par. 1): added; united; attached
innate (par. 1): inborn
subtleties (par. 1): fine distinctions
baste (par. 1): to sew with long stitches
treadle (par. 1): a lever operated by the foot and connected to the crank of a small machine
borscht (par. 1): a Russian beet soup
stippled (par. 2): speckled; painted in dots rather than in lines
seder (par. 2): the feast commemorating the exodus of the Jews from Egypt, held on the eve of the first day of Passover
spindle (par. 2): the pin used to spin thread on a sewing machine
zeal (par. 3): passion; intense eagerness
redolent (par. 4): having a sweet scent
ominous (par. 6): hinting at a future evil event
muslin (par. 6): a thin cotton cloth used for shirts, sheets, etc.
imminent (par. 6): about to happen; threatening
yortsayt (par. 7): a memorial and prayer for the departed

dispersion (par. 8): scattering
der heym (par. 7): Yiddish for "the home"
pince-nez (par. 9): eyeglasses kept in place on the nose by means
      of a spring
sentience (par. 10): the ability to perceive, feel, and understand

In Brownsville tenements the kitchen is always the 1
largest room and the center of the household. As a child I
felt that we lived in a kitchen to which four other rooms
were annexed. My mother, a "home" dressmaker, had her
workshop in the kitchen. She told me once that she had
begun dressmaking in Poland at thirteen; as far back as I
can remember, she was always making dresses for the local
women. She had an innate sense of design, a quick eye for
all the subtleties in the latest fashions, even when she
despised them, and great boldness. For three or four dollars
she would study the fashion magazines with a customer, go
with the customer to the remnants store on Belmont Avenue
to pick out the material, argue the owner down—all remnants stores, for some reason, were supposed to be shady, as
if the owners dealt in stolen goods—and then for days would
patiently fit and baste and sew and fit again. Our apartment
was always full of women in their housedresses sitting
around the kitchen table waiting for a fitting. My little
bedroom next to the kitchen was the fitting room. The
sewing machine, an old nut-brown Singer with golden scrolls
painted along the black arm and engraved along the two
tiers of little drawers massed with needles and thread on
each side of the treadle, stood next to the window and the
great coalblack stove which up to my last year in college
was our main source of heat. By December the two outer
bedrooms were closed off, and used to chill bottles of milk
and cream, cold borscht and jellied calves' feet.

    The kitchen held our lives together. My mother 2
worked in it all day long, we ate in it almost all meals except

the Passover *seder,* I did my homework and first writing at the kitchen table, and in winter I often had a bed made up for me on three kitchen chairs near the stove. On the wall just over the table hung a long horizontal mirror that sloped to a ship's prow at each end and was lined in cherry wood. It took up the whole wall, and drew every object in the kitchen to itself. The walls were a fiercely stippled white-wash, so often rewhitened by my father in slack seasons that the paint looked as if it had been squeezed and cracked into the walls. A large electric bulb hung down the center of the kitchen at the end of a chain that had been hooked into the ceiling; the old gas ring and key still jutted out of the wall like antlers. In the corner next to the toilet was the sink at which we washed, and the square tub in which my mother did our clothes. Above it, tacked to the shelf on which were pleasantly ranged square, blue-bordered white sugar and spice jars, hung calendars from the Public National Bank on Pitkin Avenue and the Minsker Progressive Branch of the Workman's Circle; receipts for the payment of insurance premiums, and household bills on a spindle; two little boxes engraved with Hebrew letters. One of these was for the poor, the other to buy back the Land of Israel. Each spring a bearded little man would suddenly appear in our kitchen, salute us with a hurried Hebrew blessing, empty the boxes (sometimes with a sidelong look of disdain if they were not full), hurriedly bless us again for remem-bering our less fortunate Jewish brothers and sisters, and so take his departure until the next spring, after vainly trying to persuade my mother to take still another box. We did occasionally remember to drop coins in the boxes, but this was usually only on the dreaded morning of "mid-terms" and final examinations, because my mother thought it would bring me luck. She was extremely superstitious, but embar-rassed about it, and always laughed at herself whenever, on the morning of an examination, she counseled me to leave the house on my right foot. "I know it's silly," her smile seemed to say, "but what harm can it do? It may calm God down."

The kitchen gave a special character to our lives; 3 my mother's character. All my memories of that kitchen are dominated by the nearness of my mother sitting all day long at her sewing machine, by the clacking of the treadle against the linoleum floor, by the patient twist of her right shoulder as she automatically pushed at the wheel with one hand or lifted the foot to free the needle where it had got stuck in a thick piece of material. The kitchen was her life. Year by year, as I began to take in her fantastic capacity for labor and her anxious zeal, I realized it was ourselves she kept stitched together. I can never remember a time when she was not working. She worked because the law of her life was work, work and anxiety; she worked because she would have found life meaningless without work. She read almost no English; she could read the Yiddish paper, but never felt she had time to. We were always talking of a time when I would teach her how to read, but somehow there was never time. When I awoke in the morning she was already at her machine, or in the great morning crowd of housewives at the grocery getting fresh rolls for breakfast. When I returned from school she was at her machine, or conferring over *McCall's* with some neighborhood woman who had come in pointing hopefully to an illustration—"Mrs. Kazin! Mrs. Kazin! Make me a dress like it shows here in the picture!" When my father came home from work she had somehow mysteriously interrupted herself to make supper for us, and the dishes cleared and washed, was back at her machine. When I went to bed at night, often she was still there, pounding away at the treadle, hunched over the wheel, her hands steering a piece of gauze under the needle with a finesse that always contrasted sharply with her swollen hands and broken nails. Her left hand had been pierced through when as a girl she had worked in the infamous Triangle Shirtwaist Factory on the East Side. A needle had gone straight through the palm, severing a large vein. They had sewn it up for her so clumsily that a tuft of flesh always lay folded over the palm.

The kitchen was the great machine that set our lives 4 running; it whirred down a little only on Saturdays and holy days. From my mother's kitchen I gained my first picture of life as a white, overheated, starkly lit workshop redolent with Jewish cooking, crowded with women in housedresses, strewn with fashion magazines, patterns, dress material, spools of thread—and at whose center, so lashed to her machine that bolts of energy seemed to dance out of her hands and feet as she worked, my mother stamped the treadle hard against the floor, hard, hard, and silently, grimly at war, beat out the first rhythm of the world for me.

Every sound from the street roared and trembled at 5 our windows—a mother feeding her child on the doorstep, the screech of the trolley cars on Rockaway Avenue, the eternal smash of a handball against the wall of our house, the clatter of *"der Italyéner"*'s cart packed with watermelons, the sing-song of the old-clothes men walking Chester Street, the cries *"Árbes! Árbes! Kinder! Kinder! Heyse gute árbes!"* All day long people streamed into our apartment as a matter of course—"customers," upstairs neighbors, downstairs neighbors, women who would stop in for a half-hour's talk, salesmen, relatives, insurance agents. Usually they came in without ringing the bell—everyone knew my mother was always at home. I would hear the front door opening, the wind whistling through our front hall, and then some familiar face would appear in our kitchen with the same bland, matter-of-fact inquiring look: no need to stand on ceremony: my mother and her kitchen were available to everyone all day long.

At night the kitchen contracted around the blaze of 6 light on the cloth, the patterns, the ironing board where the iron had burned a black border around the tear in the muslin cover; the finished dresses looked so frilly as they jostled on their wire hangers after all the work my mother had put into them. And then I would get that strangely ominous smell of tension from the dress fabrics and the burn in the cover of the ironing board—as if each piece of cloth and paper crushed with light under the naked bulb might suddenly go up in flames. Whenever I pass some small tailoring shop still lit up at night and see the owner hunched over his steam press; whenever in some poorer neighborhood of the city I see through a window some small crowded kitchen naked under the harsh light glittering in the ceiling, I still smell that fiery breath, that warning of imminent fire. I was always holding my breath. What I must have felt most about ourselves, I see now, was that we ourselves were like kindling—that all the hard-pressed pieces of ourselves and all the hard-used objects in that kitchen were like so many slivers of wood that might go up in flames if we came too near the white-blazing filaments in that naked bulb. Our tension itself was fire, we ourselves were forever burning—to live, to get down the foreboding in our souls, to make good.

Twice a year, on the anniversaries of her parents' 7 deaths, my mother placed on top of the ice-box an ordinary kitchen glass packed with wax, the *yortsayt,* and lit the candle in it. Sitting at the kitchen table over my homework, I would look across the threshold to that mourning-glass, and sense that for my mother the distance from our kitchen to *der heym,* from life to death, was only a flame's length away. Poor as we were, it was not poverty that drove my mother so hard; it was loneliness—some endless bitter brooding over all those left behind, dead or dying or soon to die; a loneliness locked up in her kitchen that dwelt every day on the hazardousness of life and the nearness of death, but still kept struggling in the lock, trying to get us through by endless labor.

With us, life started up again only on the last shore. 8 There seemed to be no middle ground between despair and the fury of our ambition. Whenever my mother spoke of her hopes for us, it was with such unbelievingness that the likes of us would ever come to anything, such abashed hope and readiness for pain, that I finally came to see in the flame burning on top of the ice-box death itself burning away the bones of poor Jews, burning out in us everything but courage, the blind resolution to live. In the light of that mourning-candle, there were ranged around me how many dead and dying—how many eras of pain, of exile, of dispersion, of cringing before the powers of this world!

It was always at dusk that my mother's loneliness 9 came home most to me. Painfully alert to every shift in the light at her window, she would suddenly confess her fatigue by removing her pince-nez, and then wearily pushing aside the great mound of fabrics on her machine, would stare at the street as if to warm herself in the last of the sun. "How sad it is!" I once heard her say. "It grips me! It grips me!" Twilight was the bottommost part of the day, the chillest and loneliest time for her. Always so near to her moods, I knew she was fighting some deep inner dread, struggling against the returning tide of darkness along the streets that invariably assailed her heart with the same foreboding— Where? Where now? Where is the day taking us now?

Yet one good look at the street would revive her. I 10 see her now, perched against the windowsill, with her face against the glass, her eyes almost asleep in enjoyment, just as she starts up with the guilty cry—"What foolishness is this in me!"—and goes to the stove to prepare supper for us: a moment, only a moment, watching the evening crowd of women gathering at the grocery for fresh bread and milk. But between my mother's pent-up face at the window and the winter sun dying in the fabrics—"Alfred, see how beautiful!"—she has drawn for me one single line of sentience.

BUILDING VOCABULARY

1. *Denotation* refers to the "dictionary definition" of a word, and *connotation* refers to the various shades of meaning and feeling that we bring to a word. Write dictionary definitions for the following words from Kazin's essay, and then discuss some of the connotations that you associate with the words.

     a. tenement (par. 1)
     b. kitchen (par. 1)
     c. homework (par. 2)
     d. insurance agents (par. 2)
     e. twilight (par. 9)

2. Which major sense (sight, sound, smell, touch, or taste) does Kazin rely on for descriptive purposes in this essay? Find several words to illustrate this sense. Locate other words that appeal to other senses.

3. Name all the action words in paragraph 2 of the essay.

UNDERSTANDING THE WRITER'S IDEAS

1. Where does the action take place? How old is Kazin? What sort of neighborhood does he describe? Is his family rich or poor?

2. What is the importance of the kitchen in Kazin's life? What is the connection between it, the sewing machine, and Kazin's mother?

3. Why does Kazin concentrate on the activities of his mother? Why does she work so hard? Why is she so lonely? Mention specific paragraphs that give you the answer.

4. What is his mother's attitude toward the sunset in paragraphs 9 and 10?

5. Explain in your own words the meaning of the last sentence in the essay.

UNDERSTANDING THE WRITER'S TECHNIQUES

1. A unified written work never departs from its subject. In Kazin's piece everything relates directly or indirectly to the writer's subject. What are the two subjects of this selection? How many paragraphs start with a reference to one of these two things? Why does the writer use such a strategy?

2. Kazin's essay relies heavily on *figurative language*—language that is not direct or literal but which, instead, departs from normal meanings, often by making comparisons. Figurative language presents descriptive details from a fresh angle. Among the many types of figurative language a writer can use, Kazin employs *allusion*. Allusions are references to literary, historical, or cultural things. One allusion to Jewish culture in this piece is the *seder,* the feast to celebrate Passover, the period in Jewish history which preceded the exodus from Egypt. What others can you find? List several allusions that Kazin makes to Jewish culture.

3. *Metaphors* are also figurative comparisons. Here, the writer brings together two items normally not thought of as similar. Yet, his purpose is to let us see his intention more clearly. One of the key metaphors in the essay occurs in paragraph 4: "The kitchen was the great machine that kept our lives running." What details of description contribute to the development and extension of this metaphor?

4. *Imagery* is clear, vivid description, not just ordinary description. In some essays, writers create *patterns* of images, a concentration on and repetition of a single descriptive element throughout the selection. Locate examples of "machine" imagery and examples of "fire and heat" imagery in the passage. What connection (if any) do you see here between these two types of images? How does this pattern contribute to the meaning of the essay?

5. Why do writers use patterns of imagery? How can they help to organize and develop a selection?

6. Kazin's description of his childhood surroundings and his mother is not *objective* in this essay; he does not simply present factual details. Instead, he colors his description with personal emotions to create a *subjective* interpretation of the material. Locate five sentences where the description is highly subjective. Why does Kazin use so much subjective description? What impression of his mother, for example, does he try to create through subjective imagery?

7. Compare the degree of subjectivity in this essay with the subjectivity in the selections by Wong, Momaday, and Sexton.

EXPLORING THE WRITER'S IDEAS

1. America has long been termed a "melting pot," a country where people lose their varied backgrounds and form a new national character. What advantages or disadvantages do you see for different ethnic groups in a "melting pot"? What is gained or lost in the process?

2. Another aspect of the American myth involves the idea that everyone can succeed through hard work. In

part, Kazin's mother works hard so that her son can succeed in life. In the United States today, do you believe that people still escape poverty through hard work? What evidence can you suggest to support your belief? Take the question from a slightly different perspective: Does hard work guarantee success?

IDEAS FOR WRITING

Guided Writing

Select a room in your house or apartment and, in an essay of four or five paragraphs, describe it carefully in the manner of Kazin's essay.

1. Select the one room which seems to be the center of your household. Identify it as such in an opening thesis sentence.

2. If you identify this room with a special person, then describe that individual in detail.

3. Try to recapture the sights, sounds, and smells of the room as it appears at a particularly vivid time. Try to set up at least one pattern of imagery that repeats itself throughout the essay.

4. Relate the room to the rest of the home, to other people, to the neighborhood.

5. Be certain to explain completely the significance of this room in your own life, perhaps in a closing paragraph.

More Writing Projects

1. Select a special time of day (there are several such instances in Kazin's essay, notably the twilight at the end of the selection) or a special season, and write a four-paragraph theme that captures through vivid description the moods that the scene evokes in you.

2. Select a special event that is important to you, your family, and your ethnic or religious heritage, and describe it carefully in a brief paragraph or essay.

two

Narration

Narration is the telling of a story. As a technique in essay writing, it normally involves a discussion of events that are "true" or real, events that take place over a period of time. Narration helps a writer explain things and, as such, it is an important skill for the kind of writing often required of you.

Writers who use narration usually rely on descriptive details to advance their stories. Moreover, in the narrative essay, there always must be some purpose in the telling, a purpose that goes beyond mere enjoyment of the story itself. Consequently, narration in an essay advances a thesis, or main idea. For example, if you had to write an essay on the happiest event in your life, you might choose to narrate the day your team won the state championship. You would establish your thesis—your main point—quickly, and then go on to tell about the event itself. In short, you would use narration as a means to an end—to make a significant statement about an important moment in your life.

The manner in which you relate this event depends on the simplicity or complexity of the story that you want to tell. If the season before the winning game was itself filled with excitement, you certainly would want to explain that and to trace the exciting events over a period of time. If the championship itself provided most of the thrills, you would want to concentrate on a much shorter period of time, breaking your narration down to days, hours, even minutes, instead of months. Learning to present time—whether in a single personal event, a series of related events, a historical occurrence, or an aging process—is one of the key elements in narrative prose.

Normally in a narrative essay you would start at the beginning and move to the end, or from past to present, or from old to new, but there are many other ways to relate events in the narrative essay. For instance, you could begin an essay on the death of someone important to you by detailing the day of the funeral, and then moving backward in time to flesh out the events leading up to the funeral. For beginners this "flashback" technique often causes very confused writing; but skilled writers know how to "jump around" in time without confusing the reader, blurring the thesis, or destroying the progression of the essay.

As with descriptive writing, the narrative essay requires a careful selection of details. Certain moments within any time order are more important than others, and these crucial moments will be emphasized and developed fully by a good writer. Other moments, significant but less important than the main moments, will take up less space, while unimportant items will be eliminated entirely. However, the writer must connect each event in the time span to other events that come before or after. Here, transitions of time—words like "afterwards," "soon," "a day later," "suddenly"—serve as bridges to connect the various moments in the narrative pattern.

There are other aspects of narration that appear in this chapter. For example, you must select a point of view for your story—whether presenting events through your own eyes or from a more objective or detached position. You must also decide on the value of dialogue (recording of conversations). Finally, you must be aware that other techniques of prose writing (like description) can reinforce your narrative pattern. Fortunately, most individuals have a basic storytelling ability and know how to develop stories that make a point. Once you master narration as a writing pattern, you will be able to use it in a variety of situations.

Langston Hughes

SALVATION

For more than forty years, Langston Hughes (1902–1967) was a major figure in American literature. In poetry, essays, drama, and fiction he attempted, as he said himself, "to explain and illuminate the Negro condition in America." This selection from his autobiography, *The Big Sea* (1940), tells the story of his "conversion" to Christ. Salvation was a key event in the life of his community, but Hughes tells comically how he bowed to pressure by permitting himself to be "saved from sin."

Words to Watch

dire (par. 3): terrible; disastrous
gnarled (par. 4): knotty; twisted
rounder (par. 6): watchman; policeman
deacons (par. 6): clergymen or laymen appointed to help the minister
serenely (par. 7): calmly; tranquilly
knickerbockered (par. 11): dressed in short, loose trousers that are gathered below the knees

I was saved from sin when I was going on thirteen. 1
But not really saved. It happened like this. There was a big revival at my Auntie Reed's church. Every night for weeks

there had been much preaching, singing, praying, and shouting, and some very hardened sinners had been brought to Christ, and the membership of the church had grown by leaps and bounds. Then just before the revival ended, they held a special meeting for children, "to bring the young lambs to the fold." My aunt spoke of it for days ahead. That night I was escorted to the front row and placed on the mourners' bench with all the other young sinners, who had not yet been brought to Jesus.

My aunt told me that when you were saved you saw 2 a light, and something happened to you inside! And Jesus came into your life! And God was with you from then on! She said you could see and hear and feel Jesus in your soul. I believed her. I had heard a great many old people say the same thing and it seemed to me they ought to know. So I sat there calmly in the hot, crowded church, waiting for Jesus to come to me.

The preacher preached a wonderful rhythmical ser- 3 mon, all moans and shouts and lonely cries and dire pictures of hell, and then he sang a song about the ninety and nine safe in the fold, but one little lamb was left out in the cold. Then he said: "Won't you come? Won't you come to Jesus? Young lambs, won't you come?" And he held out his arms to all us young sinners there on the mourners' bench. And the little girls cried. And some of them jumped up and went to Jesus right away. But most of us just sat there.

A great many old people came and knelt around us 4 and prayed, old women with jet-black faces and braided hair, old men with work-gnarled hands. And the church sang a song about the lower lights are burning, some poor sinners to be saved. And the whole building rocked with prayer and song.

Still I kept waiting to *see* Jesus. 5

Finally all the young people had gone to the altar 6 and were saved, but one boy and me. He was a rounder's son named Westley. Westley and I were surrounded by sisters and deacons praying. It was very hot in the church, and getting late now. Finally Westley said to me in a whisper: "God damn! I'm tired o' sitting here. Let's get up and be saved." So he got up and was saved.

Then I was left all alone on the mourners' bench. 7
My aunt came and knelt at my knees and cried, while
prayers and songs swirled all around me in the little church.
The whole congregation prayed for me alone, in a mighty
wail of moans and voices. And I kept waiting serenely for
Jesus, waiting, waiting—but he didn't come. I wanted to see
him, but nothing happened to me. Nothing! I wanted something to happen to me, but nothing happened.

I heard the songs and the minister saying: "Why 8
don't you come? My dear child, why don't you come to Jesus?
Jesus is waiting for you. He wants you. Why don't you come?
Sister Reed, what is this child's name?"

"Langston," my aunt sobbed. 9

"Langston, why don't you come? Why don't you come 10
and be saved? Oh, Lamb of God! Why don't you come?"

Now it was really getting late. I began to be ashamed 11
of myself, holding everything up so long. I began to wonder
what God thought about Westley, who certainly hadn't seen
Jesus either, but who was now sitting proudly on the
platform, swinging his knickerbockered legs and grinning
down at me, surrounded by deacons and old women on their
knees praying. God had not struck Westley dead for taking
his name in vain or for lying in the temple. So I decided that
maybe to save further trouble, I'd better lie, too, and say
that Jesus had come, and get up and be saved.

So I got up. 12

Suddenly the whole room broke into a sea of shouting, 13
as they saw me rise. Waves of rejoicing swept the place.
Women leaped in the air. My aunt threw her arms around
me. The minister took me by the hand and led me to the
platform.

When things quieted down, in a hushed silence, 14
punctuated by a few ecstatic "Amens," all the new young
lambs were blessed in the name of God. Then joyous singing
filled the room.

That night, for the last time in my life but one—for 15
I was a big boy twelve years old—I cried. I cried, in bed
alone, and couldn't stop. I buried my head under the quilts,
but my aunt heard me. She woke up and told my uncle I was
crying because the Holy Ghost had come into my life, and

because I had seen Jesus. But I was really crying because I couldn't bear to tell her that I had lied, that I had deceived everybody in the church, that I hadn't seen Jesus, and that now I didn't believe there was a Jesus any more, since he didn't come to help me.

BUILDING VOCABULARY

1. Throughout this essay, Hughes selects words dealing with religion to emphasize his ideas. Look these words up in a dictionary. Then tell what *connotations* the following words have for you. (See page 381.)

    a. sin (par. 1)
    b. mourner (par. 1)
    c. lamb (par. 3)
    d. salvation (title)

2. Locate additional words that deal with religion.

3. When Hughes talks about lambs in the fold—and lambs in general—he is using a figure of speech, a comparison. What is being compared? How does religion enter into the comparison? Why is it useful as a figure of speech?

UNDERSTANDING THE WRITER'S IDEAS

1. According to Hughes' description, what is a revival meeting like? What is the effect of the "preaching, singing, praying, and shouting" on the "sinners" and the "young lambs"?

2. Why does Westley "see" Jesus? Why does Langston Hughes come to Jesus?

3. How does the author feel after his salvation? Does Hughes actually believe in Christ after his experience? How do you know?

UNDERSTANDING THE WRITER'S TECHNIQUES

1. Is there a thesis statement in the essay? Where is it located?

2. How does the first paragraph serve as an introduction to the narrative?

3. What is the value of description in this essay? List several instances of vivid description that contribute to the narrative.

4. Where does the main narration begin? How much time passes in the course of the action?

5. In narration, it is especially important to have effective *transitions*—or word bridges—from stage to stage in the action. Transitions help the reader shift easily from idea to idea, event to event. List several transition words that Hughes uses.

6. A piece of writing has *coherence* if all its parts relate clearly and logically to each other. Each sentence grows naturally from the sentence before it; each paragraph grows naturally from the paragraph before it. Is Hughes' essay coherent? Which transitions help advance the action and relate the parts of a single paragraph to each other? Which transitions help connect paragraphs together? How does the way Hughes organized this essay help establish coherence?

7. A story (whether it is true or fiction) has to be told from the first-person ("I, we"), second-person ("you"), or third-person ("he, she, it, they") *point of view*. Point of view in narration sets up the author's position in regard to the action, making him either a part of the action or an observer of it.

a. What is the point of view in "Salvation"—is it first, second, or third person?

b. Why has Hughes chosen this point of view instead of any other? Can you think of any advantages to this point of view?

8. What is your opinion about the last paragraph, the conclusion of this selection? What does it suggest about the mind of a twelve-year-old boy? What does it say about adults' misunderstanding of the activities of children?

9. What does the word "conversion" mean? What conversion really takes place in this piece? How does that

compare to what people usually mean when they use "conversion" in a religious sense?

EXPLORING THE WRITER'S IDEAS

    1.   Hughes seems to suggest that we are forced to do things because of social pressures. Do you agree with his suggestion? Do people do things because their friends or families expect them to? To what extent are we part of the "herd"? Is it possible for a person to retain individuality under pressure from a group? When did you bow to group pressures? When did you resist?

    2.   Do you find the religious experience in Hughes' essay unusual or extreme? Why or why not? How do *you* define religion?

    3.   Under what circumstances might a person lie in order to satisfy others? Try to recall a specific episode in which you or someone you know was forced to lie in order to please others.

IDEAS FOR WRITING

Guided Writing

Narrate an event in your life where you (or someone you know) gave in to group pressure or were forced to lie in order to please those around you.

    1.   Start with a thesis statement.

    2.   Set the stage for your narrative in the opening paragraph by telling where and when the incident took place. Use specific names for places.

    3.   Try to keep the action within as brief a time period as possible. If you can write about an event that took no more than a few minutes, so much the better.

    4.   Use description to sketch in the characters around you. Use colors, actions, sounds, smells, sensations of touch to fill in details of the scene.

    5.   Use effective transitions of time to link sentences and paragraphs.

6. Use the last paragraph to explain how you felt immediately after the incident.

More Writing Projects

1. Explain an abstract word like "salvation," "sin," "love," or "hatred" by narrating an event that reveals the meaning of the word to you.

2. Narrate an important event that affected your relationship to family, friends, or your community during your childhood.

3. Tell about an important religious experience you remember. You might want to narrate an event about your own "conversion."

Penelope Maunsell

MAU MAU

Although many narrative essays are highly personal accounts similar to that by Langston Hughes, there is another type of narrative. In "Mau Mau," Penelope Maunsell presents a historical account of a group of freedom fighters in Africa. She tells us events as they occur over a period of time. Maunsell, who was an editorial assistant in the preparation of the ten-volume *Purnell's History of the Twentieth Century,* uses narrative to provide us with basic information. As you read this short essay, concentrate on the way that she organizes her material.

Words to Watch

emerged (par. 2): came forth into view; became known
prolonged (par. 2): lengthened; drawn out
evolved (par. 2): unfolded; developed gradually
arson (par. 3): the crime of setting fire to property
exorcizers (par. 3): people who drive out evil spirits
eradicate (par. 5): get rid of; destroy
amnesties (par. 5): pardons

In September 1948, the government of the British 1
colony of Kenya received the first official report of a 'new movement' among the 1¼ million strong Kikuyu tribe. The

movement was Mau Mau, the focus of Kikuyu protests against the presence of white farmer-settlers on their lands. Between 1952 and 1956, Mau Mau was to cost the British and Kenyan governments £55 million.

Mau Mau emerged as a secret society as a result of 2 a prolonged breakdown of Kikuyu tribal life under European influence: the name is a corruption of *'Uma Uma'* (Out! Out!)—given as a warning when police were approaching. In 1902 the Kenya-Uganda railway opened up Kikuyu territory to British farmers who settled there, taking over Kikuyu lands and bringing customs and religions which clashed with Kikuyu traditions. The Kikuyu Central Association (KCA) was formed to recover the 'lost lands' and acquired Jomo Kenyatta as general secretary. It was banned in 1940 but four years later another political party was formed—the Kenyan African Union (KAU) which had the same objectives and members as the KCA. Mau Mau evolved under the cover of the KAU, aiming to drive out all foreigners, recover their lost lands, obtain self-government, and restore ancient customs.

Violence broke out in 1952 with arson attacks 3 against non-Mau Mau Kikuyu and European settlers. The government realized that direct action would be necessary. The first major step was to mount a campaign to urge medicine men—who acted as doctors, diviners, and exorcizers—to release Mau Mau members from their oaths. This was intended to strike at the heart of the movement, for oath-taking was a very important part of Kikuyu tribal life. But the arson attacks grew and assassinations began. On 21st October 1952 the new governor, Sir Evelyn Baring, imposed a state of emergency. The turning point came in March 1953 when an enormous massacre occured at Lari in the Rift Valley, in which 84 people died and huts and cattle were burnt. Uncommitted Kikuyu joined in to defeat Mau Mau and Kenyatta was convicted of 'managing' the movement and sentenced to seven years' imprisonment. Although only sixty-eight Europeans were killed altogether, the assassinations were so savage and senseless that they provoked a hatred of Mau Mau which was sometimes as difficult to control as Mau Mau's hatred of Europeans.

Mopping-up operations were organized to flush Mau 4
Mau from their hideouts, but bombing wounded more wild-
life than rebels. Eventually special teams composed of ex-
Mau Mau hunted down and killed half of the fifty major
Mau Mau leaders.

By the end of the emergency in 1960, 10,000 Mau 5
Mau had been killed—almost half by Kikuyu Home Guard
and tribal police. Even Kenya's independence in 1963 and
Jomo Kenyatta's appointment as Prime Minister did not
eradicate the movement. Two amnesties were declared
before hundreds of Mau Mau surrendered, and even now
the movement may still survive.

BUILDING VOCABULARY

1.   Select five words or phrases from this essay which
seem to have clear *denotations* (see page 381). Why should
an essay of this type rely more on denotative than on
connotative vacabulary?

2.   Write definitions for the following words:

a. corruption (par. 2)
b. territory (par. 2)
c. acquired (par. 2)
d. secretary (par. 2)
e. banned (par. 2)
f. restore (par. 2)

Check your definitions against their usage in the essay.

3.   Maunsell puts certain phrases like "new movement" and "lost lands" in quotes. What do these two terms
mean? Why do you think the author put them in quotes?

UNDERSTANDING THE WRITER'S IDEAS

1.   Which paragraph(s) tells how Mau Mau
emerged? Restate this emergence in your own words. What
was the "new movement" protesting?

2.   What were the goals of Mau Mau? Who was the

primary leader? What do we learn about him in the course of the essay?

3. What was the turning point in the battle against Mau Mau?

4. How does Maunsell describe the violence that occurred during the Mau Mau uprising?

5. Why did Mau Mau fail? Was the movement destroyed entirely?

UNDERSTANDING THE WRITER'S TECHNIQUES

1. What is Maunsell's reason for using narration in this essay? Does she want to inform, to instruct, to simply tell a story, or to delight? Defend your choice.

2. Analyze the historical *chronology* (the sequence of events and the order in which they occurred) in this essay. Does Maunsell move from earlier to later, or does she move back and forth in historical time? How clear and effective is the chronological order in this selection?

3. *Flashback* is a narrative technique in which the writer begins at some point in the main action and then moves back in time in order to provide important information. Where does the writer use flashback in this essay? Why is it effective?

4. What is the point of view in this essay? How does it differ in effect from the first-person point of view used in Hughes' essay? Would it be possible to narrate a historical event from a first-person point of view? If so, who might the narrator be?

5. How would you explain the *tone* (see page 391) of this essay? What words in the essay best suggest that tone? What events contribute to the tone?

6. Study the author's conclusion (par. 5). In what way does it grow out of paragraph 4? Does it summarize earlier information or provide a few final points of information? Why is the last sentence especially effective?

7. Would you say that Maunsell is objective or subjective in her narrative of the Mau Mau movement? Why?

EXPLORING THE WRITER'S IDEAS

1.   What is meant by the terms "colonialism" and "imperialism"? Would you say that the United States, like England, has been an imperial power in the twentieth century? Why?

2.   Under what circumstances would you defend your country? Do you think that the Mau Mau movement was "legitimate defense of country"? How do you evaluate Mau Mau methods of achieving independence?

3.   Maunsell describes several forms of violence in this essay. Can violence ever be justified? If so, under what circumstances or conditions?

4.   How does this essay explain the difficulties African tribal leaders have in trying to achieve independence for their people?

IDEAS FOR WRITING

Guided Writing

Select an event or period in history, a movement, or a famous historical figure, and write a short narrative on the subject.

1.   Begin by consulting a good encyclopedia or other source book for basic information.

2.   Consult textbooks, magazines, or newspapers if you need more information. In your essay give information about the main sources you consulted.

3.   Take brief notes on your subject. Be certain to record all important dates and all major facts. Do not copy material word for word.

4.   Plan the chronology that you want to use.

5.   Write a four to six paragraph narrative account of the subject.

6.   As you write, try to be as objective as possible.

7.   Write a conclusion that deals with the last years of your subject.

More Writing Projects

1.   Take a current event familiar to you and write a short narrative essay on it. You might want to examine

the account of the same event in different newspapers and magazines in order to get a clear picture.

2. Bring to class examples of historical narrative that you found in newspapers or magazines. Rewrite one such account in your own words.

3. Watch some form of entertainment—a sports contest, a film, a concert—and then write a narrative in which you highlight the major events.

Jose Yglesias

THE DEPRESSION

Jose Yglesias's account of life during the Depression (1929–1940) appears in *Hard Times* by Studs Terkel. A noted author whose books include *The Goodbye Land* and *An Orderly Life,* Yglesias uses narration to show what it means to be a Latin, a worker, and a member of a union family during the troubled years of the 1930s. In this selection, look for the way Yglesias uses chronology to advance both a personal and a historical account of the 1930s.

Words To Watch

imperceptibly (par. 1): not noticeably
satanic (par. 3): devilish; wicked
deprivation (par. 3): a loss
ardent (par. 4): passionate; eager
apprentices (par. 8): beginners or trainees
anarchist (par. 12): a person who believes that all forms of government are bad and should be eliminated
bonus march (par. 12): A march on Washington, D.C. in 1932 by 15,000 World War I veterans demanding immediate payment of life insurance certificates
radical (par. 13): favoring extreme change
indicted (par. 16): accused of or charged with a crime
La huelga do los lectores (par. 17): "the strike of the readers"
militancy (par. 17): fighting spirit
wildcat strike (par. 17): a labor strike that has not been authorized by the union
foyer (par. 19): an entrance hall or lobby
derogatory (par. 23): belittling; weakening

In the sunlit town, the Depression came impercep- 1
tibly. The realization came to me when Aunt Lila said
there's no food in the house. My aunt, who owned the house
we lived in, would no longer charge rent. It would be
shameful to charge rent with $9 a week coming in.

The grocery man would come by and take a little 2
order, which he would bring the next day. When my mother
would not order anything because she owed, he'd insist:
Why are you cutting down on the beans?

There was a certain difference between the Depres- 3
sion in my home town than elsewhere. They weren't dark,
satanic mills. The streets were not like a city ghetto. There
were poor homes, that hadn't been painted in years. But it
was out in the open. You played in the sunlight. I don't
remember real deprivation.

Ybor City was an island in the South. When an 4
American got mad at any Latin, he called him a Cuban
nigger. This was one of the first feelings I remember: I want
to be an American. You become ashamed of the community.
I was an ardent supporter of Henry Ford at the age of
twelve.

The strike of 1931 revolved around readers in the 5
factory. The workers themselves used to pay twenty-five to
fifty cents a week and would hire a man to read to them
during work. A cigar factory is one enormous open area,
with tables at which people work. A platform would be
erected, so that he'd look down at the cigar makers as he
read to them some four hours a day. He would read from
newspapers and magazines and a book would be read as a
serial. The choice of the book was democratically decided.
Some of the readers were marvelous natural actors. They
wouldn't just read a book. They'd act out the scenes. Consequently, many cigar makers, who were illiterate, knew
the novels of Zola and Dickens and Cervantes and Tolstoy.
And the works of the anarchist, Kropotkin. Among the
newspapers read were *The Daily Worker* and the *Socialist
Call*.

The factory owners decided to put an end to this, 6
though it didn't cost them a penny. Everyone went on strike

when they arrived one morning and found the lecture platform torn down. The strike was lost. Every strike in my home town was always lost. The readers never came back.

The Depression began in 1930, with seasonal un- 7 employment. Factories would close down before Christmas, after having worked very hard to fill orders throughout late summer and fall. Only the cheaper grade cigars would be made. They cut off the more expensive type. Regalia.

My uncle was a foreman. He was ill-equipped for 8 the job because he couldn't bear to fire anybody. He would discuss it with his wife: We have to cut off so many people. What am I going to do? My aunt would say: You can't fire him. They have twelve children. You'd hear a great deal of talk. You knew things were getting worse. No more ap- prentices were taken in. My sister was in the last batch.

The strike left a psychological scar on me. I was in 9 junior high school and a member of the student patrol. I wore an arm band. During the strike, workers marched into the schools to close them down, bring the children out. The principal closed the gates, and had the student patrols guard them. If they come, what do I do? My mother was in the strike.

One member of the top strike committee was a 10 woman. That day I stood patrol, she was taken off to jail. Her daughter was kept in the principal's office. I remember walking home from school, about a block behind her, trying to decide whether to tell her of my sympathies, to ask about her mother. I never got to say it. I used to feel bad about that. Years later, in New York, at a meeting for Loyalist Spain, I met her and told her.

Everybody gave ten percent of their pay for the 11 Republic. It was wild. The total community was with Loyalist Spain. They used to send enormous amounts of things. It was totally organized. The song "No passarán" that was taken to be Spanish was really by a Tampa cigar maker.

It was an extraordinarily radical strike. The cigar 12 makers tried to march to City Hall with red flags, singing the old Italian anarchist song, "Avanti popolo," "Scarlet Banner." I thought it was Spanish because we used to sing

"Avanca pueblo." You see, the bonus march made them feel the revolution was here.

It was a Latin town. Men didn't sit at home. They 13 went to cafes, on street corners, at the Labor Temple, which they built themselves. It was very radical talk. The factory owners acted out of fright. The 1931 strike was openly radical. By then, there was a Communist Party in Ybor City. Leaflets would be distributed by people whom you knew. They'd come down the street in the car with their headlights off. And then onto each porch. Everybody knew who it was. They'd say, "Oh, *cómo está,* Manuel."

During the strike, the KKK would come into the 14 Labor Temple with guns, and break up meetings. Very frequently, they were police in hoods. Though they were called the Citizens' Committee, everybody would call them Los Cuckoo Klan. The picket lines would hold hands, and the KKK would beat them and cart them off.

The strike was a ghastly one. When the factories 15 opened, they cut off many workers. There was one really hated manager, a Spaniard. They would say, "It takes a Spaniard to be that cruel to his fellow man." He stood at the top of the stairs. He'd hum "The Scarlet Banner": "You—you can come in." Then he'd hum "The Internationale": "You—you can come in." Then he'd turn his back on the others. They weren't hired. Nobody begged him, though.

When the strike was lost, the Tampa paper published 16 a full page, in large type: the names of all the members of the strike committee. They were indicted for conspiracy and spent a year in jail. None of them got their jobs back.

The readers' strike lasted only a couple of weeks: *La* 17 *huelga de los lectores.* I just don't know how they kept up their militancy. There were, of course, many little wildcat strikes. Cigar makers were just incredible. If they were given a leaf that would crumble: "Too dry—out!" When cigar makers walked out, they didn't just walk out at the end of a day. They'd walk out on the day the tobacco had been moistened, laid out. The manufacturer lost a few hundred dollars, in some cases, a thousand.

There were attempts to organize the CIO. I remember 18

one of my older cousins going around in a very secretive manner. You'd think he was planning the assassination of the czar. He was trying to sign people up for the CIO. The AF of L International was very conservative and always considered as an enemy. They never gave the strike any support. It was considered the work of agitators.

People began to go off to New York to look for jobs. 19 Almost all my family were in New York by 1937. You'd take that bus far to New York. There, we all stayed together. The only place people didn't sleep in was the kitchen. A bed was even in the foyer. People would show up from Tampa, and you'd put them up. We were the Puerto Rican immigrants of that time. In any cafeteria, in the kitchen, the busboys, the dishwashers, you were bound to find at least two from Ybor City.

Some would drift back as jobs would open up again 20 in Tampa. Some went on the WPA. People would put off governmental aid as long as possible. Aunt Lila and her husband were the first in our family, and the last, to go on WPA. This was considered a terrible tragedy, because it was charity. You did not mention it to them.

That didn't mean you didn't accept another thing. 21 There was no payday in any cigar factory that there wasn't a collection for anyone in trouble. If a father died, there was a collection for the funeral. When my father went to Havana for an operation, there was a collection. That was all right. You yourself didn't ask. Someone said: "Listen, so and so's in trouble." When Havana cigar makers would go on strike, it was a matter of honor: you sent money to them. It has to do with the Spanish-Cuban tradition.

Neighbors have always helped one another. The 22 community has always been that way. There was a solidarity. There was just something very nice. . . .

People working in the cigar industry no longer have 23 the intellectual horizons that my parents had, and my aunts and uncles. They were an extraordinarily cultivated people. It makes it very difficult for me today to read political analysts, even those of the New Left, who talk in a derogatory way of the "glorification" of the working class. The working class I knew was just great.

BUILDING VOCABULARY

1. Yglesias employs a number of literary, political, and historical allusions (see page 379) in this essay. List all the allusions that you can find. How many of them do you know? What do they contribute to the essay?

2. Is the use of foreign words justified in this essay? How many foreign words can you find? Which ones can you figure out? Does Yglesias ever provide hints about their meaning?

3. Use the following words in sentences of your own:

a. realization (par. 1)
b. ghetto (par. 3)
c. serial (par. 5)
d. psychological (par. 9)
e. incredible (par. 16).

UNDERSTANDING THE WRITER'S IDEAS

1. Where does the action of this narrative take place? Why does the action shift from one city to another? What years are covered in this narrative?

2. How would you describe the economic condition of the Yglesias family? Read aloud specific passages. In what kind of work is the family involved?

3. Why do the workers employ "readers" in the factory? Why do you suppose that the owners of the factory wanted to get rid of the readers?

4. How old was Yglesias when the 1931 strike occurred? How does he describe himself? What does the author mean when he says that the strike "left a psychological scar" (par. 9) on him?

5. Do you think that Yglesias is proud of his parents and community for their actions during the 1930s? Why? Which paragraph best shows his attitude?

UNDERSTANDING THE WRITER'S TECHNIQUES

1. How would you explain the *tone* (see page 391) of this essay? Which statements best suggest the tone? Is Yglesias as subjective as Hughes or as objective as Maunsell?

2. Explain the author's use of time in this essay. Does Yglesias employ a strict chronological order? Does he move forward in time from day to day? Does he employ a variety of methods? Read aloud parts of specific paragraphs to support your explanation of Yglesias's use of time.

3. In narration, it is important to maintain *proportion*—in other words, to concentrate on major events and either ignore or devote less space to minor events. In this essay, what is the major event? Which paragraphs discuss it? What minor events are sketched by Yglesias? Does he maintain proportion in his description of events?

4. Where does the author come closest to stating his central thesis? Why does he place it where he does?

5. What is the function of paragraphs 1 to 4? Why does Yglesias wait until paragraph 5 to *introduce* the main event into the narrative?

6. What is the point of view (see page 388) in this narrative? What is the relationship between the author's use of point of view and the tone of the essay?

EXPLORING THE WRITER'S IDEAS

1. Yglesias raises important social and political issues here. What are they? Would you say that these issues are the same today as they were in the 1930s? Why?

2. The author finds great strength in his neighborhood. Do you think that one's neighborhood is still a source of value and communal strength in today's world? Use your own neighborhood to support your comments.

3. Yglesias, in paragraph 4, uses the term "Cuban nigger." Clearly the word "nigger" has developed expanded meanings in modern times. For example, essays have been written on "the student as nigger" and on "the woman as nigger." What connotations are now brought to this particular word? Is it being overused or misused, or does it still have value?

4. How do you feel about labor unions? Do you find them as radical today as the cigar maker's union was in Yglesias's town?

5. At the conclusion of his essay Yglesias writes that his parents and relatives who worked in the factories "were extraordinarily cultivated people." He also says that today the "intellectual horizons" of the American worker are much lower. Would you agree or disagree with this statement? Why? Could a system of "readers" be set up in factories today? How do you think workers would react to readers on the job? Why? What other method for personal development would you suggest for workers while they work?

IDEAS FOR WRITING

Guided Writing

Discuss some work problems in America by writing about an episode that happened to you, your parents, or others whom you know. (You might want to focus on a job you had, on a strike you remember, on a period of unemployment and the difficulties of looking for work, and so forth.)

1. Establish the time and place of the action in your opening paragraph.

2. Maintain good proportion by focusing on key events.

3. Try to cover a period of weeks, months, or years; however, if you prefer, concentrate on a shorter period of time, but provide a few episodes within this time frame.

4. Describe the important people around you.

5. If possible, relate your personal experience to the conditions of the times, and make historical references as Yglesias did in his narrative.

6. Use details rich in sensory language. Show colors, name sounds and actions. Try to let the reader see details of the scene exactly as you saw them.

7. Write a conclusion similar to that of Yglesias, which summarizes your attitude toward work in America as it affects you and others.

More Writing Projects

1.   Yglesias's narrative is actually an example of "oral history." It was told to Studs Terkel, who recorded it on tape. Ask your parents, relatives, or older friends what they remember about the Depression (or any other historical period) and try to write down their stories. Bring these written narratives to class for discussion. You, too, might want to use a tape recorder from which to copy parts of the most interesting stories.

2.   Explain community "togetherness" (or the lack of it) by narrating an event that drew your neighborhood together (or divided it) over a common problem.

3.   If you work, write a five-day account of key events on the job. Be sure to use clear sensory details. Show people, places, and actions as exactly as you can.

George Orwell

A HANGING

One of the masters of English prose, George Orwell
(1903–1950) often used narration of personal events to
explore important social issues. Notice here how he involves the reader in a simple yet fascinating and tragic
story, almost as if he were writing fiction. Orwell takes
a brief time span and expands that moment with specific
language. At one point, as you will see, the purpose of the
narrative comes into sharp focus.

Words to Watch

sodden (par. 1): heavy with water
absurdly (par. 2): ridiculously
desolately (par. 3): gloomily; lifelessly; cheerlessly
prodding (par. 3): poking or thrusting at something
Dravidian (par. 4): any member of a group of intermixed races of
      southern India and Burma
pariah (par. 6): outcast; a member of a low caste of southern India
      and Burma
servile (par. 11): slave-like; lacking spirit or independence
reiterated (par. 12): repeated
abominable (par. 13): hateful; disagreeable; unpleasant
timorously (par. 15): fearfully
oscillated (par. 16): moved back and forth between two points
garrulously (par. 20): in a talkative manner
refractory (par. 22): stubborn
amicably (par. 24): friendly; peaceably

It was in Burma, a sodden morning of the rains. A 1
sickly light, like yellow tinfoil, was slanting over the high
walls into the jail yard. We were waiting outside the
condemned cells, a row of sheds fronted with double bars,
like small animal cages. Each cell measured about ten feet
by ten and was quite bare within except for a plank bed and
a pot of drinking water. In some of them brown silent men
were squatting at the inner bars, with their blankets draped
round them. These were the condemned men, due to be
hanged within the next week or two.

One prisoner had been brought out of his cell. He 2
was a Hindu, a puny wisp of a man, with a shaven head and
vague liquid eyes. He had a thick, sprouting moustache,
absurdly too big for his body, rather like the moustache of
a comic man on the films. Six tall Indian warders were
guarding him and getting him ready for the gallows. Two
of them stood by with rifles with fixed bayonets, while the
others handcuffed him, passed a chain through his handcuffs
and fixed it to their belts, and lashed his arms tight to his
sides. They crowded very close about him, with their hands
always on him in a careful, caressing grip, as though all the
while feeling him to make sure he was there. It was like
men handling a fish which is still alive and may jump back
into the water. But he stood quite unresisting, yielding his
arms limply to the ropes, as though he hardly noticed what
was happening.

Eight o'clock struck and a bugle call, desolately thin 3
in the wet air, floated from the distant barracks. The
superintendent of the jail, who was standing apart from the
rest of us, moodily prodding the gravel with his stick, raised
his head at the sound. He was an army doctor, with a grey
toothbrush moustache and a gruff voice. "For God's sake
hurry up, Francis," he said irritably. "The man ought to
have been dead by this time. Aren't you ready yet?"

Francis, the head jailer, a fat Dravidian in a white 4
drill suit and gold spectacles, waved his black hand. "Yes
sir, yes sir," he bubbled. "All iss satisfactorily prepared. The
hangman iss waiting. We shall proceed."

"Well, quick march, then. The prisoners can't get their breakfast till this job's over."

We set out for the gallows. Two warders marched on either side of the prisoner, with their files at the slope; two others marched close against him, gripping him by arm and shoulder, as though at once pushing and supporting him. The rest of us, magistrates and the like, followed behind. Suddenly, when we had gone ten yards, the procession stopped short without any order or warning. A dreadful thing had happened—a dog, come goodness knows whence, had appeared in the yard. It came bounding among us with a loud volley of barks, and leapt round us wagging its whole body, wild with glee at finding so many human beings together. It was a large woolly dog, half Airedale, half pariah. For a moment it pranced round us, and then, before anyone could stop it, it had made a dash for the prisoner, and jumping up tried to lick his face. Everyone stood aghast, too taken aback even to grab at the dog.

"Who let that bloody brute in here?" said the superintendent angrily. "Catch it, someone!"

A warder, detached from the escort, charged clumsily after the dog, but it danced and gambolled just out of his reach, taking everything as part of the game. A young Eurasian jailer picked up a handful of gravel and tried to stone the dog away, but it dodged the stones and came after us again. Its yaps echoed from the jail walls. The prisoner, in the grasp of the two warders, looked on incuriously, as though this was another formality of the hanging. It was several minutes before someone managed to catch the dog. Then we put my handkerchief through its collar and moved off once more, with the dog still straining and whimpering.

It was about forty yards to the gallows. I watched the bare brown back of the prisoner marching in front of me. He walked clumsily with his bound arms, but quite steadily, with that bobbing gait of the Indian who never straightens his knees. At each step his muscles slid neatly into place, the lock of hair on his scalp danced up and down, his feet printed themselves on the wet gravel. And once, in spite of the men who gripped him by each shoulder, he stepped slightly aside to avoid a puddle on the path.

It is curious, but till that moment I had never 10 realised what it means to destroy a healthy, conscious man. When I saw the prisoner step aside to avoid the puddle, I saw the mystery, the unspeakable wrongness, of cutting a life short when it is in full tide. This man was not dying, he was alive just as we were alive. All the organs of his body were working—bowels digesting food, skin renewing itself, nails growing, tissues forming—all toiling away in solemn foolery. His nails would still be growing when he stood on the drop, when he was falling through the air with a tenth of a second to live. His eyes saw the yellow gravel and the grey walls, and his brain still remembered, foresaw, reasoned—reasoned even about puddles. He and we were a party of men walking together, seeing, hearing, feeling, understanding the same world; and in two minutes, with a sudden snap, one of us would be gone—one mind less, one world less.

The gallows stood in a small yard, separate from the 11 main grounds of the prison, and overgrown with tall prickly weeds. It was a brick erection like three sides of a shed, with planking on top, and above that two beams and a crossbar with the rope dangling. The hangman, a grey-haired convict in the white uniform of the prison, was waiting beside his machine. He greeted us with a servile crouch as we entered. At a word from Francis the two warders, gripping the prisoner more closly than ever, half led, half pushed him to the gallows and helped him clumsily up the ladder. Then the hangman climbed up and fixed the rope round the prisoner's neck.

We stood waiting, five yards away. The warders had 12 formed in a rough circle round the gallows. And then, when the noose was fixed, the prisoner began crying out on his god. It was a high, reiterated cry of "Ram! Ram! Ram! Ram!", not urgent and fearful like a prayer or a cry for help, but steady, rhythmical, almost like the tolling of a bell. The dog answered the sound with a whine. The hangman, still standing on the gallows, produced a small cotton bag like a flour bag and drew it down over the prisoner's face. But the sound, muffled by the cloth, still persisted, over and over again: "Ram! Ram! Ram! Ram! Ram!"

The hangman climbed down and stood ready, holding 13 the lever. Minutes seemed to pass. The steady, muffled crying from the prisoner went on and on, "Ram! Ram! Ram!" never faltering for an instant. The superintendent, his head on his chest, was slowly poking the ground with his stick; perhaps he was counting the cries, allowing the prisoner a fixed number—fifty, perhaps, or a hundred. Everyone had changed colour. The Indians had gone grey like bad coffee, and one or two of the bayonets were wavering. We looked at the lashed, hooded man on the drop, and listened to his cries—each cry another second of life; the same thought was in all our minds: oh, kill him quickly, get it over, stop that abominable noise!

Suddenly the superintendent made up his mind. 14 Throwing up his head he made a swift motion with his stick. "Chalo!" he shouted almost fiercely.

There was a clanking noise, and then dead silence. 15 The prisoner had vanished, and the rope was twisting on itself. I let go of the dog, and it galloped immediately to the back of the gallows; but when it got there it stopped short, barked, and then retreated into a corner of the yard, where it stood among the weeds, looking timorously out at us. We went round the gallows to inspect the prisoner's body. He was dangling with his toes pointed straight downwards, very slowly revolving, as dead as a stone.

The superintendent reached out with his stick and 16 poked the bare body; it oscillated, slightly. "*He's* all right," said the superintendent. He backed out from under the gallows, and blew out a deep breath. The moody look had gone out of his face quite suddenly. He glanced at his wristwatch. "Eight minutes past eight. Well, that's all for this morning, thank God."

The warders unfixed bayonets and marched away. 17 The dog, sobered and conscious of having misbehaved itself, slipped after them. We walked out of the gallows yard, past the condemned cells with their waiting prisoners, into the big central yard of the prison. The convicts, under the command of warders armed with lathis, were already receiving their breakfast. They squatted in long rows, each man holding a tin pannikin, while two warders with buckets marched round ladling out rice; it seemed quite a homely, jolly scene, after the hanging. An enormous relief had come upon us now that the job was done. One felt an impulse to sing, to break into a run, to snigger. All at once everyone began chattering gaily.

The Eurasian boy walking beside me nodded towards 18 the way we had come, with a knowing smile: "Do you know, sir, our friend (he meant the dead man), when he heard his appeal had been dismissed, he pissed on the floor of his cell. From fright.—Kindly take one of my cigarettes, sir. Do you not admire my new silver case, sir? From the boxwallah, two rupees eight annas. Classy European style."

Several people laughed—at what, nobody seemed 19 certain.

Francis was walking by the superintendent, talking 20 garrulously: "Well, sir, all hass passed off with the utmost satisfactoriness. It wass all finished—flick! like that. It iss not always so—oah, no! I have known cases where the doctor wass obliged to go beneath the gallows and pull the prisoner's legs to ensure decease. Most disagreeable!"

"Wriggling about, eh? That's bad," said the super- 21 intendent.

"Ach, sir, it iss worse when they become refractory! 22 One man, I recall, clung to the bars of hiss cage when we went to take him out. You will scarcely credit, sir, that it took six warders to dislodge him, three pulling at each leg. We reasoned with him. 'My dear fellow,' we said, 'think of all the pain and trouble you are causing to us!' But no, he would not listen! Ach, he wass very troublesome!"

I found that I was laughing quite loudly. Everyone 23 was laughing. Even the superintendent grinned in a tolerant way. "You'd better all come out and have a drink," he said quite genially. "I've got a bottle of whisky in the car. We could do with it."

We went through the big double gates of the prison, 24
into the road. "Pulling at his legs!" exclaimed a Burmese
magistrate suddenly, and burst into a loud chuckling. We
all began laughing again. At that moment Francis's anecdote
seemed extraordinarily funny. We all had a drink together,
native and European alike, quite amicably. The dead man
was a hundred yards away.

BUILDING VOCABULARY

1.   It is often possible to figure out the meaning of
a difficult word by using context clues—clues in surrounding
words and sentences. Without a dictionary, make an "edu-
cated guess" on the definitions of the words in italics below.
Before you guess, look back to the paragraph for clues.
Afterward, check your guess in a dictionary.

>   a. *condemned* men (par. 1)
>   b. puny *wisp* of a man (par. 2)
>   c. Indian *warders* (par. 2)
>   d. careful *caressing* grip (par. 2)
>   e. stood *aghast* (par. 6)
>   f. it danced and *gambolled* (par. 7)
>   g. *solemn* foolery (par. 10)
>   h. armed with *lathis* (par. 17)
>   i. a tin *pannikin* (par. 17)
>   j. quite *genially* (par. 23)

2.   What are definitions for the words below? Look
at words within them which you may be able to recognize.

>   a. moodily
>   b. dreadful
>   c. Eurasian
>   d. incuriously
>   e. formality

3.   a. Select any five words from the Words to Watch
section on page 55 and write a sentence of your own for
each.

b.   Select any five words from Exercises 1 and 2 above
and write a sentence of your own for each.

UNDERSTANDING THE WRITER'S IDEAS

1. What is the main point that the writer wishes to make in this essay? Which paragraph tells the author's purpose most clearly? Which sentence in that paragraph best states the main idea of the essay?

2. The events in the essay occur in Burma, a country in Asia. Describe in your own words the specific details of the action.

3. Who are the major characters in this essay? Why might you include the dog as a major character?

4. In a narrative essay the writer often tells the events in *chronological order*—that is, according to the way they occur in time. Examine the following events from "A Hanging." Arrange these events in the order in which they occurred.

   a. A large wooly dog tries to lick the prisoner's face.

   b. A Eurasian boy talks about his silver case.

   c. The superintendent signals "Chalo!" to the hangman.

   d. One prisoner, a Hindu, is brought from his cell.

   e. Francis discusses with the superintendent a prisoner who had to be pulled off the bars of his cage.

   f. The prisoner steps aside to avoid a puddle as he marches to the gallows.

5. What is the author's opinion of *capital punishment* (legally killing someone who has disobeyed the laws of society)? How does the incident with the puddle suggest that opinion, even indirectly?

UNDERSTANDING THE WRITER'S TECHNIQUES

1. In the first paragraph of the essay, we see clear images such as "brown silent men were squatting at the inner bars, with their blankets draped around them." The use of color and action make an instant appeal to our sense of sight.

   a. What images in the rest of the essay do you find most vivid?

b. Which sentence gives the best details of sound?

c. What word pictures suggest action and color?

d. Where do you find words that describe a sensation of touch?

2. In order to make their images clearer, writers use *figurative language* (see page 383). "A Hanging" is especially rich in *similes,* which are comparisons using the word *like* or *as.*

a. What simile does Orwell use in the first paragraph in order to let us see how the light slants over the jail yards walls? How does the simile make the scene clearer?

b. What other simile does Orwell use in the first paragraph?

c. Discuss the similes in the paragraphs listed below. What are the things being compared? Are the similes, in your opinion, original? How do they contribute to the image the author intends to create?

(1) "It was like man handling a fish. . . ." (par. 2)

(2) "A thick sprouting moustache . . . rather like the moustache of a comic man in the films." (par. 2)

(3) "It was a high, reiterated cry . . . like the tolling of a bell." (par. 12)

(4) "The Indians had gone grey like bad coffee. . . ." (par. 13)

(5) "He was dangling with his toes pointed straight downwards, slowly revolving, as dead as a stone." (par. 15)

3. You know that an important feature of narration is the writer's ability to look at a brief span of time and to expand that moment with specific language.

a. How has Orwell limited the events in "A Hanging" to a specific moment in time and place?

b. How does the image "a sodden morning of the rains" in paragraph 1 set the mood for the main event portrayed in the essay? What is the effect of the image "brown silent men"? Why does Orwell describe the prisoner as "a puny wisp of a man, with a shaven head and vague liquid eyes"? (par. 2) Why does the author present him in almost a comic way?

c. What is the effect of the image about the bugle call in paragraph 3, line 1? Why does Orwell create the image of the dog licking the prisoner's face (par. 6)? How does it contribute to his main point? In paragraph 12, Orwell tells us that the dog whines. Why does he give that detail? Discuss the value of the images about the dog in paragraphs 15 and 17.

d. Why does Orwell offer the image of the prisoner stepping aside "to avoid a puddle on the path"? How does it advance the point of the essay? What is the effect of the image of the superintendent poking the ground with his stick (par. 13)?

e. What is the importance of the superintendent's words in paragraph 3? What is the value of the Eurasian boy's conversation in paragraph 18? How does the dialogue in paragraphs 20 to 24 contribute to Orwell's main point?

f. Why has Orwell left out information about the crime the prisoner committed? How would you feel about the prisoner if you knew he were, say, a rapist, a murderer, a molester of children, or a heroin supplier?

4. Analyze the point of view in the essay. Is the "I" narrator an observer, a participant, or both? Is he neutral or involved? Support your opinion.

5. In "A Hanging," Orwell skillfully uses several forms of *irony* to support his main ideas. Irony, in general, is the use of language to suggest the opposite of what is said. First, there is *verbal irony,* which involves a contrast between what is said and what is actually meant. Second, there is *irony of situation,* where there is a contrast between what is expected or thought appropriate and what actually happens. Then, there is *dramatic irony,* in which there is a contrast between what a character says and what the reader (or the audience) actually knows or understands.

a. Look at paragraph 2. Why does Orwell describe the prisoner as a *comic* type? Why does he emphasize the prisoner's *smallness?* Why does Orwell write that the prisoner "hardly noticed what was happening"? Why might this be called ironic?

b. When the dog appears in paragraph 6, how is its behavior described? How do the dog's actions contrast with the situation?

c. What is the major irony that Orwell analyzes in paragraph 10?

d. In paragraph 11, how does the fact that one prisoner is being used to execute another prisoner strike you?

e. Why is the Superintendent's remark in paragraph 11—"*He's* all right"—a good example of verbal irony?

f. After the hanging, the men engage in seemingly normal actions. However, Orwell undercuts these actions through the use of irony. Find at least three examples of irony in paragraphs 17 to 24.

EXPLORING THE WRITER'S IDEAS

1. Orwell is clearly against capital punishment. Why might you agree or disagree with him? Are there any crimes for which capital punishment is acceptable to you? If not, what should society do with those convicted of serious crimes?

2. Do you think the method used to perform capital punishment has anything to do with the way we view it? Is death by hanging or firing squad worse than death by gas or by the electric chair? Or are they all the same? Socrates— a Greek philosopher convicted of conspiracy—was forced to drink *hemlock,* a fast acting poison. Can you accept that?

3. Orwell shows a variety of reactions people have to an act of execution. Can you believe the way the characters behave? Why? How do you explain the large crowds that gathered to watch public executions in Europe in the sixteenth and seventeenth centuries?

IDEAS FOR WRITING

Guided Writing

Write a narrative theme of four or five paragraphs in which you tell about a punishment you either saw or received. Use sensory language, selecting your details carefully. At one point in your paper—as Orwell does in paragraph 10—state your opinion or interpretation of the punishment clearly.

1. Use a number of images that name colors, sounds, smells, and actions.

2. Try to write at least three original similes. Think through your comparisons carefully. Make sure they are logical. Avoid overused comparisons like "He was white as a ghost."

3. Set your narrative in time and place. Tell the season of the year and the place in which the event occurred.

4. Fill in details of the setting. Show what the surroundings look like.

5. Name people by name. Show details of their actions. Quote some of their spoken dialogue.

6. Use the first-person point of view.

More Writing Projects

1. Write a narrative essay in which you tell the story of an execution from the point of view of either the executioner or the person condemned to die. Focus on the last moments before the execution.

2. Write an essay in which you narrate an event that turned out differently from what you expected—a blind date, a picnic, a holiday. Try to stress the irony of the situation.

3. Write a narrative that describes a vivid event in which you hid your true feelings about the event, such as a postelection party, the wedding of someone you disliked, a job interview, a visit to the doctor.

three

Illustration

One convenient way for writers to present and to support a point is through *illustration*—that is, by means of several examples to back up an idea. Illustration helps a writer put general or abstract thoughts into specific examples. It also holds a reader's interest: We all respond to concrete instances when we are trying to understand a point. Certainly, you are no stranger to illustration as a way to present information. Every time you try to explain why you believe or feel something to be true, and you give more than one case to back it up, you are using this technique.

Suppose you want to share with a friend your belief that the Los Angeles Dodgers are a great baseball team. First you might point out the pitching staff; then you might bring up the quality hitters; then the fielders; then the management. Your friend would, no doubt, expect you to explain each of those illustrations by giving some details. And so you would name a couple of first-rate pitchers, perhaps describe them and state their won-lost record; you would tell which of the hitters you thought outstanding and point out their runs-batted-in and their hitting averages; you would describe a good fielder or two in action, even telling a story, perhaps, of one really first-rate play you saw when the Dodgers pounded the Reds.

When you present illustrations, it is best to have *several* reasons which lead you to a certain conclusion. A single, isolated example might not convince anyone easily, unless it is a strong, extended example. You have to make decisions, of course, about the number and kinds of details to offer for each example. Sometimes each illustration will itself require a few different examples to make the point. And you have to decide which illustration to give first: No doubt you would save the most important for last.

As you have probably guessed, when you write an essay of illustration you will be using much of what you have already learned so far. Techniques of description and narration will help you support and organize your examples clearly and strongly. In fact, a number of ways to develop essays discussed later on—comparison, cause and effect, process analysis, definition, and classification—lend themselves to development by illustration. The selections you will read in this section show how four writers use illustration to advance their ideas.

Randall Williams

DADDY TUCKED THE BLANKET

Randall Williams was a reporter for *The Alabama Journal* when he wrote this autobiographical essay. He is trying here to show how the social conditions of the poor have an ugly effect upon personal relationships. A number of examples point out how his family reacted to each other and to the environment created by poverty.

Words to Watch

humiliating (par. 5): lowering the pride or dignity of someone
shiftless (par. 7): incapable; inefficient; lazy
articulate (par. 7): able to speak clearly
teetering (par. 8): wavering; moving unsteadily
deteriorating (par. 12): becoming worse
futility (par. 13): the quality of being useless
abuse (par. 16): mistreatment
psyche (par. 20): the mind
affluent (par. 21): wealthy
grandeur (par. 23): magnificence

About the time I turned 16, my folks began to 1 wonder why I didn't stay home any more. I always had an excuse for them, but what I didn't say was that I had found my freedom and I was getting out.

I went through four years of high school in semirural 2
Alabama and became active in clubs and sports; I made a
lot of friends and became a regular guy, if you know what
I mean. But one thing was irregular about me: I managed
those four years without ever having a friend visit at my
house.

I was ashamed of where I lived. I had been ashamed 3
for as long as I had been conscious of class.

We had a big family. There were several of us 4
sleeping in one room, but that's not so bad if you get along,
and we always did. As you get older, though, it gets worse.

Being poor is a humiliating experience for a young 5
person trying hard to be accepted. Even now—several years
removed—it is hard to talk about. And I resent the weakness
of these words to make you feel what it was really like.

We lived in a lot of old houses. We moved a lot 6
because we were always looking for something just a little
better than what we had. You have to understand that my
folks worked harder than most people. My mother was
always at home, but for her that was a full-time job—and
no fun, either. But my father worked his head off from the
time I can remember in construction and shops. It was hard,
physical work.

I tell you this to show that we weren't shiftless. No 7
matter how much money Daddy made, we never made much
progress up the social ladder. I got out thanks to a college
scholarship and because I was a little more articulate than
the average.

I have seen my Daddy wrap copper wire through the 8
soles of his boots to keep them together in the wintertime.
He couldn't buy new boots because he had used the money
for food and shoes for us. We lived like hell, but we went to
school well-clothed and with a full stomach.

It really is hell to live in a house that was in bad 9
shape 10 years before you moved in. And a big family puts
a lot of wear and tear on a new house, too, so you can
imagine how one goes downhill if it is teetering when you
move in. But we lived in houses that were sweltering in
summer and freezing in winter. I woke up every morning

for a year and a half with plaster on my face where it had fallen out of the ceiling during the night.

This wasn't during the Depression; this was in the late 60's and early 70's. 10

When we boys got old enough to learn trades in school, we would try to fix up the old houses we lived in. But have you ever tried to paint a wall that crumbled when the roller went across it? And bright paint emphasized the holes in the wall. You end up more frustrated than when you began, especially when you know that at best you might come up with only enough money to improve one of the six rooms in the house. And we might move out soon after, anyway. 11

The same goes for keeping a house like that clean. If you have a house full of kids and the house is deteriorating, you'll never keep it clean. Daddy used to yell at Mama about that, but she couldn't do anything. I think Daddy knew it inside, but he had to have an outlet for his rage somewhere, and at least yelling isn't as bad as hitting, which they never did to each other. 12

But you have a kitchen which has no counter space and no hot water, and you will have dirty dishes stacked up. That sounds like an excuse, but try it. You'll go mad from the sheer sense of futility. It's the same thing in a house with no closets. You can't keep clothes clean and rooms in order if they have to be stacked up with things. 13

Living in a bad house is generally worse on girls. For one thing, they traditionally help their mother with the housework. We boys could get outside and work in the field or cut wood or even play ball and forget about living conditions. The sky was still pretty. 14

But the girls got the pressure, and as they got older it became worse. Would they accept dates knowing they had to "receive" the young man in a dirty hallway with broken windows, peeling wallpaper and a cracked ceiling? You have to live it to understand it, but it creates a shame which drives the soul of a young person inward. 15

I'm thankful none of us ever blamed our parents for this, because it would have crippled our relationships. As it 16 worked out, only the relationship between our parents was damaged. And I think the harshness which they expressed to each other was just an outlet to get rid of their anger at the trap their lives were in. It ruined their marriage because they had no one to yell at but each other. I knew other families where the kids got the abuse, but we were too much loved for that.

Once I was about 16 and Mama and Daddy had had 17 a particularly violent argument about the washing machine, which had broken down. Daddy was on the back porch— that's where the only water faucet was—trying to fix it and Mamma had a washtub out there washing school clothes for the next day and they were screaming at each other.

Later that night everyone was in bed and I heard 18 Daddy get up from the couch where he was reading. I looked out from my bed across the hall into their room. He was standing right over Mama and she was already asleep. He pulled the blanket up and tucked it around her shoulders and just stood there and tears were dropping off his cheeks and I thought I could faintly hear them splashing against the linoleum rug.

Now they're divorced.   19

I had courses in college where housing was discussed, 20 but the sociologists never put enough emphasis on the impact living in substandard housing has on a person's psyche. Especially children's.

Small children have a hard time understanding 21 poverty. They want the same things children from more affluent families have. They want the same things they see advertised on television, and they don't understand why they can't have them.

Other children can be incredibly cruel. I was in 22 elementary school in Georgia—and this is interesting because it is the only thing I remember about that particular school—when I was about eight or nine.

After Christmas vacation had ended, my teacher 23 made each student describe all his or her Christmas presents. I became more and more uncomfortable as the privilege passed around the room toward me. Other children were reciting the names of the dolls they had been given, the kinds of bicycles and the grandeur of their games and toys. Some had lists which seemed to go on and on for hours.

It took me only a few seconds to tell the class that 24 I had gotten for Christmas a belt and a pair of gloves. And then I was laughed at—because I cried—by a roomful of children and a teacher. I never forgave them, and that night I made my mother cry when I told her about it.

In retrospect, I am grateful for that moment, but I 25 remember wanting to die at the time.

BUILDING VOCABULARY

1. For each expression in italics in Column A select from Column B the best definition. On a separate sheet of paper, write the correct letter after each number.

Column A	Column B
a. one thing was *irregular* about me	1. absolute
b. *conscious* of class	2. object to
c. I *resent* the weakness	3. way to express anger
d. houses that were *sweltering*	4. are expected to
e. an *outlet for his rage*	5. force
f. the *sheer* sense of futility	6. not correct
g. they *traditionally* help mother	7. very hot
h. the *impact* living in substandard housing has	8. unbelievably
i. *incredibly* cruel	9. aware
j. in *retrospect*	10. looking back

UNDERSTANDING THE WRITER'S IDEAS

1. Why did the author never have a friend visit his house? How did he explain to his parents the fact that, at sixteen, he did not stay home any more?

2. Describe some of the situations Williams remembers about the houses in which he lived as a child. Why

was it hard to keep the houses clean? Why was living in such a house so bad for the author's sisters? Why did the family keep moving around?

3. Why did the Williams family never "progress up the social ladder"? Why does he stress the idea that the family was not shiftless?

4. Why, according to the author, was his parent's relationship damaged? Why were they frequently having violent arguments? How does Williams show the love his father had for his mother?

5. Why does the author believe that children can be incredibly cruel?

6. What is the meaning of the last paragraph? For which moment do you think the author is grateful, the moment in school or the moment in which his mother cried? Why would he be grateful for either of those moments?

UNDERSTANDING THE WRITER'S TECHNIQUES

1. What is Williams's main point in this essay? Which sentence expresses the writer's *thesis?*

2. What details does Williams offer to illustrate the fact that he lived in bad houses? Which details are clearest to you?

3. How does Williams illustrate how little money his father had for himself?

4. How does Williams illustrate the way his parents argued? What elements of narration do you find in that example? Where else does the author use narrative as part of an illustration?

5. In which illustrations does the author use description? Where do you find good descriptive details in this essay? On the whole, though, the author has not used descriptive language very much. Why? Where would you have liked to see more concrete detail?

6. One way that the author has for tying together his ideas is by frequently reminding the reader of his thesis. Review your response to question 1 above; then, find words or word groups later on in the essay that repeat the main

point, either through the same words or through words that mean the same or similar things.

7. This essay is written in a very simple style. How does the author achieve this simplicity? Is it the vocabulary? How would you describe it? Is it the sentence structure? What kinds of sentences does Williams write most of the time? What is the effect of the numerous short paragraphs? What is your reaction to the two paragraphs that have only one sentence in each of them?

8. Do the author's illustrations support his main point successfully? Why do you think he chose illustration as a way to develop his idea? Which illustration do you find most effective? Why does he tell the story about his experience in school after Christmas one year at the *end* of the essay?

9. When a writer exaggerates emotions, he is often accused of *sentimentality*. In sentimental writing the author plays with the reader's emotions simply for their own sake. Would you call Williams sentimental? Why? Which images deliberately convey an emotional stance? Do you feel as if he is exaggerating emotions here? Where has he *avoided* sentimentality when he might have played up the scene for its emotional content?

EXPLORING THE WRITER'S IDEAS

1. Williams says that it is hard to talk about his humiliating past experiences, and then he says, "I resent the weakness of these words to make you feel what it was really like." Do you agree that words are weak in conveying feeling to someone who might not have experienced that feeling? Williams is talking about *humiliation* and how words are not strong enough to make people feel it. What other feeling have you had that might be hard to convey in words? Despite the fact that the author complains about words, he writes, nonetheless, about his experiences. How do you explain that?

2. Has Williams fairly presented the condition of poverty in America? How does his own situation show some

ways that a family or an individual may overcome certain features of poverty? Would you say that poverty in a rural area is the same as poverty in a large city like Atlanta, or Chicago, or New York?

3. Do you agree with Williams' analysis that his father and mother yelled at each other because they needed an outlet for their anger? Do you think the need for such an outlet can force apart two people who love each other? Is it possible for people to fight constantly and still to love each other? What instances from your own experience can you quote to demonstrate these points? How do you account for the fact that despite poverty and frequent fights, some parents stay together without divorcing?

4. The author suggests that housing plays an important part in the development of a person's psyche. Do you agree? Why? What ingredients would you list for perfect home conditions? Would you include anything other than simple physical conditions like walls that do not crumble or washing machines that work?

5. Williams' father and mother obviously sacrificed many of their own needs and comforts for their children. Do you believe that parents should make such sacrifices? Why or why not?

6. Do you agree that living in a bad house is more difficult for girls than boys? Why?

IDEAS FOR WRITING

Guided Writing

On a separate sheet of paper, fill in the blanks in this sentence and then write an essay of 350 to 500 words in which you use illustration to present your ideas:

Being _____ is a _____
experience for a young person.

1. For the blank spaces select words which reflect important aspects of your own experiences. You do not have to pick negative qualities: You might say, "Being *free* is an *important* experience for a young person." Or, you might

follow one of these other suggestions if you cannot think of one of your own. But be sure to avoid overused words like *good, bad, nice, fantastic,* or *interesting.*

     a. Being *lonely* is a *terrible* experience for a young person.

     b. Being *frightened* is an *unforgetable* experience for a young person.

     c. Being *loved* is a *vital* experience for a young person.

     d. Being *"different"* is a *sad* experience for a young person.

     2.   Use the sentence you have written as the thesis sentence of your paragraph. Build an introduction around it.

     3.   Illustrate your thesis with examples drawn from your own experience. Provide at least three illustrations.

     4.   If your illustrations require narrative, follow the techniques you learned in Chapter 2 about good narration.

     5.   If you have to use description, make sure you follow the suggestions in Chapter 1 about good description. Use concrete, sensory language to help your reader see your points clearly.

     6.   Connect the different illustrations in your essay by referring to the main point in your thesis sentence.

More Writing Projects

     1.   Write an essay of illustration in which you show how certain conditions affected your parents' relationship. You might show the effect of *poverty* on their lives; or you might show the effect of a *city, love, religion, education, superstition, fear, children* on their lives. Feel free to name any condition you choose.

     2.   Write an essay in which you provide illustrations to show the nature of poverty in your neighborhood, city, or state. You may want to select illustrations from your own experience or observation. Or, you might want to use other sources, like newspaper articles, books, magazines, presentations on radio or television.

Ray Bradbury

TRICKS! TREATS! GANGWAY!

Ray Bradbury (1920–   ) is noted for his science fiction
writing—you may have read *Farenheit 451* or have seen
the movie—but in this piece he is recalling a special time
of year for a boy who grew up in the midwest in the 1920s
and 1930s. Illustrations drawn from his childhood show
what a grand time Halloween really was in Illinois.

Words to Watch

corrupted (par. 2): spoiled; ruined
induce (par. 2): cause; bring about
climax (par. 6): the highest point of interest or excitement
corn shocks (par. 7): a bunch of corn sheaves drawn together to
     dry
grisly renderings (par. 8): terrifying examples
crump-backed (par. 8): creased; humpbacked
caldron (par. 10): a large kettle
banshee (par. 10): a female spirit that warns of death
bereavements (par. 10): losses of people through death
serpentines (par. 10): coils
papier-mâché (par. 10): a material made of paper pulp that can
     be molded into objects when moist
vulnerable (par. 15): open to attack
disemboweled (par. 17): with the bowels or entrails removed

Halloweens I have always considered wilder and richer and more important than even Christmas morn. The dark and lovely memories leap back at me as I see once again my ghostly relatives, and the lurks and things that creaked stairs or sang softly in the hinges when you opened a door.

For, you see, I have been most fortunate in the selection of my aunts and uncles and midnight-minded cousins. My grandma gave me her old black-velvet opera cape to cut into batwings and fold about myself when I was eight. My aunt gave me some white candy fangs to stick in my mouth and make delicious and most terrible smiles. A great-aunt encouraged me in my withcrafts by painting my face into a skull and stashing me in closets to induce cardiac arrest in passing cousins or upstairs boarders. My mother corrupted me completely by introducing me to Lon Chaney in *The Hunchback of Notre Dame* when I was three.

In sum, Halloween has always been *the* celebration for me and mine. And those Halloweens in the late 1920s and early '30s come back to me now at the least scent of candlewax or aroma of pumpkin pies.

Autumns were a combination of that dread moment when you see whole windows of dime stores full of nickel pads and yellow pencils meaning School is Here—and also the bright promise of October, that stirring stuff which lurks in the blood and makes boys break out in joyful sweats, planning ahead.

For we *did* plan ahead in the Bradbury houses. We were three families on one single block in Waukegan, Ill. My grandma and, until he died in 1926, grandpa, lived in the corner house; my mom and dad, and my brother Skip and I, in the house next south of that; and around the block my Uncle Bion, whose library was wise with Edgar Rice Burroughs and ancient with H. Rider Haggard.

1928 was one of the prime Halloween years. Everything that was grandest came to a special climax that autumn.

My Aunt Neva was 17 and just out of high school, and she had a Model-A Ford. "Okay, kiddo," she said around about October 20. "It's coming fast. Let's make plans. How do we use the attics? Where do we put the witches? How many corn shocks do we bring in from the farms? Who gets bricked up in the cellar with the Amontillado?"

"Wait, wait, wait!" I yelled—and we made a list. 8 Neva drew pictures and made paintings of the costumes we would all wear to make the holiday truly fascinating and horrible. That was Costume Painting Night. When Neva finished, there were sketches of Grandma as the nice mother in "The Monkey's Paw," paintings of my dad as Edgar Allan Poe, some fine grisly renderings of my brother as crumpbacked Quasimodo, and myself playing my own xylophone skeleton as Dr. Death.

After that came, in one flying downpour, Costume 9 Cutting Night, Mask Painting Night, Cider Making Night, Candle Dippling and Taffy Pulling Night, and Phonograph Playing Night, when we picked the spookiest music. Halloween, you see, didn't just stroll into our yards. It had to be seized and shaped and *made* to happen!

My grandparents' home, then, was a caldron to 10 which we might bring hickory sticks that looked like witches' broken arms and leaves from the family graveyard out where the banshee trains ran by at night souling the air with bereavements. To their house, upstairs and down, must be fetched corn shocks from fields just beyond the burying tombs, and pumpkins. And from Woolworth's, orange-black crepe serpentines, and bags of black confetti which you tossed on the wind, yelling, "A witch just sneezed!" and papier-mâché masks that smelled like a sour dog's fur after you had snuffed in and out while running. All of it had to be fetched, carried, touched, held, sniffed, crunched along the way.

October 29 and 30 were almost as great as October 11 31, for those were the late afternoons, the cool, spicy dusks when Neva and Skip and I went out for the Slaughter and final Gathering.

"Watch out, pumpkins!" 12

I stood by the Model A as the sun furnaced the 13 western sky and vanished, leaving spilled-blood and burnt-pumpkin colors behind. "Pumpkins, if they had any brains, would hide tonight!" said I.

"Yeah," said Skip. "Here comes the Smiler with the 14 Knife!" I beamed, feeling my Boy Scout knife in my pocket.

We reached our uncles' farms and went out to dance 15 around the corn shocks and grab great armfuls and wrestle them like dry Indian ghosts back to the rumble seat. Then we went back to get the harvest-moon pumpkins. They burrowed in the cereal grass, but they could not escape the Smiler and his friends. Then home, with the cornstalks waving their arms wildly in the wind behind us, and the pumpkins thudding and running around the floorboards trying to escape. Home toward a town that looked vulnerable under burning clouds, home past real graveyards with real cold people in them, your brother and sister, and you thinking of them suddenly and knowing the true, deep sense of Halloween.

The whole house had to be done over in a few short, 16 wildly laughing hours. All staircases must be eliminated by grabbing leaves out of dining-room tables and covering the steps so you could only scrabble and slip up and then slide, shrieking, down, down, down into night. The cellar must be mystified with sheets hung on lines in a ghostly maze through which giggling and screaming banshees must blunder and flee, children suddenly searching for mothers, and finding spiders. The icebox must be stashed with chicken viscera, beef hearts, ox tongues, tripe, chicken legs and gizzards, so that at the height of the party the participants, trapped in the coal cellar, might pass around the "parts" of the dead witch: "Here's her heart! . . . Here's her finger! . . . Here's her eyeball!"

Then, everything set and placed and ready, you run 17 out late from house to house to make certain-sure that each boy-ghost remembers, that each girl-become-witch will be there tomorrow night. Your gorilla fangs in your mouth, your winged cape flapping, you come home and stand in front of your grandparents' house and look at how great and spooky it has become, because your sappy aunt and your loony brother and you yourself have magicked it over, doused the lights, lit all the disemboweled pumpkins and got it ready like a dark beast to devour the children as they arrive through its open-mouth door tomorrow night.

You sneak up on the porch, tiptoe down the hall, peer into the dim pumpkin-lit parlor and whisper: "Boo." 18

And that's *it*. 19

Oh, sure, Halloween arrived. Sure, the next night 20 was wild and lovely and fine. Apples swung in doorways to be nibbled by two dozen hungry mice-children. Apples and gargling kids almost drowned in water tubs while ducking for bites.

But the party was almost unimportant, wasn't it? 21 Preparation was 70 percent of the lovely, mad game. As with most holidays, the getting set, the gathering sulfur for the explosion, was sweeter, sadder, lovelier than the stampede itself.

That Halloween of 1928 came like the rusted moon 22 up in the sky—sailing, and then down like that same moon. And it was over. I stood in the middle of my grandma's living room and wept.

On the way home across the lawn to my house, I 23 saw the pile of leaves I had made just that afternoon. I ran and dived in, and vanished. I lay there under the leaves, thinking. This is what it's like to be dead. Under grass, under dirt, under leaves. The wind blew and stirred the grand pile. Way out in farm country, a train ran past, wailing its whistle. The sound cut my soul. I felt the tears start up again. I knew if I stayed I would never get out of the grass and leaves; I would truly be dead. I jumped up, yelling, and ran in the house.

Later, I went to bed. "Darn," I said in the middle of 24 the night.

"Darn what?" asked my brother, awake in bed beside 25 me.

"365 darn days until Halloween again. What if I die, 26 waiting?"

"Why, then," said my brother, after a long silence, 27 "you'll *be* Halloween. Dead people *are* Halloween."

"Hey," said I, "I never *thought* of that." 28

"Think," said my brother. 29

I thought: 365 days from now . . . 30

Gimme a pad, some paper. Neva, rev up that Model 31
A! Skip, hunch your back! Farmyards, grow pumpkins!
Graveyards, shiver your stones! Moon, rise! Wind, hit the
trees, blow up the leaves! Up, now, run! Tricks! Treats!
Gangway!

And a small boy in midnight Illinois, suddenly glad 32
to be alive, felt something on his face. Between the snail-
tracks of his tears . . . a smile.

And then he slept. 33

BUILDING VOCABULARY

1. Bradbury has often used informal expressions
in this essay. First, explain the meaning of the words in
italics in each group below. Then suggest a word or phrase
that an author who wished to be more formal might have
used instead.

    a. *"Okay, kiddo"* (par. 7)
    b. When we picked the *spookiest* music (par. 9)
    c. Your *sappy* aunt and your *loony* brother and
       yourself have *magicked* it over (par. 17)
    d. *Gangway!* (par. 31)

2. A number of figurative expressions (see page
383) spark this essay. In the list of examples of simile,
metaphor, and *personification* below, explain each figure.
(Personification is giving an object, thing, or idea lifelike or
human qualities.) What is being compared to what? What
other figures can you find in the essay?

    a. "Halloween, you see, didn't just stroll into our
yards. It had to be seized and shaped and made to happen"
(*personification*) (par. 9)
    b. "My grandparents' home was a caldron (*meta-
phor*) to which we might bring hickory sticks that looked
like witches' broken arms" (*simile*) (par. 10)

c. "Where *banshee* trains *ran* by at night" (*metaphor*) (par. 10)

d. "papier mâché masks that smelled *like* a *sour dog's fur*" (*simile*) (par. 10)

e. "The sun *furnaced* the Western sky (*personification*) and vanished, leaving *spilled blood* and *burnt pumpkin colors* behind" (*metaphor*) (par. 13)

UNDERSTANDING THE WRITER'S IDEAS

1. What part of the essay most clearly states the author's purpose?

2. What two things did autumn signify to Bradbury?

3. What were some of the various activities for the Bradburys before October 29?

4. Why were October 29 and 30 almost as great as October 31? What did Bradbury and Neva and Skip do?

5. What is the "true, deep sense of Halloween"?

6. How did the young Bradburys change the house into a Halloween place?

7. How do the activities before Halloween compare with the activities after it? Which activities did the narrator prefer?

8. Why does the author say "Darn" in the middle of the night after Halloween? Why is he unhappy?

9. How does his brother ease Bradbury's unhappiness?

10. Why does the author smile just before he goes to sleep?

UNDERSTANDING THE WRITER'S TECHNIQUES

1. How is this essay an example of *illustration?* What examples does Bradbury give to show he has been lucky to have Halloween-minded relatives? How does he illustrate that "1928 was one of the prime Halloween years"?

2. The examples Bradbury offers to show the quality of the 1928 Halloween vary in their length and degree of development. Which examples are developed most fully?

3. In any essay of illustration the writer will often provide a simple listing of examples to demonstrate a point he is trying to make. Paragraph 15 offers a listing of details, but none of the examples is fully developed. Why does Bradbury use this technique here? What other paragraphs offer a listing of details to illustrate a point?

4. Check your responses to the question in Building Vocabulary 2. How do all the figurative expressions contribute to Bradbury's topic? How are most of the metaphors and similes related to the topic and to each other?

5. Underline some sentences that you think have the best sensory details. Where does the author use color? action? sound? smell?

6. Look at the last sentence in paragraph 9: "All of it had to be fetched, curried, touched, held, sniffed, crunched along the way." Why has Bradbury used so many verbs? What is the effect upon the reader?

7. It is clear that the style here is simple, direct, and informal. Why has the writer chosen such a style? How is it related to the topic of the essay? to the character represented in it?

8. What is the meaning of the title? Why do you think the author selected it? How does it reflect the personality of a young boy?

9. To enrich the meaning of an essay, a writer will often use *allusion,* a reference to some other work in literature (see page 379). The statement made by Aunt Neva, "Who gets bricked up in the cellar with the Amontillado?" is an allusion to a short story by Edgar Allan Poe, "The Cask of Amontillado." What is that brief story about? Why would Bradbury want to allude to Poe in this essay about Halloween? What other references to literature does the writer make (see paragraphs 2 and 8)? Explain them, or ask your instructor to if you are not familiar with them.

10. In what sequence has Bradbury presented the events in this essay? How has he used the order he selects

to create a kind of suspense, a building up from minor events to major ones?

11. Before he states his purpose in this essay, Bradbury offers a couple of paragraphs of introduction. What information does he deal with in his introduction? How does that information set the stage for the real point of the essay?

EXPLORING THE WRITER'S IDEAS

1. It is a strong statement to make that Halloween is "wilder and richer and more important than Christmas morn." Does Bradbury support his point well? In your experience, is Halloween so wild, so rich, and so important a holiday? Why? In your family, is there a special holiday for which everyone makes grand preparations? Describe it.

2. Bradbury's wild view of Halloween was, to a large degree, encouraged by his relatives' reaction to the holiday, too. How do your views about some holiday—like the Fourth of July, Thanksgiving, even Halloween—compare with or differ from the views of your relatives? In what cases do your relatives enrich your appreciation? detract from it?

3. What is the real significance of Halloween (check the dictionary or encyclopedia)? Why does that holiday still have a hold on the imagination of children today? Bradbury says that passing by a graveyard, he knew from the dead the "true deep sense of Halloween." Do you agree? Is *that* the true sense of Halloween?

4. Bradbury says in paragraph 20 that the party was less important than the preparation for it. Would you agree, in general, that the *preparation* for an event—such as a holiday, a wedding, a party—is often more important than the event itself? Explain your answer by giving a specific example from your own life.

5. How are Bradbury's feelings after Halloween is over typical of feelings any young child would have? How is he able to overcome these feelings? Are children generally able to cope with disappointment in the way young Bradbury has?

IDEAS FOR WRITING

Guided Writing

Write an essay of 500 words in which you *illustrate* the value to you of some holiday you celebrate.

    1. Write an introduction that builds up to your thesis, as Bradbury has. State in your thesis sentence just how you feel about the holiday. Is it a wild time, like Bradbury's Halloween, or deeply religious, or just a time of nonstop fun with marvelous meals and parties?

    2. Decide on an effective order for the illustrations you present. If you offer examples to support an idea about one particular holiday (the Christmas of 1977, for example) you might want to use chronology. If you present several examples (drawn over a number of years) to show why one holiday is important to you, you might again use chronology. But you might also want to tell the events according to their importance, saving the most important for last.

    3. Depending upon how many examples you offer, develop your illustrations with enough details. Some of your illustrations will require expanded treatment, others will not. In any case, offer at least three examples to support your point.

    4. Since you are drawing from your own experience, you will want to use sensory language—colors, smells, actions, sounds, images of touch. Try to use figurative expressions as effectively as Bradbury has.

    5. After you present and develop your illustrations, discuss in your conclusion how you feel after the holiday is over.

More Writing Projects

    1. In recent years, Halloween has become a rather dangerous holiday where innocent children often come to harm by thoughtless, mean adults. Write an essay of 350 to 500 words illustrating the dangers of Halloween. Or, write an essay in which you show by means of illustration what

steps your town or community takes to prevent Halloween accidents.

2. Write an essay in which you show how one relative shared in the joys or pains of your childhood experiences. Select as illustration important moments that you can narrate clearly and in concrete, sensory language.

3. Do some research about a local festival, the preparations for it, and the activities involved in its celebration. Or, you might choose to investigate a more remote festival in another part of the country, such as the chili contest in Texas, sausage festivals in Wisconsin, pie-eating contests associated with State Fairs. After you collect your research, write a four or five paragraph essay illustrating different features of this festival.

Annette Dula

NO HOME IN AFRICA

On a visit to Africa, Annette Dula, a teacher, discovered
some surprising things about her cultural roots as a black
American. Presenting a wide range of personal experiences, she develops her essay by means of illustration.
Notice how each illustration reinforces Dula's thesis in
this essay.

Words to Watch

anonymity (par. 2): not being known by others
servile (par. 4): like or characteristic of a slave
Mensaab (par. 4): a word of Hindu origin meaning "lady" or
    "mistress"
mercenary (par. 5): working for money only; greedy
rejoiced (par. 11): made glad or happy; delighted
unescorted (par. 13): not accompanied
resented (par. 14): felt displeasure
galled (par. 14): irritated; annoyed
docile (par. 17): easy to teach or discipline
typify (par. 20): to be typical of
reciprocal (par. 20): on both sides; done, felt, or given in return

I have no cultural roots in Africa nor do I want any. 1
I have discovered that Egypt is not black Africa. The skin

isn't black enough and the hair isn't kinky enough. An Egyptian merchant put his light brown arm next to my black arm and said, "My skin isn't black but I'm African, too." Sincerity was not in his voice.

In Khartoum, the Sudan, a near-riot developed 2 when I appeared to be an African woman walking down the street in a leather miniskirt. I liked melting into the anonymity of hundreds of black faces, but I also wanted the freedom that tourists enjoy.

I went to Ethiopia with Kay, who is white. The 3 people were hostile. They pelted me with rotten tomatoes. They did not bother Kay. Didn't they realize that I was black like them?

In East Africa, the Africans were too servile toward 4 whites. I got extremely angry when a gnarled little old man would bow down and call my friend "Mensaab." An African woman would not become angry.

I hated the mercenary Indians of East Africa more 5 than the Africans hated them. Two years after the incident, I can still taste the bitterness. I wanted to buy material for a blouse. At the time, most shopkeepers in East Africa were Indians. I had walked in ahead of Kay. The shopkeeper continued talking to another Indian. Kay walked in. The shopkeeper rushed up to her.

"Can I help you, madam?" he asked, with the proper 6 servility.

"My friend wants to buy material," she said. 7

"How much does she want to pay for it?" he asked. 8

"Perhaps you'd better talk to her, sir." 9

Completely ignoring her suggestion, he continued 10 explaining to Kay the virtues of expensive imported materials over cheaper native ones. "You know, these Africans are lazy. They just aren't capable of the superior quality you get in Western work!"

I walked out. I knew what prejudice was—but not 11 this kind. This was the type my parents had known in North Carolina 25 years ago. I rejoiced when the Indians were kicked out of Uganda.

I do have the appearance of a black African. I have 12

even been asked by Africans. "To what tribe do you belong?" And, "From what part of Africa do you come?" When it was to my advantage to be considered African, it pleased me. At other times, embarrassing situations could develop.

Once when I was walking from a restaurant at 13 around 9:30 P.M., four or five policemen jumped out of a squad car, surrounded me, and pointed their loaded guns at me. Though they were speaking in Swahili, I soon gathered that I was being arrested on prostitution charges. The more I protested in English, the more incensed they became. I reacted as any American woman would. "Who do you think you are? Get those guns out of my face. I am an American. I want to call the Ambassador." (Later, I learned that Kenya had a new law making it illegal for unescorted African women to be on the street after 9:30 P.M.)

More often than not, I resented being treated as an 14 African by Africans. I was truly galled at the customs station between Zaire and the Central African Republic. Tourists usually pass customs by merely showing their passports. Africans are subjected to a thorough search. As I was about to move along with other tourists, I was roughly grabbed from behind and thrust back into the crowd. I had to be freed by other tourists. The mob attitude was: "Who do you think you are? You're not a tourist! You're one of us." Why didn't I protest the preferential treatment that tourists receive? Because I felt as the American tourists do: "We are entitled to these considerations."

When I understood that the average African male 15 has little respect for the female intellect, I was surprised. Ngimbus, a close friend of mine, decided that I was a militant feminist when I lectured him on male-female equality!

"She looks like an African, but she talks nonsense," 16 he said later.

Often, I found myself defending black Americans to 17 nationalist West-Africans. A favorite question was "Why do you call yourselves *Afro*-American?" I usually answered in terms of cultural heritage, identity oppression, and other nebulous words that explain nothing. The conversation would continue: "You have forfeited the right to call yourselves *Afro*-Americans. If you were worthy of the name *Afro*-, your people would never have taken all those years of such treatment. We sympathize with you, but you're too docile for us."

"What about South Africa and Mozambique?" I would always ask. 18

The question was usually ignored or if answered, 19 the time factor was brought in: "We have accomplished more in eighty years than you have accomplished in 400 years." The conversation always left me with a need to explain our differences. But there never were acceptable explanations.

My experiences in Africa typify the reciprocal mis- 20 understandings between black Americans and Africans. Our common color is not enough. Too much time has passed.

I am not patriotic, but I am a product of America. 21 I believe in freedom of speech, even if it is only token. I take education for granted though we may not receive it equally. I believe in the working of democracy even though it never seems to work. I am forced to accept that I am an American and that here in America lie my cultural roots—whether I like it or not.

BUILDING VOCABULARY

1. For each word in italics below, select the correct meaning.

a. an Egyptian *merchant*
1. marcher   2. lover   3. businessman   4. lawyer
5. policeman

b. *sincerity* was not in his voice
1. honesty   2. sweetness   3. love   4. lust
5. hoarseness

c. the people were *hostile*
1. farmers   2. horrible   3. unconcerned
4. unfriendly   5. peculiar

d. a *gnarled* little man
1. affectionate   2. twisted   3. graceful   4. weak
5. devoted

e. the more *incensed* they became
1. insensible   2. inspired   3. silent   4. angry
5. indirect
     f. *preferential* treatment
1. special   2. predictable   3. poor   4. prejudiced
5. anonymous
     g. a *militant* feminist
1. armed   2. aggressive   3. masculine   4. ridiculous
5. attractive
     h. cultural *heritage*
1. finance   2. value   3. religion   4. fear
5. tradition
     i. other *nebulous* words
1. vague   2. strong   3. clear   4. unimportant
5. undefinable
     j. you have *forfeited*
1. fulfilled   2. forgiven   3. established   4. questioned
5. given up

UNDERSTANDING THE WRITER'S IDEAS

1. Why, according to the author, is Egypt not part of black Africa?

2. What happened in Khartoum? in Ethiopia?

3. Why would an African woman not get angry if someone called a white person "Mensaab"?

4. Why was the author bitter about the incident with East African Indians? Why did the shopkeeper ignore her? Why does Dula say that this incident reminded her of the prejudice her parents experienced in North Carolina?

5. Why was the author treated differently from other tourists at the customs station between Zaire and the Central African Republic?

6. What did Ngimbas mean when he said, "She looks like an African, but she talks nonsense"? (par. 16)

7. How did Dula defend black Americans to West Africans? Why do you think she felt it necessary to do so?

8. Why does the author say she is a product of America and that in America lie her cultural roots?

9. What is the main point of the essay? Which sentence states it most clearly?

UNDERSTANDING THE WRITER'S TECHNIQUES

1. In your own words explain the illustrations Dula offers to show that

a. it was hard to be a "free" tourist as a black in Africa

b. African men have little respect for the female intellect

c. there was hostility directed towards her

d. unescorted black women were not allowed on the streets after 9:30 p.m. in Kenya

e. she did not like being treated like an African by Africans

2. Dula developed her illustrations in different ways and with different degrees of detail. Where does she use narration? Where does she use description?

3. Which illustration does she develop with the most details? Why do you think she chose to emphasize that one? To develop the incidents in Khartoum and in Ethiopia, the author presents very few details. Why? How do they help build up to the incident with the Indians?

4. Where does Dula attempt to compare and/or contrast? How does her purpose in writing this essay almost *demand* certain comparisons and contrasts? (See pp. 107–108.)

5. Dula arranges her illustrations by *place* order; that is, she offers an example first about one geographical area and then about another. When she names a new place, it serves as a *transition* to a new example. However, she uses other techniques—words or phrases—to join her examples together smoothly. What transitions has she used in this way? Make a list of several. Where does Dula *repeat* or *refer back to* her main point in order to provide clear transitions?

6. From the kind of language and sentence struc-

ture she uses, to what kind of audience is Dula speaking? Why has she not used more informal language? How do her purpose and the quality of her style match?

EXPLORING THE WRITER'S IDEAS

1. Part of Dula's disappointment comes, it would seem, from what she expected her treatment to be like as a black in Africa. How do you think she expected to be treated?

2. Dula suggests enormous differences in the way black and white tourists are treated in Africa. Do these differences exist for black and white tourists in America? in Europe? Draw from your own experience, if you can, or check with friends or relatives who have traveled.

3. In several places (paragraphs 1, 12, 19), Dula questions the ability of skin color to join people together. Why might you agree (or disagree) with her comment, "Our common color is not enough"? Would you say that *religion* is not enough? *nationality?* What would you say *is* enough to join people together?

4. The author says, "When it was to my advantage to be considered African it pleased me." At other times she was not pleased to be considered African. How is Dula's position typical of the way most people would feel under similar circumstances? Do you think it all right to "straddle the fence," so to speak, to be one thing at a time when it serves you well and to be something else when it does not serve you well? (A black man or woman in white America is often denied that privilege. Why?)

5. Why do Africans question the phrase *Afro*-American for American blacks? Are their questions reasonable? Dula suggests that conditions in South Africa and Mozambique should be weighed against criticism that Afro-Americans are too docile. What happened in those countries? How did Africans respond to the author's point? Are their answers convincing to you? Why?

6. Do you agree with the points Dula makes in the last paragraph? How do you explain the last sentence?

IDEAS FOR WRITING

Guided Writing

Using illustration as your means of development, write an essay (500 to 750 words) in which you show how your race, religion, nationality, or sex makes people behave toward you in a special way.

    1.   Determine the way people react to you because of your race, religion, nationality or sex; try to state that reaction in a word or two. If you are black, for example, do people *fear* you or *talk down* to you? If you are a woman, do people think you are *unintelligent* or *passive*?

    2.   Make sure that the illustrations you present support your point. Draw examples from your own experience. Develop some examples more completely than others.

    3.   Use concrete, sensory detail to make your examples real for your reader.

    4.   Decide on your audience for this essay. Select your language and sentence structure to reach that audience most effectively.

    5.   Determine an effective order for the illustrations you present. You might want to discuss things according to time order, taking the incident or situation that occurred first. Or, you might want to arrange the examples, saving the most important for last. If you are drawing incidents from different geographical areas, you may want to use place order.

More Writing Projects

    1.   Write an illustrative essay in which you discuss disappointments you experienced as a traveler.

    2.   Write an essay in which you illustrate how your view of certain things is different from the view of most people of your age, sex, religion, race, or nationality.

Betty Friedan

THE HAPPY HOUSEWIFE HEROINE

Betty Friedan has been a strong supporter of women's rights and one of the most active leaders in the American feminist movement. In her book, *The Feminine Mystique,* she deals with stereotypes of the woman's role and with the problems created by those stereotypes. In this selection Friedan uses several types of illustration—drawn from letters, magazines, historical occurrences, and other places—to explore the condition of the housewife.

Words to Watch

oddity (par. 1): strangeness; peculiarity
Victorian (par. 2): a period in English history (1831–1901), characterized by middle-class respectability and stuffiness
geiger counter (par. 3): an instrument used to detect radiation
discrepancy (par. 3): disagreement; difference; inconsistency
desperation (par. 3): the state of having so little hope as to cause despair
primer-size (par. 4): the size of a textbook
chicanery (par. 4): trickery
commuting (par. 4): moving; traveling
frivolous (par. 6): not serious; silly
hegemony (par. 6): departure from the regular or normal
anomaly (par. 6): something out of the ordinary; unusual

Why have so many American wives suffered this 1
nameless aching dissatisfaction for so many years, each one
thinking she was alone? "I've got tears in my eyes with
sheer relief that my own inner turmoil is shared with other
women," a young Connecticut mother wrote me when I first
began to put this problem into words. A woman from a town
in Ohio wrote: "The times when I felt that the only answer
was to consult a psychiatrist, times of anger, bitterness and
general frustration too numerous to even mention, I had no
idea that hundreds of other women were feeling the same
way. I felt so completely alone." A Houston, Texas, housewife
wrote: "It has been the feeling of being almost alone with
my problem that has made it so hard. I thank God for my
family, home and chance to care for them, but my life
couldn't stop there. It is an awakening to know that I'm not
an oddity and can stop being ashamed of wanting something
more."

That painful guilty silence, and that tremendous 2
relief when a feeling is finally out in the open, are familiar
psychological signs. What need, what part of themselves,
could so many women today be repressing? In this age after
Freud, sex is immediately suspect. But this new stirring in
women does not seem to be sex; it is, in fact, much harder
for women to talk about than sex. Could there be another
need, a part of themselves they have buried as deeply as the
Victorian women buried sex?

If there is, a woman might not know what it was, 3
any more than the Victorian woman knew she had sexual
needs. The image of a good woman by which Victorian ladies
lived simply left out sex. Does the image by which modern
American women live also leave something out, the proud
and public image of the high-school girl going steady, the
college girl in love, the suburban housewife with an up-and-
coming husband and a station wagon full of children? This
image—created by the women's magazines, by advertisements, television, movies, novels, columns and books by
experts on marriage and the family, child psychology, sexual
adjustment and by the popularizers of sociology and psychoanalysis—shapes women's lives today and mirrors their

dreams. It may give a clue to the problem that has no name, as a dream gives a clue to a wish unnamed by the dreamer. In the mind's ear, a geiger counter clicks when the image shows too sharp a discrepancy from reality. A geiger counter clicked in my own inner ear when I could not fit the quiet desperation of so many women into the picture of the modern American housewife that I myself was helping to create, writing for the women's magazines. What is missing from the image which shapes the American woman's pursuit of fulfillment as a wife and mother? What is missing from the image that mirrors and creates the identity of women in America today?

In the early 1960's *McCall's* has been the fastest 4 growing of the women's magazines. Its contents are a fairly accurate representation of the image of the American woman presented, and in part created, by the large-circulation magazines. Here are the complete editorial contents of a typical issue of *McCall's* (July, 1960):

1. A lead article on "increasing baldness in women," caused by too much brushing and dyeing.
2. A long poem in primer-size type about a child, called "A Boy Is A Boy."
3. A short story about how a teenager who doesn't go to college gets a man away from a bright college girl.
4. A short story about the minute sensations of a baby throwing his bottle out of the crib.
5. The first of a two part intimate "up-to-date" account by the Duke of Windsor on "How the Duchess and I now live and spend our time. The influence of clothes on me and vice versa."
6. A short story about a nineteen-year-old girl sent to a charm school to learn how to bat her eyelashes and lose at tennis. ("You're nineteen, and by normal American standards, I now am entitled to have you taken off my hands, legally and financially, by some beardless youth who will spirit you away to a one-and-a-half-room apartment in the Village while he

learns the chicancry of selling bonds. And no beardless youth is going to do that as long as you volley
to his backhand.")
7. The story of a honeymoon couple commuting
between separate bedrooms after an argument over
gambling at Las Vegas.
8. An article on "how to overcome an inferiority
complex."
9. A story called "Wedding Day."
10. The story of a teenager's mother who learns how
to dance rock-and-roll.
11. Six pages of glamorous pictures of models in
maternity clothes.
12. Four glamorous pages on "reduce the way the
models do."
13. An article on airline delays.
14. Patterns for home sewing.
15. Patterns with which to make "Folding Screens—
Bewitching Magic."
16. An article called "An Encyclopedic Approach to
Finding a Second Husband."
17. A "barbecue bonanza," dedicated "to the Great
American Mister who stands, chef's cap on head,
fork in hand, on terrace or back porch, in patio or
backyard anywhere in the land, watching his roast
turning on the spit. And to his wife, without whom
(sometimes) the barbecue could never be the smash-
ing summer success it undoubtedly is . . ."

There were also the regular front-of-the-book "serv- 5
ice" columns on a new drug and medicine developments,
childcare facts, columns by Clare Luce and by Eleanor
Roosevelt, and "Pots and Pans," a column of readers' letters.
    The image of woman that emerges from this big, 6
pretty magazine is young and frivolous, almost childlike;
fluffy and feminine; passive; gaily content in a world of
bedroom and kitchen, sex, babies, and home. The magazine
surely does not leave out sex; the only passion, the only
pursuit, the only goal a woman is permitted is the pursuit

of a man. It is crammed full of food, clothing, cosmetics, furniture, and the physical bodies of young women, but where is the world of thought and ideas, the life of the mind and spirit? In the magazine image, women do no work except housework and work to keep their bodies beautiful and to get and keep a man.

This was the image of the American in the year 7 Castro led a revolution in Cuba and men were trained to travel into outer space; the year that the African continent brought forth new nations, and a plane whose speed is greater than the speed of sound broke up a Summit Conference; the year artists picketed a great museum in protest against the hegemony of abstract art; physicists explored the concept of anti-matter; astronomers, because of new radio telescopes, had to alter their concepts of the expanding universe; biologists made a breakthrough in the fundamental chemistry of life; and Negro youth in Southern schools forced the United States, for the first time since the Civil War, to face a moment of democratic truth. But this magazine, published for over 5,000,000 American women, almost all of whom have been through high school and nearly half to college, contained almost no mention of the world beyond the home. In the second half of the twentieth century in America, woman's world was confined to her own body and beauty, the charming of man, the bearing of babies, and the physical care and serving of husband, children, and home. And this was no anomaly of a single issue of a single women's magazine.

BUILDING VOCABULARY

1. Friedan uses several words related to psychology and emotional and mental states of people. Check the words below in a dictionary and write a clear meaning for each. Then write a sentence of your own in which you use the word correctly.

      a. turmoil (par. 1)
      b. frustration (par. 1)
      c. repressing (par. 2)

d. image (par. 3)
e. reality (par. 3)
f. fulfillment (par. 3)
g. psychoanalysis (par. 3)
h. identity (par. 3)

2. Use five words from the Words to Watch section in sentences of your own.

UNDERSTANDING THE WRITER'S IDEAS

1. What is the problem the author tried to put into words? What is the general point that the women from Connecticut, Ohio, and Texas all seem to be making?

2. According to the author, what is the image by which modern American women live? How does this image (in Friedan's opinion) compare with the image that emerges from *McCall's*, a women's magazine? What has been left out of both of these images?

3. What does Friedan see as the image of the housewife and the reality of a housewife's situation?

4. Why does Friedan name *McCall's* instead of some other magazine for women? Discuss in your own words the contents of the July 1960 issue. What impression do you have of the materials *McCall's* was trying to present to the American woman? What impression of the American woman of the 1960s do you get from the contents?

5. What does Friedan say was missing from the contents of the magazine? Why do you think the editors did not include articles like the ones Friedan suggests?

UNDERSTANDING THE WRITER'S TECHNIQUES

1. As you probably realized, *illustration* may serve as a way to organize information in a sentence, in a paragraph, or in an entire essay. In paragraph 3, which sentences give several illustrations (explain what you think the sentences are trying to illustrate)? How is paragraph 1 a good example of the technique of illustration? What three

examples does Friedan use there? What point is she trying to illustrate? What other paragraph offers illustrations?

2. The writers of the other essays in this section all use the first person ("I") as does Friedan, and their own personal experience to support their points. Where does Friedan use her own experience? What other kinds of supporting details does she use?

3. You learned earlier about "listing" as a kind of illustration: The writer will present a series of examples (none of which is developed to any degree) to support an idea. Friedan, instead of offering several examples in a paragraph to illustrate the "complete editorial contents" of *McCall's,* gives the reader a numbered list. Why do you think she chooses this method of illustration? What effect does it have upon the reader? How does the numbered list compare with the illustrations in the last paragraph of this selection?

4. In this short selection the author asks some questions. Why does she ask so many?

5. Look at the title. What does it mean? How is it *ironic?* (See p. 386.) What effect does repetition of the "h" sound at the start of each word have on the *tone?* (See p. 391.) How happy *is* the housewife heroine?

EXPLORING THE WRITER'S IDEAS

1. Make a list of the questions the author raises. How would you answer some of them? Why has Friedan herself not answered many of them?

2. Would you agree that many American wives suffer from "the nameless aching dissatisfaction" Friedan sees? Can you name the dissatisfaction? What would you name it? Is it possible for some women not to be dissatisfied in their roles as housewives? How?

3. What were some of the qualities of a "good" woman by Victorian standards? What difficulties did Victorian women have in meeting those standards (check an encyclopedia or some book in your library)?

4. How does the image of the modern American woman today compare with the image Friedan saw that existed in the sixties? What changes in that image do you see around you? Would you say those changes are for the better or for the worse? Why?

5. Look at a current issue of *McCall's*. Make a list of the editorial contents (in your own words) of the magazine. How is it different from or similar to the issue Friedan used? What image of the American woman does today's *McCall's* present? Look at some other magazines for women—*Ms.*, *Madamoiselle*, *Good Housekeeping*—and explain the image they portray of the modern female.

6. Friedan says that, according to the image set by *McCall's*, "the only pursuit, the only goal a woman is permitted is the pursuit of a man." Do women today still have that goal? Why? How has the "Total Woman" concept supported that goal? Why have many feminists opposed it?

7. What is Friedan's implied attitude about men?

IDEAS FOR WRITING

Guided Writing

Write an essay in which you illustrate the advances (or lack of advances) made by today's woman.

1. Select either one area—politics, jobs, education, status, for example—or two or three areas. The quantity and kind of detail you want to offer should tell you how many areas to cover.

2. Make your point clearly and strongly in the first paragraph.

3. Try not to draw from your own personal experience in offering details in this essay. You might want to consider one (or more) of these suggestions for gathering detail.

    a. conduct personal interviews with women in your neighborhood or in the area where you work or go to school.

    b. quote (or paraphrase—that is, tell in your own

words) from an interview you saw on television, heard on the radio, at a lecture, or at a rally.

    c. quote or paraphrase from newspaper or magazine articles you have read.

    d. study some graphs and charts which offer data on women's progress and explain the data in your own words.

    e. quote or paraphrase from current books on the feminist movement.

    4. Try to use different techniques of illustration. If your topic lends itself to a list somewhere in your essay, consider the value of offering a numbered list like Friedan's.

    5. Try raising some questions in your essay.

More Writing Projects

    1. Using illustration, write an essay in which you show today's image of the American man.

    2. Examine any "woman's" magazine of today and decide on three or four qualities of the modern woman you think it is trying to suggest. Illustrate those qualities by drawing examples from the contents of the magazine. Quote or paraphrase articles; describe advertisements or layouts; discuss photographs—use any of these to help make your point.

    3. Select a magazine from the 1940s and another from the 1970s. Leaf through the contents of both and make a list of comparisons and contrasts. How are the women dressed? What activities are they involved in? What *aren't* the women doing? Keep accurate records of the sources you use. After examining both magazines, develop a five-paragraph essay contrasting the presentation of women in the 1940s and 1970s.

four

Comparison and Contrast

Comparison and contrast is a method of analyzing likenesses and differences between two or more subjects. Writers use comparison and contrast simply because it is often the best way to explain something. An object or an idea can often be better understood only when its features stand next to those of another object or idea. We appreciate soccer when we compare it with football; we understand communism when we see it in the light of capitalism.

In *comparison,* the likenesses or similarities appear in a carefully organized manner. In *contrast,* the approach centers on the differences between two items. Often you will employ only comparison or only contrast in an essay, but it is also possible to combine both methods in the same paper.

You frequently make comparisons and contrasts in the course of your daily life. If you have to select an accounting course during registration, you might find out about the instructors for the various sections before making a choice. If you are in the market for a new car, you might locate comparative performance ratings for models that interest you most. If you are planning to buy ten packages of hot dogs for a barbecue, you might check prices, product quality, and other details before choosing one brand over another. In all these cases, you employ a thought pattern that sorts out likenesses and differences and arrives at a decision based on a comparative analysis of items.

The pattern of comparison and contrast in writing is more carefully organized than the comparative pattern we employ in everyday situations. Yet both circumstances demand common sense. For one thing, any strong pattern of comparison and contrast treats items that are only in the same category or class. It makes little or no sense to compare an accounting teacher with a history teacher, a car with an ant, or a hot dog with a head of lettuce. Second, there always has to be a basis for your comparison; in other words, you compare or contrast two items in order to make a decision or choice about them. And third, you always try to deal with all important aspects of the things being compared before arriving at a final determination. These common-sense characteristics of comparison and contrast apply to our pattern of thought as well as to our pattern of writing.

When you write a comparison and contrast essay, you should begin by identifying clearly the subjects of your comparison and by establishing the basis of your comparison. The thesis sentence performs this function for you ("Professor Smith is a better accounting teacher than Professor Williams because he is more experienced, more structured, and more intelligent"). There are three main ways to present your points of comparison (block, alternating, and combination); each will be dealt with in detail in this chapter. It is necessary to note here, however, that in presenting your material you should maintain a balance in the treatment of the two subjects in your comparison. In other words you do not want to devote most of your essay to subject A, and only a small fraction to subject B. Proper arrangement and balance of items in a comparative essay is a major requirement.

Rachel Carson

A Fable For Tomorrow

Rachel Carson wrote a number of books and articles in
the 1950s and 1960s that alerted Americans to dangers
facing our natural environment. In this section from *Silent
Spring* (1962), look for the ways in which Carson establishes a series of contrasts for her imaginary American
town.

Words to Watch

migrants (par. 2): people, animals, or birds that move from one
    place to another
blight (par. 3): a disease or condition that kills or checks growth
maladies (par. 3): illnesses
moribund (par. 4): dying
pollination (par. 5): the transfer of pollen (male sex cells) from
    one part of the flower to another
granular (par. 7): consisting of grains
specter (par. 9): a ghost; an object of fear or dread
stark (par. 9): bleak; barren; standing out in sharp outline

There was once a town in the heart of America 1
where all life seemed to live in harmony with its surroundings. The town lay in the midst of a checkerboard of

prosperous farms, with fields of grain and hillsides of orchards where, in spring, white clouds of bloom drifted above the green fields. In autumn, oak and maple and birch set up a blaze of color that flamed and flickered across a backdrop of pines. Then foxes barked in the hills and deer silently crossed the fields, half hidden in the mists of the fall mornings.

Along the roads, laurel, viburnum and alder, great 2 ferns and wildflowers delighted the traveler's eye through much of the year. Even in winter the roadsides were places of beauty, where countless birds came to feed on the berries and on the seed heads of the dried weeds rising above the snow. The countryside was, in fact, famous for the abundance and variety of its bird life, and when the flood of migrants was pouring through in spring and fall people traveled from great distances to observe them. Others came to fish the streams, which flowed clear and cold out of the hills and contained shady pools where trout lay. So it had been from the days many years ago when the first settlers raised their houses, sank their wells, and built their barns.

Then a strange blight crept over the area and 3 everything began to change. Some evil spell had settled on the community: mysterious maladies swept the flocks of chickens; the cattle and sheep sickened and died. Everywhere was a shadow of death. The farmers spoke of much illness among their families. In the town the doctors had become more and more puzzled by new kinds of sickness appearing among their patients. There had been several sudden and unexplained deaths not only among adults but even among children, who would be stricken suddenly while at play and die within a few hours.

There was a strange stillness. The birds, for exam- 4 ple—where had they gone? Many people spoke of them, puzzled and disturbed. The feeding stations in the backyards were deserted. The few birds seen anywhere were moribund; they trembled violently and could not fly. It was a spring without voices. On the mornings that had once throbbed with the dawn chorus of robins, catbirds, doves, jays, wrens, and scores of other bird voices there was now no sound; only silence lay over the fields and woods and marsh.

On the farms the hens brooded, but no chicks 5 hatched. The farmers complained that they were unable to raise any pigs—the litters were small and the young survived only a few days. The apple trees were coming into bloom but no bees droned among the blossoms, so there was no pollination and there would be no fruit.

The roadsides, once so attractive, were now lined 6 with browned and withered vegetation as though swept by fire. These, too, were silent, deserted by all living things. Even the streams were now lifeless. Anglers no longer visited them, for all the fish had died.

In the gutters under the eaves and between the 7 shingles of the roofs, a white granular powder still showed a few patches; some weeks before it had fallen like snow upon the roofs and the lawns, the fields and streams.

No witchcraft, no enemy action had silenced the 8 rebirth of new life in this stricken world. The people had done it themselves.

This town does not actually exist, but it might easily 9 have a thousand counterparts in America or elsewhere in the world. I know of no community that has experienced all the misfortunes I describe. Yet every one of these disasters has actually happened somewhere, and many real communities have already suffered a substantial number of them. A grim specter has crept upon us almost unnoticed, and this imagined tragedy may easily become a stark reality we all shall know.

BUILDING VOCABULARY

1. In the second paragraph, find at least five concrete words that relate to trees, birds, and vegetation. How many of these objects could you identify? Look in a dictionary for the meanings of those words you do not know.

2. Try to identify the italicized words through the

context clues (see page 6) provided by the complete sentence.

  a. half-hidden in the *mists*. (par. 1)
  b. when the first settlers *raised* their houses. (par. 2)
  c. *stricken* suddenly at play. (par. 3)
  d. the hens *brooded*, but no chicks hatched. (par. 5)
  e. *Anglers* no longer visited them, for all the fish had died. (par. 6)

UNDERSTANDING THE WRITER'S IDEAS

  1. What is the quality of the world that Carson describes in her opening paragraph? If you had to describe it in just one or two words, which would you use?

  2. What are some of the natural objects that Carson describes in her first two paragraphs? Why does she not focus on simply one aspect of nature—like animals, trees, or flowers?

  3. How does Carson describe the "evil spell" that settles over the countryside?

  4. What does Carson mean when she declares, "It was a spring without voices?" (par. 4) Why does she show that the critical action takes place in the springtime?

  5. What do you think is the "white granular powder" that Carson refers to in paragraph 7? Why does she not explain what it is or where it came from?

  6. In paragraph 9, the author states her basic point. What is it? Does she offer a solution to the problem that she poses?

UNDERSTANDING THE WRITER'S TECHNIQUES

  1. What is the purpose of the description in this essay? Why does the writer use such vivid and precise words?

  2. A *fable* is a story with a moral; in other words, a fable is a form of teaching narrative. How does Carson structure her narrative in this essay?

3. Where in this essay does Carson begin to shift from an essentially optimistic tone to a negative one?

4. Does Carson rely on comparison or contrast in this essay?

5. In this selection Carson uses what we call *the block method* of comparison and contrast. The writer presents all information about one subject, and then all information about a second subject, as in the diagram below:

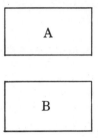

a. How does Carson use this pattern in her essay?

b. Are there actually two subjects in this essay, or two different aspects of one subject? How does chronology relate to the block structure?

c. Are the two major parts of Carson's essay equally weighted? Why or why not?

d. In the second part of the essay, does Carson ever lose sight of the objects introduced in the first part? What new terms does she introduce?

6. How can you explain paragraphs 8 and 9—which do not involve narration, description, or comparison and contrast—in relation to the rest of the essay? What is the nature of Carson's conclusion?

EXPLORING THE WRITER'S IDEAS

1. Today, chemicals are used to destroy crop insects, to color and preserve food, and to purify our water, among other things. Would Carson term this "progress"? Would you? Do you think that there are inadequate safeguards and

controls in the use of chemicals? What recent examples of chemical use have made the news?

2. Why would you agree or disagree that factories and corporations should protect the environment that they use? Should a company, for example, be forced to clean up an entire river that it polluted? What about oil spills?

3. Have there been any problems with the use of chemicals and the environment in your own area? Describe them. How do local citizens feel about these problems?

4. Do you think that it will be possible in the future for Americans "to live in harmony" with their natural surroundings? Why do you believe what you do?

IDEAS FOR WRITING

Guided Writing

Write a fable (an imaginary story) in which you contrast one aspect of the life of a person, community, or nation with another.

1. Begin with a phrase similar to Carson's "There was once. . . ." so that the reader knows you are writing a narrative fable.

2. Relate your story to an American problem.

3. Use the block method in order to establish your contrast. Write first about one aspect of the topic and then about the other.

4. Use sensory detail in order to make your narrative clear and interesting.

5. Make certain that you establish an effective transition as you move into the contrast.

6. In the second part of your essay, be sure to refer to the same points you raised in the first part.

7. Use the conclusion to establish the "moral" of your fable.

More Writing Projects

1. Write an essay that contrasts the behavior of a person you knew sometime ago with his or her current behavior.

2.   Develop a contrastive essay on a place you know well, one that has changed for better or worse. Explain the place as it once was, and as it is now. Use concrete images that appeal to color, action, sound, smell, and touch.

3.   Examine the two extremes of the ecology issue today.

4.   Using the block method, compare and contrast Carson's fable with the fable you wrote in Guided Writing.

J. William Fulbright

THE TWO AMERICAS

J. William Fulbright, a former senator from Arkansas, had great influence on the U. S. Congress during the 1960s. As an early opponent of the Vietnam War, he used his position as Chairman of the Senate Foreign Relations Committee to look carefully at American conduct and policies overseas. His book *The Arrogance of Power* examines the American character and politics. In this selection, Fulbright tells of two visions of America that he thinks are still in conflict.

Words to Watch

egotistical (par. 1): self-centered or selfish
solemn (par. 1): serious; sacred; according to strict form
pontificating (par. 1): speaking like a high priest or pope
judicious (par. 1): having sound judgement
arrogant (par. 1): full of pride and self-importance; overbearing
magnanimity (par. 2): the quality of being noble or generous
apprehension (par. 2): fear; anxiety
moralism (par. 3): moral teaching; moralizing
exemplified (par. 3): shown by example
impotence (par. 3): weakness; helplessness
intervention (par. 3): interference; a coming between
predominate (par. 4): to have influence or authority over others; to be dominant over others

There are two Americas. One is the America of 1 Lincoln and Adlai Stevenson; the other is the America of Teddy Roosevelt and the modern superpatriots. One is generous and humane, the other narrowly egotistical; one is self-critical, the other self-righteous; one is sensible, the other romantic; one is good-humored, the other solemn; one is inquiring, the other pontificating; one is moderate, the other filled with passionate intensity; one is judicious and the other arrogant in the use of great power.

We have tended in the years of our great power to 2 puzzle the world by presenting to it now the one face of America, now the other, and sometimes both at once. Many people all over the world have come to regard America as being capable of magnanimity and farsightedness but no less capable of pettiness and spite. The result is an inability to anticipate American actions which in turn makes for apprehension and a lack of confidence in American aims.

The inconstancy of American foreign policy is not 3 an accident but an expression of two distinct sides of the American character. Both are characterized by a kind of moralism, but one is the morality of decent instincts tempered by the knowledge of human imperfection and the other is the morality of absolute self-assurance fired by the crusading spirit. The one is exemplified by Lincoln, who found it strange, in the words of his second Inaugural Address, "that any man should dare to ask for a just God's assistance in wringing their bread from the sweat of other men's faces," but then added: "let us judge not, that we be not judged." The other is exemplified by Theodore Roosevelt, who in his December 6, 1904, Annual Message to Congress, without question or doubt as to his own and his country's capacity to judge right and wrong, proclaimed the duty of the United States to exercise an "internal police power" in the hemisphere on the ground that "Chronic wrongdoing, or an impotence which results in a general loosening of the ties of civilized society, may in America . . . ultimately require intervention by some civilized nation. . . ." Roosevelt of course never questioned that the "wrongdoing" would be done by our Latin neighbors and we of course were the "civilized nation" with the duty to set things right.

After twenty-five years of world power the United 4
States must decide which of the two sides of its national
character is to predominate—the humanism of Lincoln or
the arrogance of those who would make America the world's
policeman. One or the other will help shape the spirit of the
age—unless of course we refuse to choose, in which case
America may come to play a less important role in the
world, leaving the great decisions to others.

BUILDING VOCABULARY

1. Without checking your dictionary, try to figure
out the meanings of the words in italics from the way the
writer uses them in the sentences of his essay.

  a. one is generous and *humane* (par. 1)
  b. one is moderate, the other filled with *passionate
intensity* (par. 1)
  c. *tempered* by the knowledge of human imperfection
(par. 3)
  d. fired by the *crusading* spirit (par. 3)
  e. *exemplified* by Lincoln (par. 3)
  f. his own or his country's *capacity* (par. 3)

2. You can sometimes figure out the meaning of a
difficult word if you know what some prefixes and suffixes
mean. In each of these words from Fulbright's essay, certain
prefixes and suffixes are underlined. On a separate piece of
paper, write the meaning of the prefix or suffix, and give the
meaning of the word.

  a. superpatriots
  b. self-critical
  c. farsightedness
  d. pettiness
  e. imperfection
  f. proclaimed
  g. hemisphere
  h. impotence
  i. predominate

UNDERSTANDING THE WRITER'S IDEAS

1. Explain what Fulbright means when he states, "There are two Americas."

2. Why does America frequently "puzzle the world"?

3. What are the two definitions that Fulbright gives for "moralism"?

4. What did Lincoln mean when he declared it strange "that any man should dare to ask for a just God's assistance in wringing their bread from the sweat of other men's faces"? This statement Fulbright quotes is a figurative statement (see page 383). Why is Lincoln talking of *bread* and *sweat*?

UNDERSTANDING THE WRITER'S TECHNIQUES

1. How does Fulbright organize the first paragraph? What is its function? Why does he use so many semicolons? What effect do they have on the style?

2. Identify the topic sentences for paragraphs 2, 3, and 4. What is their function? Which of these sentences best captures Fulbright's main point for the essay?

3. Along with the block method (see page 380), the *alternating method* is a helpful way to organize comparison and contrast essays. With the alternating method, the writer gives a point-by-point treatment of both subjects A and B. The effect looks like this:

| A |
| B |

| A |
| B |

| A |
| B |

In other words, both subjects A and B are presented in each paragraph. Something is said about one and then about the other as the writer discusses some feature of his topic.

a. Examine the first paragraph. List all the aspects of the America of Lincoln and Stevenson, and then all the aspects of the America of Teddy Roosevelt and the super-patriots. Is Fulbright dealing with similarities or differences?

b. How is the long third sentence in paragraph 1 (beginning "One is generous and humane . . .") a good example in itself of the alternating method?

c. Identify sentences in paragraphs 2 and 3 that reflect the alternating method.

d. Can you think of any advantages that the alternating method might have over the block method? any disadvantages?

4. What are the key transitional words that Fulbright uses in his essay? How do these transitional words (like his use of semicolons) permit him to achieve an interesting balance in arranging parts of his sentences?

5. How effective is Fulbright's use of quotation in paragraph 3? Why doesn't he simply *paraphrase,* that is, say in his own words, what Lincoln and Roosevelt said?

EXPLORING THE WRITER'S IDEAS

1. To what extent do you agree with Fulbright that there are "two Americas"?

2. What examples of America's "arrogant" use of great power can you think of? Would the Vietnam War or the Watergate break-in qualify as examples? Do you think we have learned anything from these events?

3. What do you think foreigners believe about the American character? Have you ever had an opportunity to speak with someone from another country about his or her attitude toward America? What did that person think was the main *strength* or *weakness* of the American character?

4. Is there such a thing as "false" morality? How do you distinguish it from "true" morality?

5. What do you think are the best qualities in the American experience?

6. Fulbright hints that in the future America might play a less important role in world affairs. Do you think that this is a real possibility? Are there any indications that it is already happening?

IDEAS FOR WRITING

Guided Writing

Write an essay on the thesis: "There are two Americas."

1. Base your essay on your own personal observations or on things you have read or heard from reliable sources.

2. Plan to use the alternating method of development in the essay.

3. Pick out at least three points of comparison or contrast for development. For instance, the contrast between wealth and poverty in America could be one useful subtopic.

4. Write clear topic sentences for your middle paragraphs.

5. Use effective transitional words that aid you in swinging back and forth between your subjects.

6. Try to use at least one exact quotation which helps support a point you wish to make. Go back to the third paragraph in Fulbright's essay and study the way the quotes are punctuated. Where do the commas and periods stand in relation to the quotation marks?

7. In your concluding paragraph, either offer a solution to the problem of the "two Americas," or indicate the future direction the problem might take.

More Writing Projects

1. Using the alternating method, compare three or four features of life in America today with life in another country.

2. Write an essay in which you compare and contrast by the alternating method Fulbright's essay with Carson's.

3. Write an essay in which you compare and contrast your view of America in 2000 A.D. with your view of America today. Use the alternating method.

John Lame Deer

THE GREEN FROG SKIN

Many essays involving comparison and contrast are organized in a less formal way than the block method seen in Rachel Carson's "A Fable For Our Time," or the alternating method in Fulbright's "The Two Americas." In this essay, John Lame Deer, a Sioux Indian, examines white and Indian attitudes toward a common subject. John Lame Deer's plan of organization seems to fit the subject naturally; he does not force any one method of comparison and contrast, but the resulting essay is convincing and well unified. As you read, try to discover how John Lame Deer lets the reader see the similarities and differences so basic to his subject.

Words to Watch

gally-hooting (par. 2): racing
buffalo chips (par. 3): buffalo droppings that are permitted to dry and are then used as fuel.

The green frog skin—that's what I call a dollar bill. 1
In our attitude toward it lies the biggest difference between Indians and whites. My grandparents grew up in an Indian world without money. Just before the Custer battle the

white soldiers had received their pay. Their pockets were full of green paper and they had no place to spend it. What were their last thoughts as an Indian bullet or arrow hit them? I guess they were thinking of all that money going to waste, of not having had a chance to enjoy it, of a bunch of dumb savages getting their paws on that hardearned pay. That must have hurt them more than the arrow between their ribs.

The close hand-to-hand fighting, with a thousand horses gally-hooting all over the place, had covered the battlefield with an enormous cloud of dust, and in it the green frog skins of the soldiers were whirling around like snowflakes in a blizzard. Now, what did the Indians do with all that money? They gave it to their children to play with, to fold those strange bits of colored paper into all kinds of shapes, making them into toy buffalo and horses. Somebody was enjoying that money after all. The books tell of one soldier who survived. He got away, but he went crazy and some women watched him from a distance as he killed himself. The writers always say he must have been afraid of being captured and tortured, but that's all wrong. 2

Can't you see it? There he is, bellied down in a gully, watching what is going on. He sees the kids playing with the money, tearing it up, the women using it to fire up some dried buffalo chips to cook on, the men lighting their pipes with green frog skins, but mostly all those beautiful dollar bills floating away with the dust and the wind. It's this sight that drove that poor soldier crazy. He's clutching his head, hollering, "Goddam, Jesus Christ Almighty, look at them dumb, stupid, red sons of bitches wasting all that dough!" He watches till he can't stand it any longer, and then he blows his brains out with a six-shooter. It would make a great scene in a movie, but it would take an Indian mind to get the point. 3

The green frog skin—that was what the fight was all about. The gold of the Black Hills, the gold in every clump of grass. Each day you can see ranch hands riding over this land. They have a bagful of grain from their saddle horns, and whenever they see a prairie-dog hole they toss 4 a handful of oats in it, like a kind little old lady feeding the pigeons in one of your city parks. Only the oats for the prairie dogs are poisoned with strychnine. What happens to the prairie dog after he has eaten this grain is not a pleasant thing to watch. The prairie dogs are poisoned, because they eat grass. A thousand of them eat up as much grass in a year as a cow. So if the rancher can kill that many prairie dogs he can run one more head of cattle, make a little more money. When he looks at a prairie dog he sees only a green frog skin getting away from him.

For the white man each blade of grass or spring of 5 water has a price tag on it. And that is the trouble, because look at what happens. The bobcats and coyotes which used to feed on prairie dogs now have to go after a stray lamb or a crippled calf. The rancher calls the pest-control officer to kill these animals. This man shoots some rabbits and puts them out as bait with a piece of wood stuck in them. That stick has an explosive charge which shoots some cyanide into the mouth of the coyote who tugs at it. The officer has been trained to be careful. He puts a printed warning on each stick reading, "Danger, Explosive, Poison!" The trouble is that our dogs can't read, and some of our children can't either.

And the prairie becomes a thing without life—no 6 more prairie dogs, no more badgers, foxes, coyotes. The big birds of prey used to feed on prairie dogs, too. So you hardly see an eagle these days. The bald eagle is your symbol. You see him on your money, but your money is killing him. When a people start killing off their own symbols they are in a bad way.

The Sioux have a name for white men. They call 7 them *wasicun*—fat-takers. It is a good name, because you have taken the fat of the land. But it does not seem to have agreed with you. Right now you don't look so healthy— overweight, yes, but not healthy. Americans are bred like stuffed geese—to be consumers, not human beings. The moment they stop consuming and buying, this frog-skin world has no more use for them. They have become frogs themselves. Some cruel child has stuffed a cigar into their mouths and they have to keep puffing and puffing until they explode. Fat-taking is a bad thing, even for the taker. It is especially bad for Indians who are forced to live in this frog-skin world which they did not make and for which they have no use.

BUILDING VOCABULARY

1.   The author refers to money as "the green frog skin." Check your dictionary or thesaurus under "money" and make a list of several other words and terms that we use for money. From your list, select any five and explain their similarities and differences.

2.   In this piece, Lame Deer uses some slang expressions. *Slang* is an informal vocabulary, usually colorful and lively. Explain each use of slang in italics below; then rewrite the statement in standard English:

a.   "I guess they were thinking . . . of *a bunch of dumb* savages *getting their paws* on that *hard-earned pay*." (par. 1)

b.   "he *blows his brains out* with a six-shooter." (par. 3)

c.   "they are in a *bad way*." (par. 6)

UNDERSTANDING THE WRITER'S IDEAS

1.   What is the Indian attitude toward money? How does the term "green frog skin" suggest this attitude? What is the white American's attitude toward it?

2.   Why does Lame Deer refer to Custer? What happened to Custer and his men? How does Lame Deer explain the fate of the lone survivor? Does Lame Deer's justification for the suicide appear a sensible or exaggerated one? Explain.

3.   Explain in your own words what happens once the modern day rancher drops strychnine pellets down the prairie-dog holes.

4.   Why do the Sioux call the white men "fat-takers"?

5.   What is Lame Deer's main point in this essay? Which sentence or sentences come closest to stating that point most clearly?

6.   What does Lame Deer mean when he says that Americans "have become frogs themselves"?

UNDERSTANDING THE WRITER'S TECHNIQUES

1.   How does the author develop comparison and contrast in this essay? Does he use the block or alternating method?

2.   At what point does he move from past to present? How does the present compare with the past?

3.   List several sentences that contain especially vivid description.

4.   Examine paragraph 3. How does Lame Deer maintain a focus on both the white man and the Indian? Does the writer expect you to believe his account of the survivor's last end? Why does he offer it?

5.   How would you define the tone of this essay? How is the tone established through situations described by Lame Deer?

6.   Is there any irony (see page 386) in this selection? At what point or points? Is the irony bitter at any time? If so, give examples.

7.   Lame Deer uses a number of figurative expressions, especially *similes* and *metaphors* (see pages 387 and 389). Make a list of a few that are most clear.

8.   What effect do the use of figures of speech and the use of slang have on the author's style? Do they make it *informal, silly, unserious?* Why does the author avoid "highbrow" language?

9.   A *symbol* is normally a concrete object, a thing in itself, which stands for something else. When a word functions as a symbol, it moves our understanding from the concrete to the abstract (see page 390). Thus a wooden cross might symbolize the idea of Christianity; the American flag the idea of patriotism, and so forth.

a.   What is the main symbol in Lame Deer's essay?

b.   Is there another symbol in this essay? In what paragraph does it occur?

c.   What do frogs suggest to you? Does the use of a frog betray the author's attitude toward white men?

EXPLORING THE WRITER'S IDEAS

1. Do you agree with Lame Deer's idea that Americans, more so than people of other nations, love money too much? Does the love of money depend on some racial or ethnic quality; or, would you say that the love of money grows from social or economic conditions and attitudes? Defend your opinion.

2. What would it be like to grow up in a world without money? How would you eat and clothe yourself? How would you be rewarded for your labor? Make a list of some problems and some positive effects you can imagine.

3. Lame Deer says at the very end of this selection, "It is especially bad for Indians who are forced to live in this frog-skin world which they did not make and for which they have no use." Do you think that this is a fair explanation of the difficulties in the Indian's relationship to American society today? Was the Indian world before the white man came completely free of "money" in any sense?

4. Does the author idealize Indians? Why or why not?

5. What similar ideas do Rachel Carson and John Lame Deer share about the American land? Do you agree with them?

IDEAS FOR WRITING

Guided Writing

Write an essay to compare or contrast the younger and older generation's attitude toward money.

1. Establish the topic common to your two groups in the first sentence of the essay. Make the first sentence your thesis sentence.

2. Feel free to invent situations that reveal the attitudes of your subjects toward the common topic or problem.

3. Make your own attitude apparent throughout the essay.

4. Just as Lame Deer uses "green frog skin" throughout the essay in order to maintain a constant focus, try to achieve a similar effect by repeating a phrase that illuminates your topic.

5. Save one last important point for the concluding paragraph. Write at least six sentences in this paragraph.

6. Use figurative expressions (and slang) that effectively serve your purpose. Adjust your style to an informal audience (college newspaper, local newspaper, students in a local auditorium).

More Writing Projects

1. Explain the changes in the attitudes concerning a "practical" education of college students in the 1960s and those in the 1970s.

2. Take two groups of people, two nations, two political systems, or the two sexes and compare and contrast their attitudes toward a common subject. For instance, you could compare men's and women's attitudes toward sports; black and white conceptions of "soul"; a capitalist's and a communist's attitude toward money.

Bruno Bettleheim

FAIRY TALES AND MODERN STORIES

Bruno Bettleheim was born in Austria in 1903 and came to the United States in 1939. For many years he has been one of the major child psychologists in the world. In this selection, taken from *The Uses of Enchantment* (1976), Bettleheim compares fairy tales and realistic stories, analyzing the effect that they have on both children and adults. As you read this essay, keep in mind the various stories he is comparing.

Words to Watch

realistic (par. 1): having to do with real things
props (par. 1): supports
elaboration (par. 1): a thing worked out carefully
rankled (par. 1): caused pain or resentment
idyllic (par. 2): pleasing and simple
protracted (par. 2): drawn out
gratifications (par. 2): things that cause satisfaction
sustained (par. 3): maintained; supported; comforted
effected (par. 4): brought to pass; accomplished
consolation (par. 5): comfort
vagaries (par. 5): odd notions; unexpected actions
extricating (par. 5): setting free; getting out of; releasing
prevail (par. 5): to triumph; to gain the advantage
asocial (par. 5): unsocial

The shortcomings of the realistic stories with which 1
many parents have replaced fairy tales is suggested by a
comparison of two such stories—"The Little Engine That
Could" and "The Swiss Family Robinson"—with the fairy
tale of "Rapunzel." "The Little Engine That Could" encourages the child to believe that if he tries hard and does not
give up, he will finally succeed. A young adult has recalled
how much impressed she was at the age of seven when her
mother read her this story. She became convinced that one's
attitude indeed affects one's achievements—that if she would
now approach a task with the conviction that she could
conquer it, she would succeed. A few days later, this child
encountered in first grade a challenging situation: she was
trying to make a house out of paper, gluing various sheets
together. But her house continually collapsed. Frustrated,
she began to seriously doubt whether her idea of building
such a paper house could be realized. But then the story of
"The Little Engine That Could" came to her mind; twenty
years later, she recalled how at that moment she began to
sing to herself the magic formula "I think I can, I think I
can, I think I can . . ." So she continued to work on her paper
house, and it continued to collapse. The project ended in
complete defeat, with this little girl convinced that she had
failed where anybody else could have succeeded, as the Little
Engine had. Since "The Little Engine That Could" was a
story set in the present, using such common props as engines
that pulled trains, this girl had tried to apply its lesson
directly in her daily life, without any fantasy elaboration,
and had experienced a defeat that still rankled twenty years
later.

Very different was the impact of "The Swiss Family 2
Robinson" on another little girl. The story tells how a
shipwrecked family manages to live an adventurous, idyllic,
constructive, and pleasurable life—a life very different from
this child's own existence. Her father had to be away from
home a great deal, and her mother was mentally ill and
spent protracted periods in institutions. So the girl was
shuttled from her home to that of an aunt, then to that of
a grandmother, and back home again, as the need arose.

During these years, the girl read over and over again the story of this happy family who lived on a desert island, where no member could be away from the rest of the family. Many years later, she recalled what a warm, cozy feeling she had when, propped up by a few large pillows, she forgot all about her present predicament as she read this story. As soon as she had finished it, she started to read it over again. The happy hours she spent with the Family Robinson in that fantasy land permitted her not to be defeated by the difficulties that reality presented to her. She was able to counteract the impact of harsh reality by imaginary gratifications. But since the story was not a fairy tale, it merely gave her a temporary escape from her problems; it did not hold out any promise to her that her life would take a turn for the better.

Consider the effect that "Rapunzel" had on a third 3 girl. This girl's mother had died in a car accident. The girl's father, deeply upset by what had happened to his wife (he had been driving the car), withdrew entirely into himself and handed the care of his daughter over to a nursemaid, who was little interested in the girl and gave her complete freedom to do as she liked. When the girl was seven, her father remarried, and, as she recalled it, it was around that time that "Rapunzel" became so important to her. Her stepmother was clearly the witch of the story, and she was the girl locked away in the tower. The girl recalled that she felt akin to Rapunzel because the witch had "forcibly" taken possession of her, as her stepmother had forcibly worked her way into the girl's life. The girl felt imprisoned in her new home, in contrast to her life of freedom with the nursemaid. She felt as victimized as Rapunzel, who, in her tower, had so little control over her life. Rapunzel's long hair was the key to the story. The girl wanted her hair to grow long, but her stepmother cut it short; long hair in itself became the symbol of freedom and happiness to her. The story convinced her that a prince (her father) would come someday and rescue her, and this conviction sustained her. If life became too difficult, all she needed was to imagine herself as Rapunzel, her hair grown long, and the prince loving and rescuing her.

"Rapunzel" suggests why fairy tales can offer more 4
to the child than even such a very nice children's story as
"The Swiss Family Robinson." In "The Swiss Family Robinson," there is no witch against whom the child can discharge
her anger in fantasy and on whom she can blame the father's
lack of interest. "The Swiss Family Robinson" offers escape
fantasies, and it did help the girl who read it over and over
to forget temporarily how difficult life was for her. But it
offered no specific hope for the future. "Rapunzel," on the
other hand, offered the girl a chance to see the witch of the
story as so evil that by comparison even the "witch" stepmother at home was not really so bad. "Rapunzel" also
promised the girl that her rescue would be effected by her
own body, when her hair grew long. Most important of all,
it promised that the "prince" was only temporarily blinded—
that he would regain his sight and rescue his princess. This
fantasy continued to sustain the girl, though to a less intense
degree, until she fell in love and married, and then she no
longer needed it. We can understand why at first glance the
stepmother, if she had known the meaning of "Rapunzel" to
her stepdaughter, would have felt that fairy tales are bad
for children. What she would not have known was that
unless the stepdaughter had been able to find that fantasy
satisfaction through "Rapunzel," she would have tried to
break up her father's marriage and that without the hope
for the future which the story gave her she might have gone
badly astray in life.

It seems quite understandable that when children 5
are asked to name their favorite fairy tales, hardly any
modern tales are among their choices. Many of the new tales
have sad endings, which fail to provide the escape and
consolation that the fearsome events in the fairy tale require
if the child is to be strengthened for meeting the vagaries
of his life. Without such encouraging conclusions, the child,
after listening to the story, feels that there is indeed no
hope for extricating himself from his despairs. In the traditional fairy tale, the hero is rewarded and the evil person
meets his well-deserved fate, thus satisfying the child's deep
need for justice to prevail. How else can a child hope that
justice will be done to him, who so often feels unfairly

treated? And how else can he convince himself that he must act correctly, when he is so sorely tempted to give in to the asocial proddings of his desires?

BUILDING VOCABULARY

1. *Jargon* is specialized vocabulary that appears in a certain profession or discipline. Bettleheim might be expected to use a certain amount of jargon from psychology (fortunately, he keeps it to a minimum). Try to figure out what Bettleheim means by the following terms:

    a. fantasy elaboration (par. 1)
    b. imaginary gratifications (par. 2)
    c. escape fantasies (par. 4)
    d. fantasy satisfaction (par. 4)
    e. asocial proddings (par. 5)

2. Write sentences in which you use the following words correctly:

    a. *impressed* (par. 1)
    b. *conviction* (par. 1)
    c. *impact* (par. 2)
    d. *predicament* (par. 2)
    e. *victimized* (par. 3)
    f. *astray* (par. 4)
    g. *sorely* (par. 5)

3. Would you say that the level of vocabulary in this essay is concrete or abstract? Why?

UNDERSTANDING THE WRITER'S IDEAS

1. Check in the children's book section of your library to summarize the stories and fairy tales Bettleheim discusses. How many stories is he examining in this essay?

2. What is the most important similarity between *The Little Engine That Could* and *The Swiss Family Robinson?*

3. What is the effect on children of *The Little Engine That Could*? How does it influence the adult whom Bettleheim introduces in paragraph 1?

4. How does Bettleheim summarize the story of *The Swiss Family Robinson*? Does this story, according to the author, have a beneficial effect on adults with problems?

5. Explain why "Rapunzel" was so important to the girl who had lost her mother in the car accident.

6. Why do fairy tales benefit readers more than modern fairy tales and realistic stories do? What do traditional fairy tales provide?

7. What does Bettleheim mean by his last sentence, "And how else can he convince himself that he must act correctly, when he is so sorely tempted to give in to the asocial proddings of his desires?"

UNDERSTANDING THE WRITER'S TECHNIQUES

1. Where does Bettleheim state his main point? How clear is his statement of it? Does he indicate in his thesis sentence his plan of development for the essay?

2. How does Bettleheim order his essay in terms of comparison and contrast? What is interesting about the pattern he chooses?

3. Where does the writer use narration? Why does he use it? How does it support the technique of comparison and contrast?

4. What is the function of paragraph 1? of paragraph 2? of paragraph 3?

5. How does the writer organize paragraph 4?

6. Is the same amount of emphasis given to "Rapunzel" as to the two "realistic" tales? Why or why not?

7. In concluding paragraphs of comparison and contrast papers, it is common to bring the two subjects together for a final observation. Does Bettleheim follow this strategy? How does he organize his subjects in the last paragraph?

8. How does Bettleheim achieve clear transitions from paragraph to paragraph? Discuss some of the words he uses so that his ideas are connected together clearly.

EXPLORING THE WRITER'S IDEAS

1.   Bettleheim suggests that certain types of fairy tales help us to cope with problems. Do you agree or disagree? What particular fairy tale do you remember that might help a child deal with his or her problems?

2.   Why do most children clearly take delight from traditional fairy tales?

3.   Look again at Bettleheim's psychoanalysis of the three children whom he uses as examples in his essay. Do you accept his explanations of their behavior? How might his ideas be criticized by other psychologists?

4.   Which fairy tales—traditional or modern—appealed to you as a child? Why were you so fond of them?

5.   If exposure to certain types of fairy tales can affect us seriously, then what can we conclude about our exposure to stories on television, film, and other types of media? Is it fair to generalize about television from Bettleheim's argument?

IDEAS FOR WRITING

Guided Writing

Write an essay in which you compare and/or contrast two or three fairy tales or stories that you remember from early childhood. Or, do the same for two films, two television programs, two newspapers, or two subjects from another media form.

1.   State the purpose of your comparison as soon as you can.

2.   Decide on the best pattern of development (block, alternating, or a combination of both) for your purposes.

3.   List the point of comparison or contrast that you plan to cover for each subject.

4.   Be certain to support each point with substantial detail. Summarize parts of stories that bear out your point. Quote where you have to.

5.   Make certain that, in the closing paragraph, you draw conclusions about all the subjects treated.

More Writing Projects

1.   Write an essay in which you compare or contrast two newspapers or magazines. Be prepared to compare and contrast their contents, and also to indicate the type of audience at which they are aimed. Write a comparative paper on your findings.

2.   Compare and contrast the style of writing of any two writers in this section.

3.   Select two heroes or heroines from popular children's stories or fairy tales; compare and contrast the two characters in regard to personality and behavior.

five

Definition

Definition is a way of explaining an important word so that the reader knows, as exactly as possible, what you mean by it. You probably have written essays requiring short "dictionary definitions" of words that were not clear to the reader. However, there are terms that require longer definitions because they may be central to the writer's thought. When an entire essay focuses on the meaning of a key word or group of related words, you will need to employ "extended definition" as a method of organization.

Words requiring extended definition tend to be abstract, controversial, or complex. Terms like "freedom," "pornography," and "communism" reflect the need for extended definition. Such words depend on extended definition because they are often confused with some other word or term; because they are easily misunderstood; or because they are of special importance to the writer, who chooses to redefine the term for his or her own purposes. We can, of course, simply offer an extended definition of a word for the sake of definition itself; this is valid. But it is normal for us to have opinions about complex and controversial words, and, consequently, to employ extended definition for the purpose of illuminating a thesis. The word "abortion" could be defined objectively, with the writer tracing its history, explaining its techniques, and describing its effects on the patient. Yet many writers asked to provide an extended definition of "abortion" would have strong personal opinions about the term. They would want to develop a thesis about it, perhaps covering much of the same ground as the objective account, but taking care that the reader understands the word as they do. It is normal for us to have our own opinion about any word, but in all instances we must make the reader understand fully what we mean by it.

Writers use several techniques to develop extended definitions. One common strategy is to define some general group to which the subject belongs (for instance, the "mallard" is a member of a larger group of ducks), and to show how the word differs from all other words in that general group. A second technique is to give the etymology of a word—its origin and history in the language—to help the reader. Yet another method of extended definition is to deal with what you do *not* mean by the term—a technique called "negation." Finally, many methods already learned can be used profitably in extended definition. You can define a word by narrating an event that reveals its meaning; you can provide specific examples, even a simple listing, to illustrate what you mean by a term; you can compare and contrast related terms; you can describe details that help to establish meaning.

Extended definition involves no single pattern of essay organization, but rather a group of available strategies that you use depending on your purpose and on the word itself. The word selected may be ordinary and relatively concrete like "chocolate," or abstract and complex like "immobilization." Often, as in the essays here on the "international insult" and on "roots," the definition is never directly stated, but is understood or put together from the information a writer gives. Because so many methods can be applied effectively in an essay of extended definition, you should be able to organize and develop this type of composition easily.

Wayne W. Dyer

IMMOBILIZATION

Dr. Wayne W. Dyer, a therapist and counselor, believes that people *can* realize their own potential if they learn to change any emotional behavior that defeats happiness. Here in a chapter from his book *Your Erroneous Zones* he explains through definition a key word in his approach to understanding feelings. Notice how he uses illustration to strengthen his definition.

Words to Watch

brood (par. 3): think about unhappily; sulk
gnawing (par. 3): eating away at; irritating
abusive (par. 3): insulting
twitching (par. 3): moving jerkily and suddenly
cut a wide swath (par. 4): create a great impression
virtually (par. 4): essentially; practically
strategy (par. 4): plan of action

As you consider your potential for choosing happiness, keep in mind the word *immobilization* as the indicator of negative emotions in your life. You might believe that anger, hostility, shyness and other similar feelings are worth having at times, and so you want to hang on to them. Your guide should be the extent to which you are in any way immobilized by the feeling.

Immobilization can range from total inaction to mild 2 indecision and hesitancy. Does your anger keep you from saying, feeling, or doing something? If so, then you are immobilized. Does your shyness prevent you from meeting people you want to know? If so, you are immobilized and missing out on experiences that are rightfully yours. Is your hate and jealousy helping you to grow an ulcer or to raise your blood pressure? Does it keep you from working effectively on the job? Are you unable to sleep or make love because of a negative present-moment feeling? These are all signs of immobilization. *Immobilization:* A state, however mild or serious, in which you are not functioning at the level that you would like to. If feelings lead to such a state, you need to look no further for a reason to get rid of them.

Here is a brief checklist of some instances in which 3 you may be immobilized. They range from minor to major states of immobility.

You are immobilized when . . .

You can't talk lovingly to your spouse and children though you want to.

You can't work on a project that interests you.

You don't make love and would like to.

You sit in the house all day and brood.

You don't play golf, tennis, or other enjoyable activities, because of a leftover gnawing feeling.

You can't introduce yourself to someone who appeals to you.

You avoid talking to someone when you realize that a simple gesture would improve your relationship.

You can't sleep because something is bothering you.

Your anger keeps you from thinking clearly.

You say something abusive to someone that you love.

Your face is twitching, or you are so nervous that you don't function the way you would prefer.

Immobilization cuts a wide swath. Virtually all 4 negative emotions result in some degree of self-immobility, and this alone is a solid reason for eliminating them entirely from your life. Perhaps you are thinking of occasions when a negative emotion has a payoff, such as yelling at a young child in an angry voice to emphasize that you do not want him to play in the street. If the angry voice is simply a device for emphasis and it works, then you've adopted a healthy strategy. However, if you yell at others not to make a point, but because you are internally upset, then you've immobilized yourself, and it's time to begin working at new choices that will help you to reach your goal of keeping your child out of the street without experiencing feelings that are hurtful to you.

BUILDING VOCABULARY

1. You have already seen how prefixes and suffixes affect the meanings of words. Each of these words from the essay you just read begins with *in*. After you check a dictionary, explain whether or not the element *in* has the same meaning or use in each word:

> indicator (par. 1)
> inaction (par. 2)
> indecision (par. 2)
> instance (par. 3)
> internally (par. 4)

2. Examine the definitions in the Words to Watch section on page 141. Write an original sentence that uses each word correctly.

UNDERSTANDING THE WRITER'S IDEAS

1. What negative feelings might be worth having at times according to Dyer?

2. How can immobilization "range from total in-action to mild indecision and hesitancy"?

3. What is Dyer's definition of *immobilization?* Quote exactly the sentence that states the definition in the essay. Which part of the definition gives the general group into which immobilization fits? Which part of the definition gives the special qualities that distinguish the word from others in the general group?

4. What specific examples of immobility does the writer offer?

5. How may the use of a negative emotion be a healthy strategy in dealing with people? How may the use of a negative emotion immobilize someone, according to the writer?

UNDERSTANDING THE WRITER'S TECHNIQUES

1. How does the opening paragraph serve as an introduction to Dyer's purpose in this brief selection? Which sentence serves as a thesis sentence?

2. Why does Dyer offer a definition of the word "immobilization" at the end of paragraph 2? Why does he ask a series of questions just before providing the definition? Do the questions lead effectively to that definition? Is it a good technique to build in this way to the word Dyer wishes to define?

3. Check the word "immobilization" in a dictionary. How does Dyer's definition contrast with the dictionary definition? How do the differences in meaning explain why Dyer wrote this chapter? If he could define the word in one sentence, why does he need four paragraphs to extend that definition?

4. Why has the writer offered a simple listing to explain states of immobility? What effect does the repetition of the word "you" have upon the reader?

5. Does the final paragraph serve as an effective conclusion? How does the discussion of the effects of negative emotion contribute to our understanding of immobilization as Dyer uses that word?

EXPLORING THE WRITER'S IDEAS

1. Do you believe that people have the potential for choosing happiness? Or, do you believe that circumstances in life (more than individual choice) create states of happiness or sadness?

2. Do you agree that there are negative feelings that are worth having at times? Give an example from your own life of how anger, hostility, or shyness may be healthy or unhealthy strategies in dealing with people.

3. Have you ever been immobilized in the sense that Dyer means? When?

4. Which items in the checklist of instances in which immobilization occurs do you think most people have experienced? Would you agree that the examples do indeed suggest immobilization?

5. In the last paragraph Dyer shows how the expression of a negative emotion "has a payoff." Do you agree that, if an angry voice is simply a device for emphasis, it is a healthy strategy? In the instance of a child playing in the street, does an angry voice serve its purpose? Would it matter, do you think, if the reasons for yelling at that moment stemmed from the person's internal feelings?

6. In general, are people's expressions of anger more a result of healthy strategies for emphasis or more a result of hurtful internal feelings? Explain your response with an example.

IDEAS FOR WRITING

Guided Writing

Write an extended definition of some negative emotion, like *fear, shyness, anger, hate, loneliness, depression,* or some other that you think needs defining.

1. In your first paragraph write an introduction which names the emotion with which you will be dealing.

2. Build up to a one-sentence definition of the word. You might want to ask a series of questions which will point out situations in which the emotion works negatively.

3. In your one-sentence definition, explain exactly and clearly your definition of the emotion. And you should also, in that sentence, be sure to name the general group to which the word belongs, and also the special qualities which distinguish the word from others in the general group. Later in the paragraph, you might want to compare your definition of the word with a definition you took from a dictionary. Although Dyer does not do this, comparison is often very helpful in the writing of an extended definition.

4. As Dyer has done, include in your essay a simple listing illustrating some feature of your definition. You might want to list different ways people express the emotion; or you might want to list ways they deal with the emotion.

5. In your final paragraph explain how negative emotion can be a healthy strategy. If you think the emotion is never a healthy strategy in dealing with people, explain *that*. But in either case, give a specific example of a situation in which the emotion might appear, in order to make your point. (Dyer discusses the example of a parent raising a voice in anger to a child playing in the street.)

More Writing Projects

1. Take any important term or concept in psychology today and write an extended definition of it. You might choose *neurosis, paranoia, therapy, guilt, Freudian, complex,* or some other word.

2. Write your own extended definition of immobilization. In this essay narrate a specific instance from your own life in which you show how you were immobilized.

Richard David Story

A HISTORY OF CHOCOLATE

Quite often a reader can learn a great deal from an extended definition of a term already well known. The term that is central to this essay by Richard Story, a senior editor for *American Way* magazine, is in such a category. Although there is nothing abstract about the word "chocolate," at the same time, there is much information about this popular food that many people do not know. In this essay, look for Story's reliance on other rhetorical patterns to develop his extended definition.

Words to Watch

infamous (par. 1): notorious; having a bad reputation
contend (par. 2): maintain; argue
pods (par. 3): cases for seeds
patron (par. 3): champion; supporter
coffers (par. 3): chests or other places where valuables are kept
goblet (par. 4): a special drinking glass, often made of precious metal
confectioner (par. 8): one who sells candies or sweets
staple (par. 9): the chief item or commodity
limoge (par. 12): fine chinaware made in Limoges, France
truffles (par. 13): mushroomlike foodstuffs that grow underground

In 1642, the infamous chief minister of France, 1
Cardinal Richelieu, made one last request of the attendants
surrounding him on his deathbed: "Chocolate, chocolate,
chocolate!" Admittedly, the authenticity of Richelieu's request may have as much to do with creative history-telling
as does the George Washington of "I shall never tell a lie"
fame, but in so doing it does indicate both the historical
longevity and the very special love affair with *Theobroma
cacao* (from the Greek words *theos* and *broma* meaning "food
of the gods"), or what we know today as the miraculous,
magical substance, chocolate. *maintain a grue'*

Some say the cocoa bean, from which the taste and 2
matter we call chocolate is made, originated in the Amazon
basin of Brazil, others place it in the Orinoco valley of
Venezuela, while others contend that it is native to Central
America. Wherever it first grew, we know only for certain
that it has been cultivated for three or four thousand years
in hot, rainy climates, not more than twenty degrees north
or south of the equator. However, no historical reference to
chocolate existed until the year 1502 when Columbus, on
his fourth voyage to the New World, came upon a cargo ship
in the Mexican Pacific filled with silver, gold, rare jewels
and food. Among the latter, cocoa beans were included.
Sensing that they somehow must be special to have been
included in such distinguished company, he took them back
to Spain and presented them at the court of King Ferdinand
and Queen Isabella. However, no one—not even Columbus—
knew what these beans could be, and they were dismissed
without a second thought. Yet Columbus officially and quite
unknowingly introduced chocolate to Western civilization.

The Aztecs long believed that the god of the air 3
brought cocoa beans down from the heavens of paradise and
planted them as testimony to the specialness of this antique
civilization. When the tree bloomed into life and bore the
miraculous pods full of crunchy, shiny, brown beans, they
were picked and eaten. Universal wisdom and knowledge,
it was believed, would spring thereafter. In fact, the Aztec
ruler Montezuma was the foremost patron of the cocoa nut.
It is recorded that he kept a supply of some two million

supporter

pounds of the beans in his *chesto* coffers. Throughout Latin America, the beans were so treasured that they were used as money. One historian notes that in sixteenth-century Nicaragua, ten beans bought a rabbit and one hundred beans, a "relatively good slave."

Although Columbus has to be credited with the 4 official introduction of cocoa beans to Europe, it was Cortez who first introduced chocolate in one of the forms we know today: hot chocolate. When he met Montezuma on his famous trip to the Aztec land, he was served *chocatl* to drink hot from a huge golden ceremonial goblet. However, the Spaniards to whom he offered the recipe upon his return found the hot liquid too bitter and soon began sweetening and flavoring the beverage with sugar, vanilla and sometimes cinnamon. It became immensely popular with the Spanish court, and ladies of fashion ordered their servants to bring piping hot bowls of the delicacy to drink during church. But for more than a century, the brew was kept secret from the rest of Europe, until Spanish monks, who served it to travelers before sleep, leaked the secret to the rest of the continent.

In 1657, chocolate gained new popularity with the 5 establishment of chocolate houses throughout London. Gentlemen came from all over London and the surrounding areas to sip the "new" beverage of hot chocolate and to discuss politics, art and religion. It was also in these establishments that the present-day word "tip" was first used. Shiny brass boxes with a slit for a monetary token were attached to the exit doors and labeled "To Insure Promptness" (abbreviated tip).

Until this time, no one had even thought of making 6 chocolate into a substance for eating, only for drinking. Nobody knows exactly when or how, but at some point around the middle of the eighteenth century, someone decided to extract the powder from the beans and mold it into a block for eating. A milestone in the history of chocolate manufacturing was reached in 1828, when C. J. Van Houten of Holland developed a process by which most of the fat could be removed from cocoa beans. The resulting by-product, cocoa butter, was mixed with finely ground sugar and cocoa and then molded into bars. Fifty years later, Daniel Peter in the tiny Swiss village of Vevey added milk to the mixture, combined forces with his friend, Henri Nestle, who had already begun to manufacture sweetened condensed milk, combined the two and created milk chocolate.

America got a slow start on both the introduction 7 and the subsequent manufacturing of chocolate. She has since made up for it, and today imports 225,000 tons of cocoa beans a year or about one-sixth of the world's supply. In fact, one American consumes about seventeen pounds of candy a year, about two-thirds of which is chocolate—a record beaten only by the Swiss who each consume some twenty-five pounds per year. Chocolate was unknown in America until 1775, when raw cocoa beans were imported for the first time by Massachusetts traders who sailed to South America and the West Indies. These beans required extensive processing, and in 1765, an Irish immigrant, John Hannon—with the financial backing of a wealthy doctor—established the first American chocolate factory in Dorchester, Massachusetts. It is not surprising that a doctor financed the first chocolate factory. For at that time, doctors were desperate to improve the taste of unpleasant medicines and hence their business. Chocolate proved the cure.

After that, chocolate spread throughout the Colonies 8 and throughout the rest of America. In the mid-nineteenth century, the age of penny candy was born. Chocolate until then had been produced in huge planks—eighteen inches long, two inches thick and twelve inches wide. Shopkeepers found the marketability of chocolate in this size unprofitable, and began hammering and chiseling the chocolate like an uncut diamond until they broke the board into bite-sized pieces and sold it in bags for a penny a chocolate. Simultaneously, chocolate-covered candies were created and shortly afterwards, the chocolate box. In 1870, a New England confectioner realized that he was going to have to close down his shop if he didn't quickly invent some way to hold his coconut creams and the like together. By the time customers brought them home, the candies were nothing but one big pool of sticky sweets. So he decided to cover them in a thick chocolate glaze and sell them this way. Richard Cadbury also had complaints from customers that the chocolate chips he sold from those huge planks were squashed and mangled by the time they were brought home. He hit upon the idea of a small box, divided into about fifteen compartments— each for a piece of his chocolate.

However, chocolate has not only been associated 9 with the sweet tooth, but as far back as 1775, General Braddock's army (in which George Washington fought) included provisions of chocolate for emotional and physical health. In 1898, during the Spanish-American War, chocolate was shipped in massive amounts to American soldiers in the Philippines. One-ounce chocolate cakes were issued as part of the "survival" kit to GIs abroad during World War I; and during World War II, four ounces of chocolate were a staple for soldiers, with U.S. manufacturers setting aside half of their production for the armed services. In 1953, when Sir Edmund Hillary and his party climbed to the top of Mount Everest, they were well equipped with chocolate as a source of high-energy. Even the *Gemini* astronauts were given chocolate in space. Moreover, research at the University of Pennsylvania School of Medicine (published in the *Journal of the American Medical Association*) showed no cause-and-effect relationship between chocolate and acne. Dental research at the University of Texas and at Harvard indicated that the consumption of chocolate milk "makes no significant difference" in the development of cavities.

It is, however, the romantic, delicious and sometimes 10 naughty connotations of chocolate that make it a weakness worldwide, and it has as many different customs and uses throughout the world as it has calories. In Mexico, chocolate is used in the preparation of a hot, spicy gravy—*molé* sauce— that is ladled, along with apples and spices, over beef, poultry and vegetables. A hot, aromatic chocolate drink is served at birthday parties in Iceland, and Vienna is famous for one of the most delectable desserts in the world: *sachertorte,* made from paper thin slices of chocolate cake, spread between layers with fruity jams. But in Honduras, chocolate probably receives its most romantic use. A man presents a chocolate box to a woman, and if she accepts the chocolate, she also has accepted his proposal of marriage.

Likewise in America, chocolate—especially choco- 11 late candy—is the stuff that dreams are made of. Fashionable Europeans have long considered fine chocolates as necessary to gracious living as fresh flowers and vintage wines. They are served not merely as an in-between-meal snack but to complement contrasting gourmet foods, while in the U.S., school children are familiar with such names as M & M, Hershey, Three Musketeers, Almond Joy and Russell Stover almost before they have learned their multiplication tables. Recently a whole new breed of chocolates and chocolatiers has suddenly sprung to life with a much more European tradition.

Godiva chocolates were born in Belgium where when 12 a baby is christened, a marriage takes place or a birthday occurs, fine chocolate is given as a gift. Each box of chocolate from the elegant boutiques is a work of art in both the quality of chocolate and in the packaging (some containers, priced up to $250, are made of Russian lacquered wood and French limoge porcelain). At first exclusively European, Godiva chocolate can now be found throughout the United States and ordered from such stores as Bloomingdale's and Neiman-Marcus.

In 1841, Domingo Ghiradelli sailed from Italy to San 13 Francisco and founded Ghiradelli Chocolate Manufactory and some of the finest chocolates in the world. They can be bought only from their original San Francisco base. In New York City, Plumbridge, a ninety-three-year-old family run confectionery, attracts an international clientele. Just around the corner from Plumbridge on Madison Avenue is Kron Chocolatier, known as the "eighth wonder of the modern world" to chocolate lovers. The romantic, aromatic little shop (more like an old-fashioned country kitchen with marble top surfaces for the making of chocolate) is run by Mr. Kron himself. His products range from giant Christmas, valentine and Easter cards made out of his own special blend of chocolate to hand-dipped strawberries and life-sized chocolate sculpture. Mr. Kron is also a professor of chocolates. Throughout the year his store offers an intensive four-week course in chocolate that includes just about everything you always wanted to know about chocolate: how to make Cognac and chocolate cherries, chocolate truffles and the like.

Today, chocolate is considerably different from the *chocatl* Cortez drank at the court of Montezuma. What began as a "food of the gods" is now a nutritional staple on all round trips to the moon. In 1785, Thomas Jefferson wrote: "The superiority of chocolate both for health and nourishment I hope will soon give it the same preference in America which it has in Europe." If he only knew. 14

BUILDING VOCABULARY

1. *Trite language* refers to words and expressions that have been overused, and, consequently, have lost much of their effectiveness. People rely on trite language in their conversation but should not use it often in writing. Of course, a good writer will be able to introduce such vocabulary at strategic points. Examples from Story's essay are given below. Explain in your words what they mean:

    a. "without a second thought" (par. 2)
    b. "a milestone in history" (par. 6)
    c. "got a slow start" (par. 7)
    d. "hit upon the idea" (par. 8)

2. What is your dictionary's meaning of "chocolate"? How does a "lexical" (or dictionary) definition differ from an extended definition?

3. What connotations do the following words, which are drawn from the first paragraph of Story's essay, have for you? Make a list of at least five for each.

    a. deathbed
    b. creative
    c. fame
    d. magical
    e. chocolate

UNDERSTANDING THE WRITER'S IDEAS

1. What connection does Story find between Cardinal Richelieu's deathbed request and George Washington's "I shall never tell a lie" statement?

2. Where is the cocoa bean grown? What conditions are necessary for its growth?

3. Who introduced cocoa beans to Europe? Who introduced hot chocolate to Europe?

4. What was the attitude of South American natives toward the cocoa bean?

5. Explain how the word "tip" originated.

6. Describe the process by which chocolate is made.

7. How did early Americans refine the process of chocolate manufacture and distribution?

8. For what purposes has chocolate been used in the United States?

9. What are some of the "romantic, delicious, and sometimes naughty" connotations associated with chocolate today?

10. Identify the following historical figures: Richelieu; King Ferdinand and Queen Isabella; Montezuma; C. J. Van Houten; Henri Nestle; John Hannon; Richard Cadbury; Domingo Ghiradelli.

UNDERSTANDING THE WRITER'S TECHNIQUES

1. What is the tone of this essay?

2. Analyze the introductory paragraph. Why does Story begin with an anecdote? How does he incorporate definition into it? In what way does the opening help set the tone of the essay?

3. What is the function of narration in the development of this essay? What time span does the writer cover? Does the essay progress in straight historical sequence? Which paragraphs seem to use historical flashbacks? Finally, how useful is narration to extended definition?

4. Is only the term "chocolate" defined in this essay, or are there other supporting definitions? What are they? Why are they defined?

5. Why does Story use so much illustration and example in this essay? Which paragraphs use multiple illustrations with special effectiveness?

6. What is the role of description in this essay? of comparison and contrast? of process analysis? (look ahead to page 215). From the many writing strategies used in this essay, what can you conclude about the technique of extended definition?

EXPLORING THE WRITER'S IDEAS

1. At one stage in the essay, Story writes, "Dental research at the University of Texas and Harvard indicated that the consumption of chocolate milk makes no significant difference in the development of cavities." (par. 9) Why is this a somewhat misleading statement? Do you think that writers (and speakers) frequently slant the statements that they make? Do you find any other slanted remarks in this essay?

2. This essay appeared in a magazine that American Airlines puts aboard its planes as reading matter for its passengers. Do you think that this essay would interest a passenger in flight? A more general audience? Is it "heavy" reading, "light" reading, or what? Is there such a form as "popular writing"? What magazines that you know include articles on popular topics?

3. Is chocolate actually as important to the health and happiness of society as Story suggests? Are there other foods that seem to have an unusual impact on or importance to a particular culture?

IDEAS FOR WRITING

Guided Writing

Select a food—for instance, hamburgers, frankfurters, cotton candy, pizza, grits, tortillas—and write an essay of definition.

1. Prepare for your essay by consulting an encyclopedia for basic information. Take notes, but make certain you write down the information in your own words.

2. In your introductory paragraph, attempt to establish the *tone* (see page 391) of your essay. Try to establish the relative importance of your subject.

3. Provide historical background for your subject.

4. Use other strategies—description, illustration, comparison and contrast, and so forth—to aid in establishing an extended definition of your topic.

5. If desirable, explain the significance of the product in terms of your own life. Also explain the significance of the product to various cultures.

6. Look again at Story's conclusion and try to pattern your own conclusion after it.

More Writing Projects

1. Select one of the following topics and write a paragraph or extended definition on it: automobile; grapes; alcohol; grass; water. Be prepared to discuss your paragraph with the class and to examine other ways to expand the composition.

2. Select a word which has a very specific denotation but which has a variety of connotations (see page 381). Write an extended definition of that word. In the first part of your essay explain and interpret the dictionary definition. In the next part of your essay show how one, or several, connotative meanings compare or contrast with the denotative meanings.

Charles F. Berlitz

THE ETYMOLOGY OF THE INTERNATIONAL INSULT

In this essay, Charles Berlitz uses a variety of examples to define the insult related to a person's race or religion, and the insult related to country of birth. The author, who founded the internationally known Berlitz School of Languages, analyzes words that have highly charged meanings and connotations for all of us. He does not use such words to insult any readers, but rather to aid us in understanding how "international insults" have developed.

Words to Watch

etymology (title): the origin and development of a word
derived (par. 2): traced from a source
perjorative (par. 2): showing disrespect for
appellation (par. 3): a name
opprobrious (par. 3): abusive; disrespecful
inversion (par. 3): a reversal
swarthy (par. 5): dark
epithets (par. 6): words or phrases that describe a particular characteristic of a person or thing
semantic (par. 7): relating to meaning in language
diminutive (par. 11): shortening (in this case, of a word)
contraction (par. 11): shortening
physiognomy (par. 12): given or done in return
sanctified (par. 15): made holy

"What is a kike?" Disraeli once asked a small 1
group of fellow politicians. Then, as his audience shifted
nervously, Queen Victoria's great Jewish Prime Minister
supplied the answer himself. "A kike" he observed, "is a
Jewish gentleman who has just left the room."

The word kike is thought to have derived from the 2
ending -ki or -ky found in many names borne by the Jews
of Eastern Europe. Or, as Leo Rosten suggests, it may come
from *kikel,* Yiddish for a circle, the preferred mark for name
signing by Jewish immigrants who could not write. This
was used instead of an X, which resembles a cross. Kikel
was not originally pejorative, but has become so through
use.

Yid, another word for Jew has a distinguished 3
historic origin, coming from the German *Jude* (through the
Russian *zhid*). *Jude* itself derives from the tribe of Judah,
a most honorable and ancient appellation. The vulgar and
opprobrious word "Sheeny" for Jew is a real inversion, as it
derives from *shaine* (Yiddish) or *schön* (German), meaning
"beautiful." How could beautiful be an insult? The answer
is that it all depends on the manner, tone or facial expression
or sneer (as our own Vice President has trenchantly observed) with which something is said. The opprobrious
Mexican word for an American—*gringo,* for example, is
essentially simply a sound echo of a song the American
troops used to sing when the Americans were invading
Mexico—"Green Grow the Lilacs." Therefore the Mexicans
began to call the Americans something equivalent to "los
green-grows" which became Hispanized to *gringo.* But from
this innocent beginning to the unfriendly emphasis with
which many Mexicans say *gringo* today there is a world of
difference—almost a call to arms, with unforgettable memories of past real or fancied wrongs, including "lost" Texas
and California.

The pejorative American word for Mexicans, Puerto 4
Ricans, Cubans and other Spanish-speaking nationals is
simply *spik,* excerpted from the useful expression "No esspick
Englitch." Italians, whether in America or abroad, have
been given other more picturesque appellations. *Wop,* an

disrespect

all-time pejorative favorite, is curiously not insulting at all by origin, as it means, in Neapolitan dialect, "handsome," "strong" or "good looking." Among the young Italian immigrants some of the stronger and more active—sometimes to the point of combat—were called *guappi*, from which the first syllable, "wop," attained an "immediate insult" status for all Italians.

travel

"Guinea" comes from the days of the slave trade and 5 is derived from the African word for West Africa. This "guinea" is the same word as the British unit of 21 shillings, somehow connected with African gold profits as well as New Guinea, which resembled Africa to its discoverers. Dark or swarthy Italians and sometimes Portuguese were called *Guineas* and this apparently spread to Italians of light complexion as well. *words*

One of the epithets for Negroes has a curious and 6 tragic historic origin, the memory of which is still haunting us. The word is "coons." It comes from *baracoes* (the o gives a nasal *n* sound in Portuguese), and refers to the slave pens or barracks ("*baracoons*") in which the victims of the slave trade were kept while awaiting transshipment. Their descendants, in their present emphasizing of the term "black" over "Negro," may be in the process of upgrading the very *show dieopsa* word "black," so often used pejoratively, as in "black-hearted," "black day," "black arts," "black hand," etc. Even some African languages use "black" in a negative sense. In Hausa "to have a black stomach" means to be angry or unhappy.

The sub-Sahara African peoples, incidentally, do not 7 think that they are black (which they are not, anyway). They consider themselves a healthy and attractive "people color," while whites to them look rather unhealthy and somewhat frightening. In any case, the efforts of African Americans to dignify the word "black" may eventually represent a semantic as well as a socio-racial triumph.

A common type of national insult is that of referring 8 to nationalities by their food habits. Thus "Frogs" for the French and "Krauts" for the Germans are easily understandable, reflecting on the French addiction to *cuisses de gren-*

quilles (literally "thighs of frogs") and that of the Germans for various kinds of cabbage, hot or cold. The French call the Italians *"les macaronis"* while the German insult word for Italians is *Katzenfresser* (cateaters), an unjust accusation considering the hordes of cats among the Roman ruins fed by individual cat lovers—unless they are fattening them up? The insult word for an English person is "limey," referring to the limes distributed to seafaring Englishmen as an antiscurvy precaution in the days of sailing ships and long periods at sea.

At least one of these food descriptive appellations 9 has attained a permanent status in English. The word "Eskimo" is not an Eskimo word at all but an Algonquin word unit meaning "eaters-of-flesh." The Eskimos naturally do not call themselves this in their own language but, with simple directness, use the word *Inuit*—"the men" or "the people."

Why is it an insult to call Chinese "Chinks"? Chink 10 is most probably a contraction of the first syllables of *Chung-Kuo-Ren*—"Middle Country Person." In Chinese there is no special word for China, as the Chinese, being racially somewhat snobbish themselves (although *not* effete, according to recent reports), have for thousands of years considered their land to be the center or middle of the world. The key character for China is therefore the word *chung* of "middle" which, added to *kuo*, becomes "middle country" or "middle kingdom"—the complete Chinese expression for "China" being *Chung Hwa Min Kuo* ("Middle Flowery People's Country"). No matter how inoffensive the origin of "Chink" is, however, it is no longer advisable for everyday or any-day use now.

Jap, an insulting diminutive that figured in the last 11 national U.S. election (though its use in the expression "fat Jap" was apparently meant to have an endearing quality by our Vice President) is a simple contraction of "Japan," which derives from the Chinese word for "sun." In fact the words "Jap" and "Nip" both mean the same thing. "Jap" comes from Chinese and "Nip" from Japanese in the following fashion: *Jihpen* means "sun origin" in Chinese, while *Ni-*

hon (Nippon) gives a like meaning in Japanese, both indicating that Japan was where the sun rose. Europeans were first in contact with China, and so originally chose the Chinese name for Japan instead of the Japanese one.

The Chinese "insult" words for whites are based on 12 the observations that they are *too* white and therefore look like ghosts or devils, *fan kuei* (ocean ghosts), or that their features are too sharp instead of being pleasantly flat, and that they have enormous noses, hence *ta-bee-tsu* (great-nosed ones). Differences in facial physiognomy have been fully reciprocated by whites in referring to Asians as "Slants" or "Slopes."

Greeks in ancient times had an insult word for 13 foreigners too, but one based on the sound of their language. This word is still with us, though its original meaning has changed. The ancient Greeks divided the world into Greeks and "Barbarians"—the latter word coming from a description of the ridiculous language the stranger was speaking. To the Greeks it sounded like the "baa-baa" of a sheep—hence "Barbarians!"

The black peoples of South Africa are not today 14 referred to as Negro or Black but as Bantu—not in itself an insult but having somewhat the same effect when you are the lowest man on the totem pole. But the word means simply "the men," *ntu* signifying "man" and *ba* being the plural prefix. This may have come from an early encounter with explorers or missionaries when Central or South Africans on being asked by whites who they were may have replied simply "men"—with the implied though probably unspoken follow-up question, "And who are you?"

This basic and ancient idea that one's group are the 15 only people—at least the only friendly or non-dangerous ones—is found among many tribes throughout the world. The Navajo Indians call themselves *Diné*—"the people"— and qualify other tribes generally as "the enemy." Therefore an Indian tribe to the north would simply be called "the northern enemy," one to the east "the eastern enemy," etc., and that would be the *only* name used for them. These ancient customs, sanctified by time, of considering people who differ in color, customs, physical characteristics and habits—and by enlargement all strangers—as potential enemies is something mankind can no longer afford, even linguistically. Will man ever be able to rise above using insult as a weapon? It may not be possible to love your neighbor, but by understanding him one may be able eventually to tolerate him. Meanwhile, if you stop calling him names, he too may eventually learn to dislike *you* less.

BUILDING VOCABULARY

1. Take any five words from the Words to Watch section (page 157) and use them in sentences of your own.

2. Many of the words that Berlitz defines in this essay (like *kike, wop, coon*) are not appropriate to formal writing or normal conversation. They are *vulgarisms*—words that exist at a level below conventional vocabulary. List five vulgarisms or slang terms from your vocabulary and try to define them on your own or by consulting a specialized dictionary of slang.

3. Define the following words from Berlitz's essay. If you are not sure of the meanings, use the dictionary:

a. *shifted* (par. 1)
b. *facial* (par. 2)
c. *excerpted* (par. 3)
d. *transshipment* (par. 5)
e. *scurvy* (par. 8)
f. *Algonquin* (par. 9)

UNDERSTANDING THE WRITER'S IDEAS

1. Who was Disraeli? Explain in your own words the meaning of Disraeli's definition of "kike."

2. Find original meanings in Berlitz's essay for the following words: *Jude; Wop; Schon; Guappi; Chung-Kuo-Ren.* What are the similarities among these five terms?

3. How does Berlitz explain the way in which something beautiful can be turned into an insult?

relating to meaning in language

4.   What does Berlitz mean when he says that "the efforts of African Americans to dignify the word 'black' may eventually represent a semantic as well as socio-racial triumph"?

5.   What is the relationship between national eating habits and the national insult?

6.   Why do white people look frightening to both sub-Sahara Africans and to Chinese?

7.   Why do we find so many tribes who refer to themselves as "the men" or "the people"?

8.   What attitude toward the national insult does Berlitz suggest in the last paragraph?

UNDERSTANDING THE WRITER'S TECHNIQUES

1.   There are many ways to develop introductory paragraphs in essays. One useful strategy is to tell a brief story or *anecdote,* as Berlitz does in this essay. Do you find Berlitz's anecdote effective? Why or why not? Why is there no thesis sentence? How does the anecdote relate to the rest of the essay?

2.   How does Berlitz create a smooth transition (see page 391) between paragraphs 2 and 3? between 3 and 4? Find other examples of skillful transitions between paragraphs.

3.   Does Berlitz ever offer a single-sentence definition of the "national insult"? Why or why not? What strategy does he employ to make the meaning of his extended definition clear? What is the relationship of the many definitions of specific national insults to the large definition that Berlitz presents?

4.   Berlitz tries hard to select examples from many races, nationalities, and geographic areas. Why does he do this? Is there any geographic pattern that you detect in the organization of the essay?

5.   Why does Berlitz withhold his thesis until the last paragraph? Do you find the last paragraph effective? Why or why not?

6.   What is the tone of the essay? Is it appropriate to the subject? Why or why not?

EXPLORING THE WRITER'S IDEAS

1. Do you think that all national and ethnic insults develop in as clear a manner as Berlitz describes it?

2. Does understanding a national insult make it any easier to accept? Why? Why not?

3. Why is it that we have so many ethnic and national insults in the American language? Why do so many individuals use these insults from time to time? Is it ever possible to use them in a joking manner? Is it possible to use them with positive rather than negative connotations? For instance, if one black person called another "nigger," what would the effect be? How would the effect differ if a white person were to use the word?

4. Do you think that ethnic insults are a form of violence with language? Why? Do you feel that all types of insults have some form of aggression behind them? How do music, film, and television contribute to the growth of ethnic insults? List some songs or films that do this.

5. Try to answer the question Berlitz raises in the last paragraph. Do you agree with the last sentence?

IDEAS FOR WRITING

Guided Writing

Write an extended definition of an insult you find especially ugly or vulgar.

1. Start with a brief anecdote that might be drawn from personal experience.

2. Try to discuss insults related to the one you have singled out. Compare or contrast them to your word.

3. Use a number of examples to support your general ideas. Be certain to define what each insult means.

4. Pay attention to transitions as you move from one example to another.

5. Reserve your thesis for the concluding paragraph of your essay.

More Writing Projects

     1. Select a racial, religious, or national insult and define it by showing what negative qualities about the race are suggested by the insult. Then, show what positive contributions the people labeled by the "insult" have made to American society.

     2. Some comedians—Groucho Marx, W. C. Fields, Don Rickels, Richard Pryor—made their fame with insults that make audiences laugh. Write an essay in which you define an insult or insults used for humorous effects. Be sure to treat this question in your essay: Is it possible *not* to offend someone with a racial or ethnic insult?

Alex Haley

ROOTS

Probably no single book or television program in recent
years has had as significant an impact on the American
mind as Alex Haley's *Roots*. In this selection, Haley
narrates the search for his own roots. Haley, who also
ghostwrote *The Autobiography of Malcolm X* (1964), mixes
autobiography and extended definition, as well as several
other writing strategies, to explain the meaning and
significance of his subject.

Words to Watch

saga (par. 4): a long story of adventure
subsequent (par. 4): coming after
encyclopedic (par. 6): comprehensive in scope
matriarch (par. 6): a woman who rules a family or tribe
quotient (par. 7): the number obtained when one quantity is
    divided by another
angular (par. 7): sharp
surname (par. 8): last name (family name)
archives (par. 9): a place where public records are kept
cumulative (par. 10): increasing in size or effect through successive
    additions
profusion (par. 16): abundant supply; a pouring forth
staccato (par. 21): made up of abrupt sounds

My earliest memory is of Grandma, Cousin Georgia, 1
Aunt Plus, Aunt Liz and Aunt Till talking on our front
porch in Henning, Tenn. At dusk, these wrinkled, graying
old ladies would sit in rocking chairs and talk, about slaves
and massas and plantations—pieces and patches of family
history, passed down across the generations by word of
mouth. "Old-timey stuff," Mama would exclaim. She wanted
no part of it.

The furthest-back person Grandma and the others 2
ever mentioned was "the African." They would tell how he
was brought here on a ship to a place called "Naplis" and
sold as a slave in Virginia. There he mated with another
slave, and had a little girl named Kizzy.

When Kizzy became four or five, the old ladies said, 3
her father would point out to her various objects and name
them in his native tongue. For example, he would point to
a guitar and make a single-syllable sound, *ko*. Pointing to
a river that ran near the plantation, he'd say "Kamby
Bolongo." And when other slaves addressed him as Toby—
the name given him by his massa—the African would
strenuously reject it, insisting that his name was "Kin-tay."

Kin-tay often told Kizzy stories about himself. He 4
said that he had been near his village in Africa, chopping
wood to make a drum, when he had been set upon by four
men, overwhelmed, and kidnaped into slavery. When Kizzy
grew up and became a mother, she told her son these stories,
and he in turn would tell *his* children. His granddaughter
became my grandmother, and she pumped that saga into
me as if it were plasma, until I knew by rote the story of the
African, and the subsequent generational wending of our
family through cotton and tobacco plantations into the Civil
War and then freedom.

At 17, during World War II, I enlisted in the Coast 5
Guard, and found myself a messboy on a ship in the Southwest
Pacific. To fight boredom, I began to teach myself to become
a writer. I stayed on in the service after the war, writing
every single night, seven nights a week, for eight years
before I sold a story to a magazine. My first story in the
Digest was published in June 1954: "The Harlem Nobody

Knows." At age 37, I retired from military service, determined to be a full-time writer. Working with the famous Black Muslim spokesman, I did the actual writing for the book *The Autobiography of Malcolm X.*

6   I remembered still the vivid highlights of my family's story. Could this account possibly be documented for a book? During 1962, between other assignments, I began following the story's trail. In plantation records, wills, census records, I documented bits here, shreds there. By now, Grandma was dead; repeatedly I visited other close sources, most notably our encyclopedic matriarch, "Cousin Georgia" Anderson in Kansas City, Kan. I went as often as I could to the National Archives in Washington, and the Library of Congress, and the Daughters of the American Revolution Library.

7   By 1967, I felt I had the seven generations of the U.S. side documented. But the unknown quotient in the riddle of the past continued to be those strange, sharp, angular sounds spoken by the African himself. Since I lived in New York City, I began going to the United Nations lobby, stopping Africans and asking if they recognized the sounds. Every one of them listened to me, then quickly took off. I can well understand: me with a Tennessee accent, trying to imitate African sounds!

8   Finally, I sought out a linguistics expert who specialized in African languages. To him I repeated the phrases. The sound "Kin-tay," he said, was a Mandinka tribe surname. And "Kamby Bolongo" was probably the Gambia River in Mandinka dialect. Three days later, I was in Africa.

9   In Banjul, the capital of Gambia, I met with a group of Gambians. They told me how for centuries the history of Africa has been preserved. In the other villages of the back country there are old men, called *griots*, who are in effect living archives. Such men know and, on special occasions, tell the cumulative histories of clans, or families, or villages, as those histories have long been told. Since my forefather had said his name was Kin-tay (properly spelled Kinte), and since the Kinte clan was known in Gambia, they would see what they could do to help me.

10   I was back in New York when a registered letter

came from Gambia. Word had been passed in the back country, and a *griot* of the Kinte clan had, indeed, been found. His name, the letter said, was Kebba Kanga Fofana. I returned to Gambia and organized a safari to locate him.

There is an expression called "the peak experience," 11 a moment which, emotionally, can never again be equaled in your life. I had mine, that first day in the village of Juffure, in the back country in black West Africa.

When our 14-man safari arrived within sight of the 12 village, the people came flocking out of their circular mud huts. From a distance I could see a small, old man with a pillbox hat, an off-white robe and an aura of "somebodiness" about him. The people quickly gathered around me in a kind of horseshoe pattern. The old man looked piercingly into my eyes, and he spoke in Mandinka. Translation came from the interpreters I had brought with me.

"Yes, we have been told by the forefathers that there 13 are many of us from this place who are in exile in that place called America."

Then the old man, who was 73 rains of age—the 14 Gambian way of saying 73 years old, based upon the one rainy season per year—began to tell me the lengthy ancestral history of the Kinte clan. It was clearly a formal occasion for the villagers. They had grown mouse-quiet, and stood rigidly.

Out of the *griot's* head came spilling lineage details 15 incredible to hear. He recited who married whom, two or even three centuries back. I was struck not only by the profusion of details, but also by the Biblical pattern of the way he was speaking. It was something like,"—and so-and-so took as a wife so-and-so, and begat so-and-so. . . ."

The *griot* had talked for some hours, and had got to 16 about 1750 in our calendar. Now he said, through an interpreter, "About the time the king's soldiers came, the eldest of Omoro's four sons, Kunta, went away from this village to chop wood—and he was never seen again. . . ."

Goose pimples came out on me the size of marbles. 17 He just had no way in the world of knowing that what he told me meshed with what I'd heard from the old ladies on the front porch in Henning, Tenn. I got out my notebook, which had in it what Grandma had said about the African. One of the interpreters showed it to the others, and they went to the *griot,* and they all got agitated. Then the *griot* went to the people, and *they* all got agitated.

I don't remember anyone giving an order, but those 18 70-odd people formed a ring around me, moving counterclockwise, chanting, their bodies close together. I can't begin to describe how I felt. A woman broke from the circle, a scowl on her jet-black face, and came charging toward me. She took her baby and almost roughly thrust it out at me. The gesture meant "Take it!" and I did, clasping the baby to me. Whereupon the woman all but snatched the baby away. Another woman did the same with her baby, then another, and another.

A year later, a famous professor at Harvard would 19 tell me: "You were participating in one of the oldest cermonies of humankind, called 'the laying on of hands.' In their way, these tribespeople were saying to you, 'Through this flesh, which is us, we are you and you are us.'"

Later, as we drove out over the back-country road, 20 I heard the staccato sound of drums. When we approached the next village, people were packed alongside the dusty road, waving, and the din from them welled louder as we came closer. As I stood up in the Land Rover, I finally realized what it was they were all shouting: "Meester Kinte! Meester Kinte!" In their eyes I was the symbol of all black people in the United States whose forefathers had been torn out of Africa while theirs remained.

Hands before my face, I began crying—crying as I 21 have never cried in my life. Right at that time, crying was all I could do.

I went then to London. I searched and searched, and 22 finally in the British Parliamentary records I found that the "king's soldiers" mentioned by the *griot* referred to a group called "Colonel O'Hare's forces," which had been sent up the Gambia River in 1767 to guard the then British-operated James Fort, a slave fort.

I next went to Lloyds of London, where doors were 23 opened for me to research among all kinds of old maritime records. I pored through the records of slave ships that had sailed from Africa. Volumes upon volumes of these records exist. One afternoon about 2:30, during the seventh week of searching, I was going through my 1023rd set of ship records. I picked up a sheet that had on it the reported movements of 30 slave ships, my eyes stopped at No. 18, and my glance swept across the column entries. This vessel had sailed directly from the Gambia River to America in 1767; her name was the *Lord Ligonier;* and she had arrived at Annapolis (Naplis) the morning of September 29, 1767.

Exactly 200 years later, on September 29, 1967, there 24 was nowhere in the world for me to be except standing on a pier at Annapolis, staring seaward across those waters over which my great-great-great-great-grandfather had been brought. And there in Annapolis I inspected the microfilmed records of the *Maryland Gazette.* In the issue of October 1, 1767, on page 3, I found an advertisement informing readers that the *Lord Ligonier* had just arrived from the River Gambia, with "a cargo of choice, healthy SLAVES" to be sold at auction the following Wednesday.

In the years since, I have done extensive research 25 in 50 or so libraries, archives and repositories on three continents. I spent a year combing through countless documents to learn about the culture of Gambia's villages in the 18th and 19th centuries. Desiring to sail over the same waters navigated by the *Lord Ligonier,* I flew to Africa and boarded the freighter *African Star.* I forced myself to spend the ten nights of the crossing in the cold, dark cargo hold, stripped to my underwear, lying on my back on a rough, bare plank. But this was sheer luxury compared to the inhuman ordeal suffered by those millions who, chained and shackled, lay in terror and in their own filth in the stinking darkness through voyages averaging 60 to 70 days.

BUILDING VOCABULARY

1. Compare Haley's use of the following words with the dictionary meaning:

    a. massa (par. 1)
    b. strenuously (par. 3)

c. Africa (par. 4)
d. riddle (par. 8)
e. ancestral (par. 17)

2. Locate five words or phrases in Haley's essay that have a conversational quality to them. Why does Haley use such words in his essay?

3. Use five of the words in the Words to Watch section in sentences of your own.

4. In paragraph 18, does Haley rely on action verbs or verbs of being? Does the rest of the essay reflect this choice or not?

UNDERSTANDING THE WRITER'S IDEAS

1. What is Haley's "earliest memory"? What is its significance?

2. Who was "the African"? What is his importance in Haley's search?

3. Explain the process of "storytelling" that Haley narrates in this essay. How much historical time passes?

4. Why did Haley decide to become a writer?

5. How did Haley research his book?

6. How do Africans preserve history? What is the importance of the *griot* in the process?

7. Describe in your own words what Haley means by "a peak experience."

8. Why do the villagers at Juffure form a ring around Haley?

9. In the last paragraph, why does Haley force himself to sleep in the cargo hold of the *African Star?*

UNDERSTANDING THE WRITER'S TECHNIQUES

1. How does Haley develop his introductory paragraph? Is there a thesis statement? Why or why not? Is there a thesis to the essay itself?

2. In paragraph 3, how does Haley handle short definitions?

3. Is narrative tone in this essay subjective or objective?

4. What is the function of paragraph 5? Does it fit with the rest of the essay?

5. Does Haley ever give a "dictionary definition" of *roots*? What are the writing strategies utilized to develop an extended definition of the term?

6. How does Haley arrange events in this essay? List the events and the paragraphs devoted to each stage of development.

7. In his conclusion, Haley uses one last example to end his essay. How effective is this example, which centers on the *African Star*? How does it serve to summarize many of the concerns of the essay?

EXPLORING THE WRITER'S IDEAS

1. Is the search for one's "roots" actually a valuable process? Do you think that the current interest in genealogy (the study of family descent) will have an important effect on Americans, or is it just a passing fad?

2. Thomas Wolfe, a famous American writer, once observed that you can never go home again. Do you agree or disagree with his statement? What do you think Haley's reply would be?

3. Many commentators today have observed that Americans lack a sense of history—ancestral, ethnic, national, or otherwise. These people believe that for Americans the past is dead. Do you agree or disagree? Why? What is the value of the past?

WRITING PROJECTS

Guided Writing

Write an extended definition of "roots" and what the term means to you.

1. Decide at the outset to relate "roots" to what you know about your own family's history.

2. Concentrate on relatives and events to help clarify meaning.

3. Use narration to insure essay progression and development. Employ any other writing strategies that you find helpful to your extended definition.

4. Try to dramatize at least one event, as Haley does in recounting the visit to his tribal village.

5. Make certain that your own feelings and emotions about the subject are clear to the reader.

6. Check to see if a thesis emerges from your essay. This thesis should indicate whether or not your own ancestry is important to you.

More Writing Projects

1. Write a short paragraph that reveals what you would want your children to understand about the term "roots."

2. Write an essay on what "roots" would mean to at least three American ethnic or racial groups—for instance, black Americans, Italian Americans, Japanese Americans, or native Americans (American Indians).

3. Define *slavery* in an essay of 500 words.

six

Classification

Classification is the arrangement of information into groups or categories in order to make clear the relationships among members of the group. Writers need to classify, because it helps them present a mass of material by means of some orderly system. Related bits of information seem clearer when presented together as parts of a group. We are always classifying things in our daily lives: We put all our text books on one shelf or in one corner of the desk; we count on similar items in the supermarket being grouped together so we can buy all our canned vegetables or snacks in a single area; we make categories in our minds of the teachers we like, of the relatives who annoy us, and of the cars that look sleekest on the road. In classifying, we show how things within a large body of information relate to each other; we organize those things into groups so that they make sense to us and to anybody else who is interested in what we are thinking, or saying, or doing.

Classification helps writers explain relationships to their readers. First, a writer will *analyze* his or her material in order to divide some large subject into categories. Called *division* or *analysis,* this first task helps split an idea or object into its parts. Then, some of the parts can serve as categories into which the writer can fit individual pieces that share some common qualities. So, if you wanted to write about sports, for example, you might first break the topic down—*divide* it—into *team sports* and *individual sports* (although there are many other ways you might have made the division). Then you could group together (*classify*) baseball, soccer, and football in the first category; and, perhaps, boxing, wrestling and tennis in the second. Your purpose in dividing or analyzing is to determine the parts of a whole (team sports and individual sports *are* very different).

Division does not always require that classification follow it. Your purpose in classifying, however, is to show how things in a group are similar (baseball, soccer, and football have interesting similarities as team sports; boxing, wrestling, and tennis—in stressing individual achievement—are related, too). Division and classification work together. If you were to empty the contents of a pocketbook onto a table, you would begin to divide those contents into groups. Through division, you would identify objects relating to finances, objects relating to personal care, objects relating to school work. Once you had the divisions clear, you would place objects in each category: money, checks, and credit cards in the first; cosmetics, a comb, perfume in the second; pens, pencils, a notebook in the third.

When you divide and classify for writing, you have to keep several things in mind. You have to think carefully about the division of the topic so that you limit the overlap from group to group. That is best achieved by creating categories different enough from each other so there is no blending. Since you, the writer, have to establish the groups (and sometimes there are many different ways to set up groups for the same topic), you need to use a principle of classification that is sensible, accurate, and complete. Do not force categories just for the sake of making groups. You have to show how things in a group relate to each other, and this you must do without ignoring their differences and without making them stereotypes. If you stereotype objects in a group (whether the objects are people, things, or ideas), you will be oversimplifying them, taking away their individuality, and forcing them to fit your categories.

Classification resembles outlining. It provides the writer with a plan of organization. Whether the subject is personal, technical, simple, complex, or abstract, the writer can organize material about it into categories, and can move carefully from one category to another in developing an essay.

Philip Agee

SECRET WRITING

Classification is an especially useful device in explaining technical subjects. In this selection from *Inside the Company: CIA Diary,* Philip Agee presents information on secret writing. Agee, a former CIA agent, caused considerable controversy with the publication of this book, which exposed in detail the secret workings of the Central Intelligence Agency.

Words to Watch

bond (par. 1): a strong, superior grade of paper
swab stick (par. 1): a small piece of cotton used normally to apply medicine
innocuous (par. 1): harmless
impregnated (par. 2): filled; saturated
tedious (par. 4): long and tiresome

Secret writing (sw) is the communications system 1 used for concealing or making invisible a secret message on an otherwise innocent letter or other cover document. sw systems are categorized as wet systems, carbons and microdot. The wet systems use chemicals, usually disguised as pills, which dissolve in water to form a clear 'ink'. The secret message is written on a sheet of paper, preferably high-quality bond, using the end of a wooden swab stick that has been tapered with a razor-blade and soaked in the 'ink' to reach the proper tip flexibility. Before and after writing the message the paper must be rubbed with a soft cloth on both sides in all four directions to help conceal the writing within the texture of the paper. The paper with the secret message is then steamed and pressed in a thick book and after drying, if no trace of the message can be seen under ultra-violet and glancing light, a cover letter or innocuous message is written.

Carbon systems consist of ordinary bond paper that 2 has been impregnated with chemicals. The carbon is placed on top of the message sheet and the secret message is written on a sheet placed on top of the carbon. Applying the proper pressure when writing the secret message with a pencil on the top sheet transfers the invisible chemical from the carbon to the message sheet on the bottom. The cover letter is then written on the opposite side of the message sheet from the secret message.

On receipt of an sw letter, an agent applies a 3 corresponding chemical developer, rolling the developer with a cotton swab on to the page, and soon the secret message appears.

The microdot system involves a small camera kit 4 with which a letter-sized page can be photographed on an area of film no larger than the dot of an 'i'. The microdot is glued over the dot of the 'i' or a period of a cover letter. Although the equipment for microdots is incriminating, the microdots themselves are very secure and practically impossible to discover. On the other hand they require very tedious processing and can only be read with a microscope.

Secret messages can be written either in clear text 5 or encoded for greater security. The sw branch of TSD* has a continuous intelligence collection program on the postal censorship procedures in most foreign countries for protective procedures in sw operations. The operational environment in which the agent works determines the other details of sw correspondence: whether the sw cover letter will be

* Technical Services Division.

posted nationally or internationally, to a post-box or a support agent serving as an accommodation address, with false or true return addresses or none at all, the content of the cover letters, signals to indicate safety or the absence of which could indicate that the writing is being done under control of a hostile service.

The sw branch also has a technique for 'lifting' sw 6 from suspect correspondence. The process involves placing a suspect letter in a letter press with sheets on either side. By cranking down pressure enough of the chemicals will come off on the steamed sheets to allow for testing with other chemicals for development. The suspect correspondence can be returned to the mails with no traces of tampering.

BUILDING VOCABULARY

1. For each word below, write a definition in your own words (use a dictionary for help).

   a. tapered (par. 1)
   b. flexibility (par. 1)
   c. incriminatory (par. 4)
   d. encoded (par. 5)
   e. censorship (par. 5)

2. Use each word above in an original sentence of your own.

UNDERSTANDING THE WRITER'S IDEAS

1. What is an "sw system"? How many sw systems are there? What are their names?
2. Explain in your own words one of the secret writing systems that Agee describes.
3. Why must paper be rubbed on both sides before applying secret writing through the wet system?
4. What is the relationship of the cover letter to the secret message in the carbon system?
5. Why is "the equipment for microdots ... incriminating"?

6.   What are the two ways secret messages can be written?

7.   Why is the "operational environment" of a secret agent important in secret writing?

8.   How is secret writing "lifted" from suspect correspondence?

UNDERSTANDING THE WRITER'S TECHNIQUES

1.   Why does Agee open this selection with a definition of *secret writing?* Does the definition serve as a good thesis statement for the topic? Why?

2.   Identify the topic sentences in paragraphs 2, 4, 5, and 6.

3.   What is the justification for Agee's third paragraph? Could it be put in a different place? Why or why not?

4.   How many basic categories does Agee create in the essay? Does he seem to cover all major categories of his subject? Is there any overlapping? Does he develop each category adequately? What other categories might he have established for secret writing?

5.   Explain the nature of the classification process in paragraph 5. Does this continue the pattern set up in paragraphs 1 to 4, or is it a new classification pattern?

6.   What is the connection between paragraphs 5 and 6? Does paragraph 6 serve as an adequate conclusion for the selection?

7.   Agee uses *process analysis* (see pages 215–216) in this selection despite the general organizing scheme of classification. Where does he explain how to do something?

8.   Discuss the tone of Agee's essay (see page 391). Is it straightforward, humorous, or ironic? Defend your choice.

EXPLORING THE WRITER'S IDEAS

1.   Do you believe that tampering with the mails by a local or national security agency is justified? If so, under what conditions?

2. To what extent should science and technology be used by government organizations like the CIA?

3. Why does Agee not deal with the moral and ethical issues (like those raised in 1 and 2 above) of his subject? Can an "objective" presentation of material sometimes be dangerous or misleading? Why?

4. Agee's revelations about CIA operations are timely. What other individuals have made revelations in the CIA that have stimulated public controversy? What is your reaction about former CIA agents making such statements? Should a domestic or national intelligence agency be subject to public scrutiny?

IDEAS FOR WRITING

Guided Writing

Select some process with which you are familiar, for instance, methods of cooking, ways to lose weight, or systems for writing shorthand. Then write an essay that uses classification to organize your material.

1. State your subject in the first sentence by writing a definition of it, as Agee has.

2. Make certain that your introductory paragraph presents the main categories in your subject. Divide your subject into all important categories or groups.

3. Devote a full paragraph to each major group. Write a topic sentence at the start of each paragraph.

4. Provide a closing paragraph that evaluates the relative benefits of each method you analyzed.

5. Provide adequate details for the reader to understand each category. In this essay you will be explaining how things in each category work, so review the section on process analysis (pages 215–248).

More Writing Projects

1. Write an extended paragraph or essay on the various methods that the government uses to spy on people.

2.   Select a highly emotional topic that can be divided into categories—for instance, types of violent crimes, types of poverty, kinds of urban decay—and then explain your categories in a detached, objective manner. Try not to inject your own opinions into the essay.

Judith Viorst

FRIENDS, GOOD FRIENDS— AND SUCH GOOD FRIENDS

In this essay Judith Viorst, who writes for numerous popular magazines, examines types of friends in her life. Her pattern of development is easy to follow, because she tends to stay on one level in the process of classification. As you read this essay, try to keep in mind the similarities and distinctions that Viorst makes among types of friends, as well as the principles of classification that she uses.

Words to Watch

nonchalant (par. 3): showing lack of interest or concern
endodontist (par. 14): a dentist specializing in diseases of dental pulp and root canals.
sibling (par. 16): brother or sister
dormant (par. 19): as if asleep; inactive
self-revelation (par. 22): self-discovery; self-disclosure
calibrated (par. 29): measured; fixed; checked carefully

Women are friends, I once would have said, when 1 they totally love and support and trust each other, and bare to each other the secrets of their souls, and run—no questions asked—to help each other, and tell harsh truths to each other (no, you can't wear that dress unless you lose ten pounds first) when harsh truths must be told.

Women are friends, I once would have said, when they share the same affection for Ingmar Bergman, plus train rides, cats, warm rain, charades, Camus, and hate with equal ardor Newark and Brussels sprouts and Lawrence Welk and camping. 2

In other words, I once would have said that a friend is a friend all the way, but now I believe that's a narrow point of view. For the friendships I have and the friendships I see are conducted at many levels of intensity, serve many different functions, meet different needs and range from those as all-the-way as the friendship of the soul sisters mentioned above to that of the most nonchalant and casual playmates. 3

Consider these varieties of friendship: 4

1. Convenience friends. These are the women with whom, if our paths weren't crossing all the time, we'd have no particular reason to be friends: a next-door neighbor, a woman in our car pool, the mother of one of our children's closest friends or maybe some mommy with whom we serve juice and cookies each week at the Glenwood Co-op Nursery. 5

Convenience friends are convenient indeed. They'll lend us their cups and silverware for a party. They'll drive our kids to soccer when we're sick. They'll take us to pick up our car when we need a lift to the garage. They'll even take our cats when we go on vacation. As we will for them. 6

But we don't, with convenience friends, ever come too close or tell too much; we maintain our public face and emotional distance. "Which means," says Elaine, "that I'll talk about being overweight but not about being depressed. Which means I'll admit being mad but not blind with rage. Which means I might say that we're pinched this month but never that I'm worried sick over money." 7

But which doesn't mean that there isn't sufficient value to be found in these friendships of mutual aid, in convenience friends. 8

2. Special-interest friends. These friendships aren't intimate, and they needn't involve kids or silverware or 9

cats. Their value lies in some interest jointly shared. And so we may have an office friend or a yoga friend or a tennis friend or a friend from the Women's Democratic Club.

"I've got one woman friend," says Joyce, "who likes, as I do, to take psychology courses. Which makes it nice for me—and nice for her. It's fun to go with someone you know and it's fun to discuss what you've learned, driving back from the classes." And for the most part, she says, that's all they discuss.

"I'd say that what we're doing is *doing* together, not being together," Suzanne says of her Tuesday-doubles friends. "It's mainly a tennis relationship, but we play together well. And I guess we all need to have a couple of playmates."

I agree.

My playmate is a shopping friend, a woman of marvelous taste, a woman who knows exactly *where* to buy *what,* and furthermore is a woman who always knows beyond a doubt what one ought to be buying. I don't have the time to keep up with what's new in eyeshadow, hemlines and shoes and whether the smock look is in or finished already. But since (oh, shame!) I care a lot about eyeshadow, hemlines and shoes, and since I don't *want* to wear smocks if the smock look is finished, I'm very glad to have a shopping friend.

3. Historical friends. We all have a friend who knew us when . . . maybe way back in Miss Meltzer's second grade, when our family lived in that three-room flat in Brooklyn, when our dad was out of work for seven months, when our brother Allie got in that fight where they had to call the police, when our sister married the endodontist from Yonkers and when, the morning after we lost our virginity, she was the first, the only, friend we told.

The years have gone by and we've gone separate ways and we've little in common now, but we're still an intimate part of each other's past. And so whenever we go to Detroit we always go to visit this friend of our girlhood. Who knows how we looked before our teeth were straightened. Who knows how we talked before our voice got un-Brooklyned. Who knows what we ate before we learned about artichokes. And who, by her presence, puts us in touch with an earlier part of ourself, a part of ourself it's important never to lose.

"What this friend means to me and what I mean to her," says Grace, "is having a sister without sibling rivalry. We know the texture of each other's lives. She remembers my grandmother's cabbage soup. I remember the way her uncle played the piano. There's simply no other friend who remembers those things." 16

4. Crossroads friends. Like historical friends, our crossroads friends are important for *what was*—for the friendship we shared at a crucial, now past, time of life. A time, perhaps, when we roomed in college together; or worked as eager young singles in the Big City together; or went together, as my friend Elizabeth and I did through pregnancy, birth and that scary first year of new motherhood. 17

Crossroads friends forge powerful links, links strong enough to endure with not much more contact than once-a-year letters at Christmas. And out of respect for those crossroads years, for those dramas and dreams we once shared, we will always be friends. 18

5. Cross-generational friends. Historical friends and crossroads friends seem to maintain a special kind of intimacy—dormant but always ready to be revived—and though we may rarely meet, whenever we do connect, it's personal and intense. Another kind of intimacy exists in the friendships that form across generations in what one woman calls her daughter-mother and her mother-daughter relationships. 19

Evelyn's friend is her mother's age—"but I share so much more than I ever could with my mother"—a woman she talks to of music, of books and of life. "What I get from her is the benefit of her experience. What she gets—and enjoys—from me is a youthful perspective. It's a pleasure for both of us." 20

I have in my own life a precious friend, a woman of 65 who has lived very hard, who is wise, who listens well; who has been where I am and can help me understand it; 21

and who represents not only an ultimate ideal mother to me but also the person I'd like to be when I grow up.

In our daughter role we tend to do more than our share of self-revelation; in our mother role we tend to receive what's revealed. It's another kind of pleasure—playing wise mother to a questing younger person. It's another very lovely kind of friendship. 22

6. Part-of-a-couple friends. Some of the women we call our friends we never see alone—we see them as part of a couple at couples' parties. And though we share interests in many things and respect each other's views, we aren't moved to deepen the relationship. Whatever the reason, a lack of time or—and this is more likely—a lack of chemistry, our friendship remains in the context of a group. But the fact that our feeling on seeing each other is always, "I'm *so* glad she's here" and the fact that we spend half the evening talking together says that this too, in its own way, counts as a friendship. 23

(Other part-of-a-couple friends are the friends that came with the marriage, and some of these are friends we could live without. But sometimes, alas, she married our husband's best friend; and sometimes, alas, she *is* our husband's best friend. And so we find ourself dealing with her, somewhat against our will, in a spirit of what I'll call *reluctant* friendship.) 24

7. Men who are friends. I wanted to write just of women friends, but the women I've talked to won't let me— they say I must mention man-woman friendships too. For these friendships can be just as close and as dear as those that we form with women. Listen to Lucy's description of one such friendship: 25

"We've found we have things to talk about that are different from what he talks about with my husband and different from what I talk about with his wife. So sometimes we call on the phone or meet for lunch. There are similar intellectual interests—we always pass on to each other the books that we love—but there's also something tender and caring too." 26

In a couple of crises, Lucy says, "he offered himself, 27 for talking and for helping. And when someone died in his family he wanted me there. The sexual, flirty part of our friendship is very small, but *some*—just enough to make it fun and different." She thinks—and I agree—that the sexual part, though small is always *some,* is always there when a man and a woman are friends.

It's only in the past few years that I've made friends 28 with men, in the sense of a friendship that's *mine,* not just part of two couples. And achieving with them the ease and the trust I've found with women friends has value indeed. Under the dryer at home last week, putting on mascara and rouge, I comfortably sat and talked with a fellow named Peter. Peter, I finally decided, could handle the shock of me minus mascara under the dryer. Because we care for each other. Because we're friends.

8. There are medium friends, and pretty good friends, 29 and very good friends indeed, and these friendships are defined by their level of intimacy. And what we'll reveal at each of these levels of intimacy is calibrated with care. We might tell a medium friend, for example, that yesterday we had a fight with our husband. And we might tell a pretty good friend that this fight with our husband made us so mad that we slept on the couch. And we might tell a very good friend that the reason we got so mad in that fight that we slept on the couch had something to do with that girl who works in his office. But it's only to our very best friends that we're willing to tell all, to tell what's going on with that girl in his office.

The best of friends, I still believe, totally love and 30 support and trust each other, and bare to each other the secrets of their souls, and run—no questions asked—to help each other, and tell harsh truths to each other when they must be told.

But we needn't agree about everything (only 12- 31 year-old girl friends agree about *everything*) to tolerate each other's point of view. To accept without judgment. To give and to take without ever keeping score. And to *be* there, as

I am for them and as they are for me, to comfort our sorrows, to celebrate our joys.

BUILDING VOCABULARY

1. Find antonyms (words that mean the opposite of given words) for the following entries:

   a. harsh (par. 1)
   b. mutual (par. 8)
   c. crucial (par. 17)
   d. intimacy (par. 29)
   e. tolerate (par. 31)

2. The *derivation* of a word—how it originated and where it came from—can make you more aware of meanings. Your dictionary normally lists abbreviations (for instance, L. for Latin, Fr. for French) for word origins, and sometimes explains fully the way a word came into use. Look up the following words to determine their origins:

   a. psychology (par. 10)
   b. historical (par. 14)
   c. sibling (par. 16)
   d. Christmas (par. 18)
   e. sexual (par. 27)

UNDERSTANDING THE WRITER'S IDEAS

1. What is Viorst's definition of friendship in the first two paragraphs? Does she accept this definition? Why or why not?

2. Name and describe in your own words the types of friends that Viorst mentions in her essay.

3. In what way are "convenience friends" and "special interest friends" alike? How are "historical friends" and "crossroads friends" alike?

4. What does Viorst mean when she writes, "In our daughter role we tend to do more than our share of self-

revelation; in our mother role we tend to receive what's revealed" (par. 22)?

5. How do part-of-a-couple friends who came with the marriage differ from primary part-of-a-couple friends?

6. Does Viorst think that men can be friends for women? Why or why not? What complicates such friendships?

7. For Viorst, who are the best friends?

UNDERSTANDING THE WRITER'S TECHNIQUES

1. Which paragraphs make up the introduction in this essay? How does Viorst organize these paragraphs? Where does she position her thesis sentence?

2. How does the thesis sentence reveal the principles of classification (the questions Viorst asks to produce the various categories) that the author employs in the essay?

3. Does Viorst seem to emphasize each of her categories equally? Is she effective in handling each category? Why or why not? Do you think that men belong in the article as a category? For what reasons?

4. Analyze the importance of illustration in this essay. From what sources does Viorst tend to draw her examples?

5. How do definition and comparison and contrast operate in the essay? Cite specific examples of these techniques.

6. The level of language in this essay tends to be informal at times, reflecting patterns that are as close to conversation as to formal writing. Identify some sentences that seem to resemble informal speech. Why does Viorst try to achieve a conversational style?

7. Which main group in the essay is further broken down into categories?

8. Analyze Viorst's conclusion. How many paragraphs are involved? What strategies does she use? How does she achieve balanced sentence structure (parallelism) in her last lines?

EXPLORING THE WRITER'S IDEAS

1. Do you accept all of Viorst's categories of friendship? Which categories seem the most meaningful to you?

2. Try to think of people you know who fit into the various categories established by Viorst. Can you think of people who might exist in more than one category? How do you explain this fact? What are the dangers in trying to stereotype people in terms of categories, roles, backgrounds, or functions?

3. Viorst maintains that you can define friends in terms of functions and needs (see paragraph 3 and paragraphs 29 to 31). Would you agree? Why or why not? What principle or principles do you use to classify friends? In fact, *do* you classify friends? For what reasons?

IDEAS FOR WRITING

Guided Writing

Using the classification method, write an essay on a specific group of individuals—for instance, *types of friends, types of enemies, types of students, types of teachers, types of politicians, types of dates*—and so forth.

1. Establish your subject in the first paragraph. Also indicate to the reader the principle(s) of classification that you plan to use. (For guidelines look again at the second sentence in paragraph 3 of Viorst's essay.)

2. Start the body of the essay with a single short sentence that introduces categories (see paragraph 4). In the body, use numbers and category headings ("Convenience friends" . . . "Special interest friends") to separate groups.

3. Try to achieve a balance in the presentation of information on each category. Define each type and provide appropriate examples.

4. If helpful, use comparison and contrast to indicate from time to time the similarities and differences among groups. Try to avoid too much overlapping of groups, since this is harmful to the classification process.

5. Employ the personal "I" and other conversational techniques to achieve an informal style.

6. Return to your principle(s) of classification and amplify this feature in your conclusion. If you want, make a value judgement, as Viorst does, about which type of person in your classification scheme is the most significant.

More Writing Projects

1. Write an essay classifying the varieties of love.

2. Classify varieties of show business comedians, singers, talk show hosts, star athletes, or the like.

Kennell Jackson, Jr.

MYTHS ABOUT AFRICA

In terms of the classification process, "myth" can be divided in a variety of ways. As you read this selection by Kennell Jackson, Jr., who is Assistant Professor of history at Stanford University, locate the principle of classification employed by the author. Moreover, pay special attention to the vocabulary in this essay, which tends to be fairly demanding of the reader.

Words to Watch

dubious (par. 1): causing doubt or skepticism
foisted (par. 1): passed off as genuine
denigrating (par. 1): blackening the name of; insulting
pernicious (par. 1): causing injury or harm
benign (par. 1): favorable; beneficial
empirical (par. 1): relying or based only on observation or practical experience
subverted (par. 1): undermined; ruined
terra incognita (par. 2): unknown land
purgatory (par. 2): a sinful place; a place of punishment
Proteus (par. 3): in Greek mythology, a sea god who was able to change his form at will
pastoral (par. 3): characteristic of a peaceful rural life
evocations (par. 3): callings forth; depictions; imaginative recreations
cartographers (par. 3): people who make maps
conjured (par. 3): called upon; appealed to; summoned
aura (par. 4): a special atmosphere or air surrounding a person or thing

idyllic (par. 4): pleasing and simple
agglomeration (par. 4): a mass, cluster, or heap
avarice (par. 4): greed; an excessive desire to get or keep money
iconoclasm (par. 4): the attacking or ridiculing of traditional ways
    or ideas
transcend (par. 4): to go beyond the limits; to overcome
presumptuous (par. 5): too bold; taking too much for granted
idiom (par. 5): language; style of expression
Cartesian (par. 6): relating to the ideas of the French philosopher
    Rene Descartes (1596–1650), who believed in the power
    of the mind to solve problems
ethnographer (par. 6): a specialist in that branch of anthropology
    that deals with specific cultures
postulated (par. 6): claimed; assumed; taken as self-evident
dichotomy (par. 6): a division
ingenuous (par. 7): frank; open; straightforward
feudalism (par. 7): a social and economic system in which people
    are bonded to the land and to an overlord
pathology (par. 8): disease
unfettered (par. 8): freed from restraint; liberated

In past centuries and during much of this one, the 1
realities of Africa have been distorted by a host of myths,
most of which were generated in Europe. Part of Africa's
burden in the world—a kind of black man's burden—has
been bearing the weight of myth. Indeed, black Africa might
have the highly dubious distinction of being one of the most
mythologized cultural regions of the globe. It would be a
mistake to assume, as it often is, that all the fictions foisted
upon Africa have been unsavory in character. Actually,
denigrating the area is a relatively late phenomenon. Nevertheless, regardless of whether past myths were pernicious
or benign, they frequently simplified reality, often lacked a
broad empirical base, and in general revealed more about
their creators than about the continent. As a consequence,
incorrect images of the region subverted much of the potential for understanding in the outside world.

Africa has been as much a landscape in the imagi- 2
nation as a real place. In almost every century, it was
reinvented. The reasons for the rise of myths have been as
varied as the fictions themselves. Occasionally it was the
fact that Africa was unknown. It was *terra incognita* and
became artificially known through the action of myth. At
other points in the history of mythical Africa, myths were
used to rationalize European actions in Africa: During the
centuries of the slave trade, Africa was consistently drawn
as a purgatory and the slave boats were pictured as rescuing
people from its depths. In still other instances, fundamental
misunderstandings of what travelers saw and encountered
in Africa were the source of myth.

Africa was Proteus, constantly being redesigned. 3
During the sixteenth and seventeenth centuries, just after
the beginning of moderate European contact with the continent, black Africa achieved symbolic significance as a
semi-pastoral place. Tinted drawings in travelogues from
the period showed lush African environments inhabited by
warmly burnished people—occasionally poised like figures
of Grecian sculpture—living out a gentle rural existence.
Tranquil and radiant, these drawings could have been easily
lifted from the easel of Pieter Brueghel, the seventeenth-
century Dutch painter. In fact, they bear a striking resem-
blance to his evocations of Holland's countryside. Italian
cartographers in these centuries conjured up another Africa.
They positioned numerous small kingdoms in the interior
of Africa, and set kings on mounds of ornate treasure in the
middle of the Sahara.

Eighteenth- and nineteenth-century images of Af- 4
rica reversed much of this. Dark, menacing Africa was
created. The black portion of the continent retained some of
the aura of an idyllic territory. Yet it was increasingly
depicted in travel reports and portrait as a gigantic agglomeration of social and cultural ills: chaotic political cultures,
naive or irrational belief systems, savage or hypnotic rituals,
and most damaging of all, a corner of the world where
societies pursued the slave trade with particular avarice.
Even a brilliant writer like the Englishman Richard Burton,
who traveled extensively in West and East Africa near the

mid-nineteenth century, could not marshal his considerable intellectual talents—or his powerful iconoclasm—to transcend the stock stereotypes. Black depravity was a favored theme in his writing. What Burton's books did not condemn was indicated by the publication in Europe of other works such as *The White Man's Grave* (1836), *Western Africa: Its Condition and Christianity, The Means of Recovery* (1844), and *Through the Dark Continent* (1878).

As the nineteenth century progressed, Africa was 5 thought in some quarters to be in serious need of systematic European improvement. This period began a peculiar age of uplift. Africa's internal political relations were to be made orderly. Customs were to be made more chaste, more Victorian in cast. Sectors of its people were to be converted to Christianity. Its hinterlands were to be opened to the redeeming forces of international trade, settler economies, and cash-crop agriculture. Presumptuous as these ideas were, they formed an ideological idiom which generation after generation of explorers, missionaries, and colonizers employed.

Not only outsiders or Westerners have been culprits 6 in molding mythical Africa. A labor as intensive and persistent as the creation of a fictional continent is not confined to a people of one hue or of a single origin! For instance, the 1940s–50s witnessed the emergence of a clique of African poets, called the Negritude poets, who championed in poignant verses natural Africa. To them, Africa was a special territory where the fundamental harmonies between man and the universe were still preserved. Leopold Senghor, a leading figure among these poets (and president of Senegal), proclaimed African man as the opposite of Western, Cartesian man whose identity was attained solely through the exercise of reason. Senghor's black man achieved identity through intuition, participated in the texture of nature, yielded to the rhythm of natural things. Ethnographer Chiekh Anta Diop—an ideological cohort of the poets—took the Senghor model several steps further. European societies, according to him, were war-bent, hostile to foreigners, drab in their present lives, and, in their after-worlds, man could be punished. By contrast, he postulated that African societies were inclined to peace, open, joyous in the here and the hereafter. Obviously, this was a fictional dichotomy.

Another ingenuous example of non-Western myths 7 of Africa can be found in the theories of the Eastern European historian André Sik. After meditating on Africa's history prior to colonialism, Sik claimed that he had discovered a course of development that duplicated Marx's scheme for the evolution of preindustrial societies. Africa began its ancient history with a stage of primitive communalism in which collective production and sharing obtained. From this early stage, the continent entered centuries of feudalism. At the crest of feudalism in Africa, the natural path of African development was interrupted by colonialism. Sik saw little that was singularly African in the continent's history.

For a long time, African intellectuals have attempted 8 to combat the pathology of myth-making. So long have they been adversaries of myth that they know its workings well. But, at the same time, combating false representations has distracted them from the more serious challenge of establishing the preconditions of an unfettered Africa. As the editor of the *Liberian Herald* lamented, in 1853, "We are caught by the view of 'Africa, the Dark' and while we must fight it, we should know that we are losing. Our continent reeks of poorness while we defend our worth."

BUILDING VOCABULARY

1. Although the vocabulary is difficult in this essay, many words can be learned through a study of their structure. One aspect of structure is the prefix—the syllable that comes before the root (or basic part) of a word in order to give it a special meaning. Such syllables as *ab, bi, de, pre,* and *sub* are examples of prefixes. Major prefixes are normally defined in your dictionary. Explain how the underlined prefixes in these words from the essay can help a reader understand meanings:

a. subverted (par. 1)

b. transcend (par. 4)
c. dichotomy (par. 6)
d. pathology (par. 8)
e. distracted (par. 8)

2. Decide the meaning of each of the italicized words from context. Do not use your dictionaries until after you try to state the definition.

a. "Part of Africa's *burden* in the world . . . has been bearing the weight of myth." (par. 1)
b. "Mounds of *ornate* treasure" (par. 3)
c. "Richard Burton . . . could not *marshal* his considered intellectual talents." (par. 4)
d. "Customs were to be made more *chaste*, more Victorian in cast." (par. 5)
e. "Africa began its ancient history with a stage of *primitive communalism* in which collective production and sharing obtained." (par. 7)

3. Use ten of the words in the Words to Watch section in sentences of your own.

UNDERSTANDING THE WRITER'S IDEAS

1. Put the numbers 1, 2, 3, and so on next to these sentences so that the following details will be in the order that they occur in the essay.

a. "During the sixteenth and seventeenth centuries . . . black Africa achieved symbolic significance as a semi-pastoral place."
b. "Africa began its ancient history with a stage of primitive communalism. . . ."
c. "During the centuries of the slave trade, Africa was consistently drawn as a purgatory. . . ."
d. ". . . the 1940's and 1950's witnessed the emergence of a clique of African poets. . . ."

e. "Eighteenth- and nineteenth-century images of Africa reversed much of this."

2. Identify the following people: Pieter Brueghel, the Negritude poets, Andre Sik, Richard Burton, Leopold Senghor.

3. Where did most of the myths about Africa arise? Have Africans invented myths of their own? Are all the myths about Africa bad?

4. Why are there so many myths about Africa?

5. Name and describe five myths about Africa.

6. How does the author define "myth"?

7. What does Professor Jackson mean when he writes, "Africa has been as much a landscape in the imagination as a real place"?

8. What is the author's attitude toward the ideas of Chiekh Anta Diop?

9. Explain the main idea of the last paragraph.

UNDERSTANDING THE WRITER'S TECHNIQUES

1. Into what two large groups has Jackson divided his topic? What further categories has he set up under each group?

2. Where does Jackson place his thesis sentence? Does his thesis sentence express an opinion? How does it help him limit his topic?

3. How does Jackson use narrative to help establish his classification pattern?

4. How does the author develop paragraph 2?

5. Analyze the method of classification in paragraphs 3 to 5.

6. Analyze vocabulary and sentence structure in paragraph 3. What does the variety of short sentences and long sentences contribute to the essay? What is the purpose of long sentences in this paragraph, and throughout the essay in general?

7. How does Jackson restate his thesis in the last paragraph? Does he also expand his thesis at this point? How effective is the concluding quotation?

EXPLORING THE WRITER'S IDEAS

1. What do most people mean when they use the word "myth"? Do you think that "myth" is always separate from reality? What can myth tell us about reality?

2. What are some definitions of myth other than that employed by Jackson? What types of myths exist? Consult a dictionary or encyclopedia for basic information.

3. State your support of or opposition to the idea that every nation or continent has a set of myths. What might be some myths about America as Americans see them? as non-Americans see them?

4. How has the "myth of Africa" been reinforced by American movies and by such fictional heroes as "Tarzan"?

IDEAS FOR WRITING

Guided Writing

Organize a classification essay around the topic, "Myths about _____." Such topics as "Myths about Religion," Myths about Sex," and "Myths about Animals" would be appropriate.

1. Place a thesis statement at the start of your essay, one that states an opinion about the topic.

2. Explain what you mean by myth and how you will use it in the essay.

3. List at least three types of myth about the subject you have selected.

4. Divide the body of the essay according to the main categories in your classification of the subject. Devote one paragraph to each type of myth.

5. Try to use in your essay at least five new words that you have learned from Jackson's selection.

6. Rephrase and expand your thesis in the concluding paragraph.

More Writing Projects

    1.   Classify Americans according to "types."

    2.   Write an extended paragraph in which you classify myths about professional athletes.

Institute for Propaganda Analysis

TYPES OF PROPAGANDA

Although this essay was prepared by the Institute for Propaganda Analysis in 1937, it is still relevant today. Written as a guide to propaganda devices, the article relies on classification to break its subject into clearly understandable parts. This is a somewhat longer essay that utilizes both classification and other important rhetorical strategies to achieve its desired effect.

Words to Watch

scrutiny (par. 3): close examination

dissented (par. 7): disagreed with; refused to accept the doctrines of

demagogue (par. 7): a person who tries to stir up people by appealing to their emotions or prejudices in order to achieve power or become a leader

pertinent (par. 8): to the point; relevant

implications (par. 8): conclusions that can be drawn from facts

comprises (par. 8): consists of; included

status quo (par. 8): the existing state of affairs

personify (par. 13): symbolize; give human qualities to

sanction (par. 15): support; authorization

revere (par. 15): to regard with great respect

titan (par. 19): giant

intervene (par. 19): to come between

artifices (par. 20): artful devices; tricks

zealots (par. 21): fanatics; people extremely devoted to a cause

espouse (par. 21): to support
attainment (par. 22): accomplishment; anything acquired
gullible (par. 22): easily cheated or tricked
adroitly (par. 23): skillfully; cleverly

If American citizens are to have clear understanding 1
of present-day conditions and what to do about them, they
must be able to recognize propaganda, to analyze it, and to
appraise it.

But what is propaganda? 2

As generally understood, *propaganda is expression* 3
of opinion or action by individuals or groups deliberately
designed to influence opinions or actions of other individuals
or groups with reference to predetermined ends. Thus propaganda differs from scientific analysis. The propagandist is
trying to "put something across," good or bad, whereas the
scientist is trying to discover truth and fact. Often the
propagandist does not want careful scrutiny and criticism;
he wants to bring about a specific action. Because the action
may be socially beneficial or socially harmful to millions of
people, it is necessary to focus upon the propagandist and
his activities the searchlight of scientific scrutiny. Socially
desirable propaganda will not suffer from such examination,
but the opposite type will be detected and revealed for what
it is.

We are fooled by propaganda chiefly because we 4
don't recognize it when we see it. It may be fun to be fooled
but, as the cigarette ads used to say, it is more fun to know.
We can more easily recognize propaganda when we see it if
we are familiar with the seven common propaganda devices.
These are:

1. The Name Calling Device
2. The Glittering Generalities Device
3. The Transfer Device

4. The Testimonial Device
5. The Plain Folks Device
6. The Card Stacking Device
7. The Band Wagon Device

Why are we fooled by these devices? Because they 5
appeal to our emotions rather than to our reason. They
make us believe and do something we would not believe or
do if we thought about it calmly, dispassionately. In examining these devices, note that they work most effectively
at those times when we are too lazy to think for ourselves;
also, they tie into emotions which sway us to be "for" or
"against" nations, races, religions, ideals, economic and
political policies and practices, and so on through automobiles, cigarettes, radios, toothpastes, presidents, and wars.
With our emotions stirred, it may be fun to be fooled by
these propaganda devices, but it is more fun and infinitely
more to our own interests to know how they work.

Lincoln must have had in mind citizens who could 6
balance their emotions with intelligence when he made his
remark: ". . . but you can't fool all of the people all of the
time."

Name Calling

"Name Calling" is a device to make us form a judgment 7
without examining the evidence on which it should be based.
Here the propagandist appeals to our hate and fear. He does
this by giving "bad names" to those individuals, groups,
nations, races, policies, practices, beliefs, and ideals which
he would have us condemn and reject. For centuries the
name "heretic" was bad. Thousands were oppressed, tortured, or put to death as heretics. Anybody who dissented
from popular or group belief or practice was in danger of
being called a heretic. In the light of today's knowledge,
some heresies were bad and some were good. Many of the
pioneers of modern science were called heretics; witness the
cases of Copernicus, Galileo, Bruno. Today's bad names

include: Fascist, demagogue, dictator, Red, financial oligarchy, Communist, muckraker, alien, outside agitator, economic royalist, Utopian, rabble-rouser, troublemaker, Tory, Constitution wrecker.

"Al" Smith called Roosevelt a Communist by impli- 8 cation when he said in his Liberty League speech, "There can be only one capital, Washington or Moscow." When "Al" Smith was running for the presidency many called him a tool of the Pope, saying in effect, "We must choose between Washington and Rome." That implied that Mr. Smith, if elected President, would take his orders from the Pope. Likewise Mr. Justice Hugo Black has been associated with a bad name, Ku Klux Klan. In these cases some propagandists have tried to make us form judgments without examining essential evidence and implications. "Al Smith is a Catholic. He must never be President." "Roosevelt is a Red. Defeat his program." "Hugo Black is or was a Klansman. Take him out of the Supreme Court."

Use of "bad names" without presentation of their 9 essential meaning, without all their pertinent implications, comprises perhaps the most common of all propaganda devices. Those who want to *maintain* the status quo apply bad names to those who would change it. . . . Those who want to *change* the status quo apply bad names to those who would maintain it. For example, the *Daily Worker* and the *American Guardian* apply bad names to conservative Republicans and Democrats.

Glittering Generalities

"Glittering Generalities" is a device by which the propa- 10 gandist identifies his program with virtue by use of "virtue words." Here he appeals to our emotions of love, generosity, and brotherhood. He uses words like truth, freedom, honor, liberty, social justice, public service, the right to work, loyalty, progress, democracy, the American way, Constitution defender. These words suggest shining ideals. All persons of good will believe in these ideals. Hence the propagandist, by identifying his individual group, nation, race, policy, practice, or belief with such ideals, seeks to win us to his cause. As Name Calling is a device to make us form a judgment to *reject and condemn,* without examining the evidence, Glittering Generalities is a device to make us *accept and approve,* without examining the evidence.

For example, use of the phrases "the right to work" 11 and "social justice" may be a device to make us accept programs for meeting labor-capital problems, which, if we examined them critically, we would not accept at all.

In the Name Calling and Glittering Generalities 12 devices, words are used to stir up our emotions and to befog our thinking. In one device "bad words" are used to make us mad; in the other "good words" are used to make us glad.

The propagandist is most effective in the use of these 13 devices when his works make us create devils to fight or gods to adore. By his use of the "bad words," we personify as a "devil" some nation, race, group, individual, policy, practice, or ideal; we are made fighting mad to destroy it. By use of "good words," we personify as a godlike idol some nation, race, group, etc. Words which are "bad" to some are "good" to others, or may be made so. Thus, to some the New Deal is "a prophecy of social salvation" while to others it is "an omen of social disaster."

From consideration of names, "bad" and "good," we 14 pass to institutions and symbols, also "bad" and "good." We see these in the next device.

Transfer

"Transfer" is a device by which the propagandist carries 15 over the authority, sanction, and prestige of something we respect and revere to something he would have us accept. For example, most of us respect and revere our church and our nation. If the propagandist succeeds in getting church or nation to approve a campaign in behalf of some program, he thereby transfers its authority, sanction, and prestige to that program. Thus we may accept something which otherwise we might reject.

In the Transfer device, symbols are constantly used. 16
The cross represents the Christian Church. The flag represents the nation. Cartoons like Uncle Sam represent a
consensus of public opinion. Those symbols stir emotions.
At their very sight, with the speed of light, is aroused the
whole complex of feelings we have with respect to church or
nation. A cartoonist by having Uncle Sam disapprove a
budget for unemployment relief would have us feel that the
whole United States disapproves relief costs. By drawing an
Uncle Sam who approves the same budget, the cartoonist
would have us feel that the American people approve it.
Thus the Transfer device is used both for and against causes
and ideas.

Testimonial

The "Testimonial" is a device to make us accept anything 17
from a patent medicine or a cigarette to a program of
national policy. In this device the propagandist makes use
of testimonials. "When I feel tired, I smoke a Camel and get
the grandest 'lift'." "We believe the John L. Lewis plan of
labor organization is splendid; C.I.O. should be supported."
This device works in reverse also; counter-testimonials may
be employed. Seldom are these used against commercial
products like patent medicines and cigarettes, but they are
constantly employed in social, economic, and political issues.
"We believe that the John L. Lewis plan of labor organization
is bad; C.I.O. should not be supported."

Plain Folks

"Plain Folks" is a device used by politicians, labor leaders, 18
businessmen, and even by ministers and educators to win
our confidence by appearing to be people like ourselves—
"just plain folks among the neighbors." In election years
especially do candidates show their devotion to little children
and the common, homey things of life. They have front porch
campaigns. For the newspapermen they raid the kitchen

cupboard, finding there some of the good wife's apple pie. They go to country picnics; they attend service at the old frame church; they pitch hay and go fishing; they show their belief in home and mother. In short, they would win our votes by showing that they're just as common as the rest of us—"just plain folks"—and, therefore, wise and good. Businessmen often are "plain folks" with the factory hands. Even distillers use the device. "It's our family's whiskey, neighbor; and neighbor, it's your price."

Card Stacking

"Card Stacking" is a device in which the propagandist 19 employs all the arts of deception to win our support for himself, his group, nation, race, policy, practice, belief, or ideal. He stacks the cards against the truth. He uses under-emphasis and over-emphasis to dodge issues and evade facts. He resorts to lies, censorship, and distortion. He omits facts. He offers false testimony. He creates a smoke screen of clamor by raising a new issue when he wants an embarrassing matter forgotten. He draws a red herring across the trail to confuse and divert those in quest of facts he does not want revealed. He makes the unreal appear real and the real appear unreal. He lets half-truth masquerade as truth. By the Card Stacking device, a mediocre candidate, through the "build-up," is made to appear an intellectual titan; an ordinary prize fighter, a probable world champion; a worthless patent medicine, a beneficent cure. By means of this device propagandists would convince us that a ruthless war of aggression is a crusade for righteousness. Some member nations of the Non-Intervention Committee send their troops to intervene in Spain. Card Stacking employs sham, hypocrisy, effrontery.

The Band Wagon

The "Band Wagon" is a device to make us follow the crowd, 20 to accept the propagandist's program en masse. Here his theme is: "Everybody's doing it." His techniques range from those of medicine show to dramatic spectacle. He hires a hall, fills a great stadium, marches a million men in parade. He employs symbols, colors, music, movement, all the dramatic arts. He appeals to the desire, common to most of us, to "follow the crowd." Because he wants us to "follow the crowd" in masses, he directs his appeal to groups held together by common ties of nationality, religion, race, environment, sex, vocation. Thus propagandists campaigning for or against a program will appeal to us as Catholics, Protestants, or Jews; as members of the Nordic race or as Negroes; as farmers or as school teachers; as housewives or as miners. All the artifices of flattery are used to harness the fears and hatreds, prejudices, and biases, convictions and ideals common to the group; thus emotion is made to push and pull the group on to the Band Wagon. In newspaper articles and in the spoken word this device is also found. "Don't throw your vote away. Vote for our candidate. He's sure to win." Nearly every candidate wins in every election—before the votes are in.

Propaganda and Emotion

Observe that in all these devices our emotion is the stuff 21 with which propagandists work. Without it they are helpless; with it, harnessing it to their purposes, they can make us glow with pride or burn with hatred, they can make us zealots in behalf of the program they espouse. As we said at the beginning, propaganda as generally understood is expression of opinion or action by individuals or groups with reference to predetermined ends. Without the appeal to our emotion—to our fears and to our courage, to our selfishness and unselfishness, to our loves and to our hates—propagandists would influence few opinions and few actions.

To say this is not to condemn emotion, an essential 22 part of life, or to assert that all predetermined ends of propagandists are "bad." What we mean is that the intelligent citizen does not want propagandists to utilize his emotions, even to the attainment of "good" ends, without knowing what is going on. He does not want to be "used" in the attainment of ends he may later consider "bad." He does not want to be gullible. He does not want to be fooled. He does not want to be duped, even in a "good" cause. He wants to know the facts and among these is included the fact of the utilization of his emotions.

Keeping in mind the seven common propaganda 23 devices, turn to today's newspapers and almost immediately you can spot examples of them all. At election time or during any campaign, Plain Folks and Band Wagon are common. Card Stacking is hardest to detect because it is adroitly executed or because we lack the information necessary to nail the lie. A little practice with the daily newspapers in detecting these propaganda devices soon enables us to detect them elsewhere—in radio, news-reel, books, magazines, and in expressions of labor unions, business groups, churches, schools, political parties.

BUILDING VOCABULARY

1. One very important aspect of vocabulary development is your ability to recognize historical names and references. There are several historical references in this essay, many of them drawn from the 1930s. Consult an encyclopedia or dictionary and identify the following:

    a. Galileo (par. 7)
    b. Utopian (par. 7)
    c. Tory (par. 7)
    d. Al Smith (par. 8)
    e. Franklin D. Roosevelt (par. 8)
    f. Hugo Black (par. 8)
    g. New Deal (par. 13)
    h. John L. Lewis (par. 17)
    i. C.I.O. (par. 17)

2. Write definitions of your own for the main propaganda devices treated in the essay:

    a. Name Calling
    b. Glittering Generalities

c. Transfer
d. Testimonial
e. Plain Folks
f. Card Stacking
g. Band Wagon.

UNDERSTANDING THE WRITER'S IDEAS

1. What idea does this essay stress in the first sentence?
2. How does propaganda differ from scientific analysis?
3. Why, according to the writer, are we easily deceived by propaganda devices?
4. What is meant by the sentence, "In the light of today's knowledge, some heresies were bad and some were good"? (par. 7)
5. What are "virtue words"?
6. What is the similarity between the devices of Name Calling and Glittering Generalities?
7. Why are symbols important in propaganda techniques?
8. Describe in your own words how the Card Stacking device works.
9. Explain the following sentence, "Nearly every candidate wins in every election—before the votes are in." (par. 20)
10. Does this essay condemn the use of emotion? Support your response with evidence from the essay.
11. How will the intelligent citizen treat propaganda devices?

UNDERSTANDING THE WRITER'S TECHNIQUES

1. What is the thesis in this essay? Where is it? Is it developed fully in the essay?
2. Why is *definition* an important rhetorical device in this essay? How do comparison and contrast operate in the selection? How does illustration operate in the essay?
3. Why does the writer use subheadings ("Name

Calling," "Glittering Generalities," etc.)? Do they help the reader? Do they damage the *coherence*—that is, the close relationship of all parts—in this essay? Why or why not?

4. Why does the essay list all seven propaganda devices in paragraph 4? Is this an effective technique?

5. Analyze the function of paragraph 14.

6. What is the purpose of classification in this article? Does the classification scheme seem to be complete? Is each group adequately developed?

7. Is the writer ever guilty of *stereotyping*? Is it possible to use "card stacking," for example, and not to resort to lies?

8. Notice the use of *parallel structure* (the use of the same pattern) in paragraph 19: "He stacks. . . . He uses. . . . He resorts. . . ." Why is this method effective here?

9. Is there any attempt to argue or persuade (see Chapter 9) in this essay?

10. Which paragraphs constitute the conclusion of this essay? Analyze the connection between each paragraph in the concluding section.

EXPLORING THE WRITER'S IDEAS

1. Think of several current examples for each of the seven propaganda devices presented in this essay.

2. Do you think that the American public is more able today to spot propaganda than when this essay was written? Why?

3. Is there such a thing as "socially desirable propaganda" (see paragraph 3)? Can you think of such examples?

4. This essay was written prior to the introduction of television to the public. Do the propaganda devices mentioned in the essay appear on television? Discuss various commercials that seem to use propaganda devices.

5. Bring to class a newspaper or magazine, and locate propaganda devices that appear in it.

IDEAS FOR WRITING

Guided Writing

Select the three categories of propaganda devices that you find most important today, and write an essay in which you illustrate the features of each category.

1. Introduce the reader to the devices in the introductory paragraph.

2. Establish a thesis in the introductory paragraph.

3. Provide your own definitions for the propaganda devices that you selected.

4. Devote at least one paragraph to each propaganda device.

5. Use examples to support your classification. Draw these examples from television, politics, newspapers, and other appropriate sources.

6. Use parallel structure (see paragraph 19) at least once in the essay.

7. Devote your conclusion to the way in which Americans should respond to propaganda devices.

More Writing Projects

1. Write an essay that classifies the types of propaganda used by governments today.

2. Select a newspaper and develop an essay that explores categories of propaganda.

3. Write an essay in which you classify the types of people apt to be fooled by propaganda devices. Do not create categories that are too obvious (like *smart* and *dumb,* or *men, women,* and *children*). Give names to the groups you establish; show the qualities that members of each group share; show how the groups are different from each other. Be careful not to stereotype the people in each group.

4. Bring to class advertisements which you find in *Esquire, Time, Newsweek, Sports Illustrated,* or other magazines. Label the propaganda devices that you see being

used in the advertisement and explain other uses that complement the propaganda devices such as arrangement, colors, personalities. From class analysis draw inferences about the advertiser's methods in selling the product. Develop a theme on classification of advertising propaganda devices in one or two advertisements. Attach the ad to your theme when you submit it to your instructor.

seven

Process Analysis

Process analysis concentrates on *how* something is done, how something works, or how something occurs. If writing aims essentially to explain things, you can see why writers need to use process analysis. Often, the major point that will impress a reader depends on his or her ability to understand the logical steps in some plan of procedure. As a method of paragraph or essay development, process analysis traces all important steps, from beginning to end, in an activity or event. The amount of detail provided for each step in the process will depend on how much the audience knows about the subject.

Whether you are dealing with such subjects as how Columbus discovered America, how a carburetor works, how to develop a good tennis serve, or how to can fruit at home, you must present all essential information to your audience. Frequently, other methods of essay development help reinforce your analysis of process. (For example, writers often use *definition* to explain terms in a technical process that might not be familiar to readers; and to relate in clear order the steps in a process, an essay might require *narrative* techniques.) These methods will serve your main objective of explaining the process from beginning to end.

Although the purpose of process analysis is to provide your audience with a step-by-step explanation of a procedure, process analysis can also inform readers about the *significance* of the process; that is, it will instruct and inform. A typical problem in explanations of process is that a writer often assumes that readers know more than they do. You can avoid this problem by defining your audience carefully. Certainly, you would use one approach to explain how to make a perfect cheese omelet to newlyweds; and you would use a completely different approach to explain it to students in advanced cooking class. Although both groups might have to follow the same sequence of steps, the kind of information you provide and the range of your explanations would be significantly different. No matter what approach you take to process analysis, remember to present material in a clear and lively manner. In reading about how something is done, or how something works, no reader wants to be bored; make an effort to keep your writing interesting.

Arthur Ashe and Clark Graebner

THE SERVE

Many people would like to develop a particular sports talent like improving their tennis game. In this selection, Arthur Ashe and Clark Graebner, both of whom were born in 1943 and who served on the U. S. Davis Cup team, show how to perfect the tennis serve. As you read this essay, notice the careful attention the writers pay to each important step in the technique.

Words to Watch

forehand grip (par. 2): the "shake hand" grip in tennis; the racket is on its edge and the player "shakes hand" with the handle
backhand grip (par. 2): here, the hand is moved an eighth-turn to the right of the forehand grip
base line (par. 3): the back line at either end of the court
service line (par. 6): the line twenty-one feet from the net that bounds the back of the service courts
trajectory (par. 7): angle of flight

The serve is the most important single shot in 1 tennis. It is the one shot you can practice by yourself any time without need of someone else. Master the serve and you have taken a big step toward being a winning player.

The beginner should hold his racket with a forehand 2
grip. Advanced players use the backhand grip to serve, and
you will too eventually, but for the time, the forehand grip
will be easier. You should develop a smooth flowing serving
stroke before attempting to use the backhand grip.

When you step up to the baseline to serve, your body 3
should be sideways to the net and your feet should be spread
perhaps 12 to 18 inches apart. When you serve in the
forehand court (the one to your left as you face the net),
your left toe should be about an inch behind the baseline,
your left heel about six inches behind it. In other words,
your feet are not parallel to the baseline. When you serve,
your left foot should not touch the line, nor should your
right foot step into the court until your racket has made
contact with the ball. Otherwise it is a footfault and the
penalty is the same as if you hit your serve into the net.

Essentially, the serving motion is the same as the 4
ball throwing motion. Pretend the racket is a ball and
"throw" it toward the service area. The first motion you
make backward transfers your weight to your back foot. As
you swing the racket forward, the weight is transferred to
the forward foot. At no point during the serve should your
arm stop moving; it is all one continuous motion.

A vital part of the serve is the toss of the ball. The 5
object is to place the ball in air exactly where you want to
hit it. You get two serves, but there is no reason why you
should have to hold two balls at once. That's what pockets
are made for. The ball should be held in the fingers of the
left hand, never in the palm. The left hand starts at the
waist, rises slowly and straightens. You should release the
ball only when the arm is fully extended. It should be thrown
just to the point where it will meet the center of the racket
when the right arm is fully extended. If you can achieve a
perfect toss, the rest should come easily. Keep this in mind.
There is no rule in tennis that says you must hit the ball
once you toss it. If by chance you make a bad toss, say, too
far behind you, stop in mid-swing and start over again.
After apologizing to your opponent, of course.

Here is a suggestion: since the fun of tennis is to be 6 able to get the ball into play as soon as possible you may enjoy learning to serve more if you start, not from the baseline, but from the service line. Once you start putting the ball into the service court from close range, keep moving back until at last you are on the baseline.

Once you have learned how to serve, how to hit the 7 ball into the court, you can try a few variations. There are, basically, three serves—the slice, twist and flat, sometimes known as cannonball. The slice is the basic delivery for all players, whether beginners or advanced. The racket face sweeps across the side of the ball furthest from you (the three o'clock side) instead of striking directly behind it, and causes the ball to move from your opponent's left to his right. The flat serve has almost no spin and no chance of going in unless you are six feet tall. The flat serve moves in a straight line from the middle of the racket down to the court, but in the process it must, of course, cross the net. Tall players can do this, but shorter ones need spin to give the ball a curved trajectory.

The twist is good only if served well. Otherwise it 8 will provide a set-up for the receiver. It must be deep and it must have a high kick to the backhand side. You can put twist on the ball by tossing it slightly behind your head (instead of in front on the slice), then bringing the racket across it from left to right. Don't try this one until you can put your regular serve into play consistently.

BUILDING VOCABULARY

1. *Jargon* is the use of words normally associated with a particular field or profession. Take five of the special tennis terms in this essay and use them in sentences of your own.

2. Take any sports activity (baseball, football, track) and make a list of its jargon (five examples will be enough). Then write definitions for these special terms that are important to the sport.

UNDERSTANDING THE WRITERS' IDEAS

1. State in your own words the main idea of this essay.

2. Why should beginners use the forehand grip when serving?

3. What is a "footfault"?

4. Explain in your own words the "continuous motion" involved in the serve.

5. Why is a perfect toss so important to a successful serve? How is the toss managed?

6. Describe the three basic types of serves.

7. Is it wise to hit directly behind the ball during the serve? Why?

UNDERSTANDING THE WRITERS' TECHNIQUES

1. Where do the authors place their thesis sentence? Is this an effective spot? Why or why not?

2. How does the introduction involve the reader? Why would any tennis player really want to read on after he or she read the first paragraph?

3. Analyze paragraphs 2 to 4. What are the specific steps in the serving process?

4. What is the function of paragraph 5? Does the step in paragraph 5 follow logically from information in paragraph 4?

5. Explain the purpose of paragraph 6. Is it necessary to the process analysis? Could it be eliminated? Why or why not?

6. How do the authors employ classification and definition in paragraphs 7 to 8?

7. Analyze the authors' concluding paragraph. What device do they use to end the selection?

8. What sort of audience have the authors written for? How is this reflected in the style, content, and organization of the essay?

9. Can you easily visualize the tennis serve as the authors describe it? Could you follow their instructions?

EXPLORING THE WRITERS' IDEAS

1. How important is technique in a sport, and how important is natural ability?

2. Based on your own knowledge of tennis, have the authors left anything out in their presentation of the tennis serve?

3. The authors assert that a good serve will help make a winning player. Is it necessary to win in order to enjoy a sport like tennis? Are all sports competitive by nature?

IDEAS FOR WRITING

Guided Writing

In an essay employing process analysis, show how to perform a specific sports activity (or series of activities).

1. In your introductory paragraph, establish your subject and explain why it is important to master this particular activity.

2. Be sure not to select too large a topic. It would be tougher to write an essay on how to play baseball than it would be to write one on how to play third base.

3. Decide beforehand on the number of steps that you plan to describe in your process. Then organize your steps in such a way as to permit a minimum of two paragraphs in the body of your essay.

4. Assume that you are writing for beginners. Make certain that you define any special terms that your audience might not know.

5. Use formal transitions (see page 391) to move from one important step in the process to the next.

6. Save the last step for the closing paragraph, and develop your conclusion around it.

More Writing Projects

1. Use process analysis to describe the way your favorite athlete performs a specific activity in the game.

2. Bring a book to class that explains how to master a particular sport. After examining it, write an essay on how the process is described in the book. Where does the author begin, and where does he or she end?

3. Observe some sport you have never played, and write a process paper in which you explain how to perform one feature of it. You might watch some children at play and then explain how they manage a certain game.

Grace Lichtenstein

COORS BEER

Process analysis often deals with mechanical or technical procedures. In this short selection by Grace Lichtenstein, who is a correspondent for *The New York Times,* the author examines a mechanical process—the brewing of beer. As you read this piece, look for the methods that the author uses to make this technical process interesting and understandable to the general reader.

Words to Watch

palate (par. 1): taste or sense of taste
mystique (par. 2): special, almost mysterious attitudes and feelings
     surrounding a person, place, or thing
Spartan (par. 3): simple and severe
rancid (par. 4): not fresh; having a bad smell
permeate (par. 4): to spread through everything
nondescript (par. 4): lacking any recognizable character or quality
cellulose (par. 5): the main substance in woody parts of plants,
     used in many manufacturing processes

Coors is a light-bodied beer, meaning it is brewed 1
with less malt, fewer hops and more rice than beers with a
tangy taste. Compared with Heineken's or other more full-

bodied foreign beers, Coors does seem almost flavorless and it is this quality that could account for its popularity among young people just starting to get acquainted with the pleasures of beer drinking. A few locals scoff at Coors, calling it "Colorado Kool-Aid." But the fact is that, according to Ernest Pyler, "if you conducted a blindfold test of the four leading beers, the chances of picking our Coors would be minimal." Indeed, one national newspaper conducted an informal test among eight beer drinkers, finding that only three could correctly identify Coors. My own admittedly uneducated palate detects no difference between Coors and Schaefer. In short, the difference between Coors and any other decent beer could be 1,800 miles. Maybe, if Paul Newman suddenly switched to Schaefer, Denverites would pay $15 a case for it.

There is one aspect to the Coors mystique that does 2 have measurable validity. Company officials make much of the fact that Coors has good mountain water and the most expensive brewing process in the country. Several elements are unusual, though not unique.

Thousands of visitors have learned about the process 3 on guided tours through the antiseptic, Spartan plant. (For out-of-towners, the tour is often a pilgrimage—but for local students of the Colorado School of Mines, it's usually more in the line of a quick belt before classes. The tour lasts 30 minutes, at the end of which visitors are invited to quaff to their heart's content in the hospitality lounge. "I've come here 50 times," boasted one student as he polished off a glass at 11:30 one morning in the lounge.) Situated in the center of town, between two high, flat mesas in the foothills of the Rockies, the plant dominates the community just as the somewhat rancid smell of malt seems to permeate the air; one-fourth of the town's families are said to owe their jobs to the factory's operations. Anyone expecting to see in Golden the foaming white waterfall amid mountain pines that is pictured on every yellow can of Coors will be disappointed. The water used in the brewing comes from nondescript wells hidden in concrete blockhouses. The brewery now puts out about 12 million barrels of beer a year, but construction sites throughout the grounds bear witness to the company's hopes for doubling that capacity by 1984.

Like other beers, Coors is produced from barley. 4 Most of the big Midwestern brewers use barley grown in North Dakota and Minnesota. Coors is the single American brewer to use a Moravian strain, grown under company supervision, on farms in Colorado, Idaho, Wyoming and Montana. At the brewery, the barley is turned into malt by being soaked in water—which must be biologically pure and of a known mineral content—for several days, causing it to sprout and producing a chemical change—breaking down starch into sugar. The malt is toasted, a process that halts the sprouting and determines the color and sweetness (the more the roasting, the darker, more bitter the beer). It is ground into flour and brewed, with more pure water, in huge copper-domed kettles until it is the consistency of oatmeal. Rice and refined starch are added to make mash; solids are strained out, leaving an amber liquid malt extract, which is boiled with hops—the dried cones from the hop vine which add to the bitterness, or tang. The hops are strained, yeast is added, turning the sugar to alcohol, and the beer is aged in huge red vats at near-freezing temperatures for almost two months, during which the second fermentation takes place and the liquid becomes carbonated, or bubbly. (Many breweries chemically age their beer to speed up production; Coors people say only naturally aged brew can be called a true "lager.") Next, the beer is filtered through cellulose filters to remove bacteria, and finally is pumped into cans, bottles or kegs for shipping.

The most unusual aspect of the Coors process is that 5 the beer is not pasteurized, as all but a half-dozen of the 90 or so American beers are. In the pasteurization process, bottles or cans of beer are passed through a heating unit and then cooled. This destroys the yeast in the brew which could cause spoilage, if the cans or bottles or barrels are unrefrigerated for any long period. However, pasteurization also changes the flavor of beer. Coors stopped pasteurizing its product 18 years ago because it decided that "heat is an enemy of beer," according to a company spokesman.

Unpasteurized beer must be kept under constant ^{6} refrigeration. Thus, Coors does not warehouse any of its finished product, as many other brewers do, but ships everything out cold, immediately. In effect, my tour guide, a young management trainee wearing a beer-can tie clip, explained as we wandered through the packaging area, watching workers in surgical masks feed aluminum lids into machines that sealed cans whirling by on conveyor belts, the six-pack you buy in a store contains not only a very fresh beer but also a beer that could be considered draft, since it has been kept cold from vat to home refrigerator.

BUILDING VOCABULARY

1. For the italicized word in each example in Column A below select a definition from Column B.

Column A	Column B
a. locals *scoff* (par. 1)	1. drink heartily
b. *informal* test (par. 1)	2. locations
c. measurable *validity* (par. 2)	3. thickness
d. the *antiseptic* Spartan plant (par. 3)	4. not according to fixed rules
e. to *quaff* to their heart's content (par. 3)	5. a line of certain species
f. flat *mesas* (par. 3)	6. a concentrated form of something
g. construction *sites* (par. 3)	7. soundness
h. a Moravian *strain* (par. 4)	8. make fun of
i. the *consistency* of oatmeal (par. 4)	9. free from infection
j. liquid malt *extract* (par. 4)	10. hills

2. Use five of the italicized words in the first exercise in sentences of your own.

UNDERSTANDING THE WRITER'S IDEAS

1. What is a "light-bodied" beer?

2. What does the author mean when she states, "In short, the difference between Coors and any other decent beer could be 1,800 miles"?

3. What *is* special about Coors beer?

4. Why do college students like to visit the Coors plant?

5. Describe the setting of the Coors brewery. How does it contrast with the picture on the Coors can?

6. Explain in your own words the process by which Coors is produced.

7. Why is the pasteurization process important to the final flavor of any beer?

8. Why can Coors almost be considered a draft beer?

UNDERSTANDING THE WRITER'S TECHNIQUES

1. How do comparison and contrast operate in the first paragraph? Does the author also use definition in this paragraph? Where? For what purpose?

2. What is the function of paragraph 2? What is the purpose of paragraph 3? How does the author develop paragraph 3?

3. Analyze the author's use of transitional devices (see page 391) between paragraphs 2 and 3?

4. Which paragraphs analyze the process of brewing Coors? Make a list of the steps on a sheet of paper. Is the process clear and complete? Does the author use process analysis simply to inform? Does she also provide commentary? Where?

5. Where does the author introduce personal or subjective elements into this essay? Why, at these points, does she provide personal rather than technical details?

EXPLORING THE WRITER'S IDEAS

1. Suppose that three unidentified brands of beer, cola, or cigarettes were placed before you. Would you be able to identify them by taste? What is the importance of "mystique" (or image) or "brand loyalty" to a product's success?

2. Can you think of other products that have a mystique associated with them? What are they, and what accounts for the mystique?

3. Would the fact that Paul Newman drinks Coors affect people's attitudes toward the brand? Why do manufacturers attempt to have certain celebrities associated with their products? Why should consumers be influenced by these associations? (Refer to testimonial device in "Types of Propaganda," p. 207.)

4. Based on this essay, what are some ways to make a technical analysis of process interesting to the reader?

IDEAS FOR WRITING

Guided Writing

Explain how to make or to assemble a particular item or product. For example, you might want to explain how to prepare a certain dish; how to assemble a piece of equipment; how to produce something in a factory. You might want to follow Lichtenstein's example: Explain how a popular drink is made.

1. Start by introducing the reader to your "perfect product," indicating how it is possible to achieve high-quality results in its preparation.

2. Use as examples of the quality of the product, positive statements made by other individuals. These may be the ideas of friends, relatives, or experts.

3. Explain the "mystique," if there is one, surrounding the product.

4. After arousing reader interest sufficiently, de-

scribe the actual process involved, concentrating on all important details in the sequence.

5. In your last paragraph, try to capture the taste, look, or feel of the final product.

More Writing Projects

1. Consult an encyclopedia or other reference book to learn about the making of some product—steel, automobiles, plywood, and so forth. Then explain this process in your own words.

2. Set up an actual testing situation in your class. Have various members test three types of a particular item, such as chocolate, diet soda, a kitchen cleanser. Then write a report describing the process involved in the testing, as well as the process by which results were obtained.

Ernest Hemingway

CAMPING OUT

In this essay by Ernest Hemingway (1898–1961), the author uses the pattern of process analysis to order his materials on the art of camping. Hemingway wrote this piece for the *Toronto Star* in the early 1920s, before he gained worldwide recognition as a major American writer. In it, we see his lifelong interest in the outdoors and in his desire to do things well.

Words to Watch

relief map (par. 2): a map that shows by lines and colors the various heights and forms of the land
Caucasus (par. 2): a mountain range in southeastern Europe
proprietary (par. 7): held under patent or trademark
rhapsodize (par. 9): to speak enthusiastically
browse bed (par. 9): a portable cot
tyro (par. 11): an amateur; a beginner in learning something
dyspepsia (par. 13): indigestion
mulligan (par. 18): a stew made from odds and ends of meats and vegetables

Thousands of people will go into the bush this 1 summer to cut the high cost of living. A man who gets his two weeks' salary while he is on vacation should be able to put those two weeks in fishing and camping and be able to save one week's salary clear. He ought to be able to sleep comfortably every night, to eat well every day and to return to the city rested and in good condition.

But if he goes into the woods with a frying pan, an 2 ignorance of black flies and mosquitoes, and a great and abiding lack of knowledge about cookery the chances are that his return will be very different. He will come back with enough mosquito bites to make the back of his neck look like a relief map of the Caucasus. His digestion will be wrecked after a valiant battle to assimilate half-cooked or charred grub. And he won't have had a decent night's sleep while he has been gone.

He will solemnly raise his right hand and inform 3 you that he has joined the grand army of never-agains. The call of the wild may be all right, but it's a dog's life. He's heard the call of the tame with both ears. Waiter, bring him an order of milk toast.

In the first place he overlooked the insects. Black 4 flies, no-see-ums, deer flies, gnats and mosquitoes were instituted by the devil to force people to live in cities where he could get at them better. If it weren't for them everybody would live in the bush and he would be out of work. It was a rather successful invention.

But there are lots of dopes that will counteract the 5 pests. The simplest perhaps is oil of citronella. Two bits' worth of this purchased at any pharmacist's will be enough to last for two weeks in the worst fly and mosquito-ridden country.

Rub a little on the back of your neck, your forehead 6 and your wrists before you start fishing, and the blacks and skeeters will shun you. The odor of citronella is not offensive to people. It smells like gun oil. But the bugs do hate it.

Oil of pennyroyal and eucalyptol are also much 7 hated by mosquitoes, and with citronella they form the basis for many proprietary preparations. But it is cheaper and better to buy the straight citronella. Put a little on the mosquito netting that covers the front of your pup tent or canoe tent at night, and you won't be bothered.

To be really rested and get any benefit out of a 8
vacation a man must get a good night's sleep every night.
The first requisite for this is to have plenty of cover. It is
twice as cold as you expect it will be in the bush four nights
out of five, and a good plan is to take just double the bedding
that you think you will need. An old quilt that you can
wrap up in is as warm as two blankets.

Nearly all outdoor writers rhapsodize over the 9
browse bed. It is all right for the man who knows how to
make one and has plenty of time. But in a succession of one-
night camps on a canoe trip all you need is level ground for
your tent floor and you will sleep all right if you have plenty
of covers under you. Take twice as much cover as you think
that you will need, and then put two-thirds of it under you.
You will sleep warm and get your rest.

When it is clear weather you don't need to pitch your 10
tent if you are only stopping for the night. Drive four stakes
at the head of your made-up bed and drape your mosquito
bar over that, then you can sleep like a log and laugh at the
mosquitoes.

Outside of insects and bum sleeping the rock that 11
wrecks most camping trips is cooking. The average tyro's
idea of cooking is to fry everything and fry it good and
plenty. Now, a frying pan is a most necessary thing to any
trip, but you also need the old stew kettle and the folding
reflector baker.

A pan of fried trout can't be bettered and they don't 12
cost any more than ever. But there is a good and bad way
of frying them.

The beginner puts his trout and his bacon in and 13
over a brightly burning fire the bacon curls up and dries
into a dry tasteless cinder and the trout is burned outside
while it is still raw inside. He eats them and it is all right
if he is only out for the day and going home to a good meal
at night. But if he is going to face more trout and bacon the
next morning and other equally well-cooked dishes for the
remainder of two weeks he is on the pathway to nervous
dyspepsia.

The proper way is to cook over coals. Have several 14
cans of Crisco or Cotosuet or one of the vegetable shortenings
along that are as good as lard and excellent for all kinds of
shortening. Put the bacon in and when it is about half
cooked lay the trout in the hot grease, dipping them in corn
meal first. Then put the bacon on top of the trout and it will
baste them as it slowly cooks.

The coffee can be boiling at the same time and in a 15
smaller skillet pancakes being made that are satisfying the
other campers while they are waiting for the trout.

With the prepared pancake flours you take a cupful 16
of pancake flour and add a cup of water. Mix the water and
flour and as soon as the lumps are out it is ready for cooking.
Have the skillet hot and keep it well greased. Drop the
batter in and as soon as it is done on one side loosen it in
the skillet and flip it over. Apple butter, syrup or cinnamon
and sugar go well with the cakes.

While the crowd have taken the edge from their 17
appetites with flapjacks the trout have been cooked and they
and the bacon are ready to serve. The trout are crisp outside
and firm and pink inside and the bacon is well done—but
not too done. If there is anything better than that combination the writer has yet to taste it in a lifetime devoted
largely and studiously to eating.

The stew kettle will cook you dried apricots when 18
they have resumed their predried plumpness after a night
of soaking, it will serve to concoct a mulligan in, and it will
cook macaroni. When you are not using it, it should be
boiling water for the dishes.

In the baker, mere man comes into his own, for he 19
can make a pie that to his bush appetite will have it all over
the product that mother used to make, like a tent. Men have
always believed that there was something mysterious and
difficult about making a pie. Here is a great secret. There
is nothing to it. We've been kidded for years. Any man of
average office intelligence can make at least as good a pie
as his wife.

All there is to a pie is a cup and a half of flour, one- 20

half teaspoonful of salt, one-half cup of lard and cold water. That will make pie crust that will bring tears of joy into your camping partner's eyes.

21 Mix the salt with the flour, work the lard into the flour, make it up into a good workmanlike dough with cold water. Spread some flour on the back of a box or something flat, and pat the dough around a while. Then roll it out with whatever kind of round bottle you prefer. Put a little more lard on the surface of the sheet of dough and then slosh a little flour on and roll it up and then roll it out again with the bottle.

22 Cut out a piece of the rolled out dough big enough to line a pie tin. I like the kind with holes in the bottom. Then put in your dried apples that have soaked all night and been sweetened, or your apricots, or your blueberries, and then take another sheet of the dough and drape it gracefully over the top, soldering it down at the edges with your fingers. Cut a couple of slits in the top dough sheet and prick it a few times with a fork in an artistic manner.

23 Put it in the baker with a good slow fire for forty-five minutes and then take it out and if your pals are Frenchmen they will kiss you. The penalty for knowing how to cook is that the others will make you do all the cooking.

24 It is all right to talk about roughing it in the woods. But the real woodsman is the man who can be really comfortable in the bush.

BUILDING VOCABULARY

1. For each word below write your own definition, based on how the word is used in the selection. Check back to the appropriate paragraph in the essay.

    a. abiding (par. 2)
    b. assimilate (par. 2)
    c. valiant (par. 2)
    d. charred (par. 2)
    e. solemnly (par. 3)
    f. requisite (par. 8)

g. succession (par. 9)

h. studiously (par. 17)

i. concoct (par. 18)

j. soldering (par. 22)

UNDERSTANDING THE WRITER'S IDEAS

1. What is Hemingway's main purpose in this essay? Does he simply want to explain how to set up camp and how to cook outdoors?

2. What, according to the writer, are the two possible results of camping out on your vacation?

3. Why is oil of citronella the one insecticide that Hemingway recommends over all others?

4. Is it always necessary to pitch a tent when camping out? What are alternatives to it? How can you sleep warmly and comfortably?

5. Explain the author's process for cooking trout. Also explain his process for baking a pie.

6. Is it enough for Hemingway simply to enjoy "roughing it" while camping out?

UNDERSTANDING THE WRITER'S TECHNIQUES

1. Identify those paragraphs in the essay that involve process analysis, and explain how Hemingway develops his subject in each.

2. What is the main writing pattern in paragraphs 1 and 2? How does this method serve as an organizing principle throughout the essay?

3. How would you characterize the author's style of writing? Is it appropriate to a newspaper audience? Is it more apt for professional fishermen?

4. In what way does Hemingway employ classification in this essay?

5. Analyze the tone of Hemingway's essay.

6. The concluding paragraph is short. Is it effective, nevertheless, and why? How does it reinforce the opening paragraph?

EXPLORING THE WRITER'S IDEAS

1. Camping out was popular in the 1920s, as it is in the 1970s. What are some of the reasons that it remains so attractive today?

2. Hemingway's essay describes many basic strategies for successful camping. He does not rely on "gadgets," or modern inventions to make camping easier. Do such gadgets make camping more fun today than it might have been in the 1920s?

3. The author suggests that there is a right way and a wrong way to do things. Does it matter if you perform a recreational activity right as long as you enjoy doing it? Why?

IDEAS FOR WRITING

Guided Writing

Write a composition on how to do something wrong, and how to do it right—going on vacation, looking for a job, fishing, or whatever.

1. Reexamine the author's first three paragraphs and imitate his method of introducing the right and wrong ways about the subject, and the possible results.

2. Adopt a simple, informal, "chatty" style. Feel free to use a few well-placed cliches and other forms of spoken English. Use several similes.

3. Divide your subject into useful categories. Just as Hemingway treated insects, sleeping, and cooking, try to cover the main aspects of your subject.

4. Explain the process involved for each aspect of your subject. Make certain that you compare and contrast the right and wrong ways of your activity.

5. Write a short, crisp conclusion that reinforces your longer introduction.

More Writing Projects

    1.   Explain how people camp out today.

    2.   Describe how to get to your favorite vacation spot, and what to do when you get there.

    3.   If you have ever camped out, write a process paper explaining one important feature of setting up camp.

LeRoi Jones

CITY OF HARLEM

In this essay by LeRoi Jones, known today as Amiri
Baraka, process analysis is based upon historical movement. The step-by-step tracing of a particular historical
action is a major form of process analysis; it is designed
to show how a situation has developed over a period of
time and, consequently, it depends on narrative techniques. As you read this essay, notice how Jones moves
from the beginning to the end of the process, how he maps
out clear stages in the process, and how he uses other
methods to reinforce the main method.

Words to Watch

vendors (par. 1): sellers of goods
mystic (par. 1): mysterious
existential (par. 2): of or based on existence
sloth (par. 2): laziness
catalysts (par. 7): things that cause a speeding up in a process
influx (par. 7): a coming in
autonomous (par. 7): independent
exodus (par. 10): a going out or departure
queues (par. 13): lines of people waiting for something
hypocrisy (par. 18): pretending to be what one is not

In a very real sense, Harlem is the capital of Black 1
America. And America has always been divided into black
and white, and the substance of the division is social,
economic, and cultural. But even the name Harlem, now,
means simply Negroes (even though some other peoples live
there too). The identification is international as well: even
in Belize, the capital of predominantly Negro British Honduras, there are vendors who decorate their carts with
flowers and the names or pictures of Negro culture heroes
associated with Harlem like Sugar Ray Robinson. Some of
the vendors even wear t-shirts that say "Harlem, U.S.A.,"
and they speak about it as a black Paris. In Havana a young
Afro-Cuban begged me to tell him about the "big leg ladies"
of Lenox Avenue, hoping, too, that I could provide some way
for him to get to that mystic and romantic place.

There are, I suppose, contained within the central 2
mythology of Harlem, almost as many versions of its glam-
our, and its despair, as there are places with people to make
them up. (In one meaning of the name, Harlem is simply a
place white cab drivers will not go.) And Harlem means not
only Negroes, but, of course, whatever other associations
one might connect with them. So in one breath Harlem will
be the pleasure-happy center of the universe, full of loud,
hippy mamas in electric colors and their fast, slick-head
papas, all of them twisting and grinning in the streets in a
kind of existential joyousness that never permits of sadness
or responsibility. But in another breath this same place will
be the gathering place for every crippling human vice, and
the black men there simply victims of their own peculiar
kind of sloth and childishness. But perhaps these are not
such different versions after all; chances are both these
stereotypes come from the same kinds of minds.

But Harlem, as it is, as it exists for its people, as an 3
actual place where actual humans live—that is a very
different thing. Though, to be sure, Harlem is a place—a
city really—where almost anything any person could think
of to say goes on, probably does go on, or has gone on, but
like any other city, it must escape *any* blank generalization

simply because it is alive, and changing each second with each breath any of its citizens take.

When Africans first got to New York, or New 4 Amsterdam as the Dutch called it, they lived in the farthest downtown portions of the city, near what is now called The Bowery. Later, they shifted, and were shifted, as their numbers grew, to the section known as Greenwich Village. The Civil War Draft Riots in 1863 accounted for the next move by New York's growing Negro population.

After this violence (a few million dollars' worth of 5 property was destroyed, and a Negro orphanage was burned to the ground) a great many Negroes moved across the river into Brooklyn. But many others moved farther uptown to an area just above what was known as Hell's Kitchen. The new Negro ghetto was known as Black Bohemia, and later, after the success of an all black regiment in the Spanish-American War, this section was called San Juan Hill. And even in the twenties when most Negroes had made their move even further uptown to Harlem, San Juan Hill was still a teeming branch office of black night life.

Three sections along the east side of Manhattan, 6 The Tenderloin, Black Bohemia, and San Juan Hill or The Jungle featured all kinds of "sporting houses," cabarets, "dancing classes," afterhours gin mills, as well as the Gumbo Suppers, Fish Fries, Egg Nog Parties, Chitterlin' Struts, and Pigfoot Hops, before the Negroes moved still farther uptown.

The actual move into what is now Harlem was 7 caused by quite a few factors, but there are a few that were particularly important as catalysts. First, locally, there were more race riots around the turn of the century between the white poor (as always) and the Negroes. Also, the Black Bohemia section was by now extremely overcrowded, swelled as it was by the influx of Negroes from all over the city. The section was a notorious red light district (but then there have only been two occupations a black woman could go into in America without too much trouble: the other was domestic help) and the overcrowding made worse by the moral squalor that poverty encourages meant that the growing local black population had to go somewhere. The immigrant groups living on both sides of the black ghetto fought in the streets to keep their own ghettoes autonomous and pure, and the Negro had to go elsewhere.

At this time, just about the turn of the century, 8 Harlem (an area which the first Africans had helped connect with the rest of the Dutch city by clearing a narrow road—Broadway—up into the woods of Nieuw Haarlem) was still a kind of semi-suburban area, populated, for the most part, by many of the city's wealthiest families. The elaborate estates of the eighteenth century, built by men like Alexander Hamilton and Roger Morris, were still being lived in, but by the descendants of wealthy merchants. (The Hamilton house still stands near Morningside Heights, as an historic landmark called The Grange. The Morris house, which was once lived in by Aaron Burr, is known as The Jumel House, and it still stands at the northern part of Harlem, near the Polo Grounds, as a museum run by the D.A.R. George Washington used it as his headquarters for a while during the Revolutionary War.) So there was still the quiet elegance of the nineteenth century brownstones and spacious apartment buildings, the wide drives, rolling greens, and huge-trunked trees.

What made the area open up to Negroes was the 9 progress that America has always been proud of—an elevated railway went up in the nineties, and the very rich left immediately and the near rich very soon after. Saint Philips Church, after having its old site bought up by a railroad company, bought a large piece of property, with large apartment buildings, in the center of Harlem, and, baby, the panic was on. Rich and famous Negroes moved into the vacated luxury houses very soon after, including the area now known as "Strivers Row," which was made up of almost one hundred brick mansions designed by Stanford White. The panic was definitely on—but still only locally.

What really turned that quiet suburb into "Black 10 Paris," was the coming of the First World War and the mass exodus of Negroes from the South to large urban centers. At the turn of the century most Negroes still lived in the South and were agricultural laborers, but the entrance of America into the War, and the desperate call for cheap unskilled labor, served to start thousands of Negroes scrambling North. The flow of immigrants from Europe had all but ceased by 1914, and the industrialists knew immediately where to turn. They even sent recruiters down into the South to entice the Negroes north. In 1900 the Negro population of New York City was 60,000; by 1920 it was 152,467; by 1930 it was 327,706. And most of these moved, of course, uptown.

It was this mass exodus during the early part of the 11 century that was responsible for most of the black cities of the North—the huge Negro sections of New York, Chicago, Philadelphia, Detroit, etc. It was also responsible for what these sections would very shortly become, as the masses of Southern Negroes piled into their new Jordans, thinking to have a go at an innocent America.

The twenties are legend because they mark Amer- 12 ica's sudden insane entrance into the 20th century. The war had brought about a certain internationalism and prosperity (even, relatively speaking, for Negroes). During the twenties Harlem was the mecca of the good time and in many ways even came to symbolize the era called the Jazz Age. Delirious white people made the trip uptown to hear Negro musicians and singers, and watch Negro dancers, and even Negro intellectuals. It was, I suppose, the black man's debut into the most sophisticated part of America. The old darkies of the plantation were suddenly all over the North, and making a whole lot of noise.

There were nightclubs in Harlem that catered only 13 to white audiences, but with the best Negro entertainers. White intellectuals made frequent trips to Harlem, not only to find out about a newly emerging black America, but to party with an international set of swinging bodies. It was the era of Ellington at The Cotton Club for the sensual, and The New Negro for the intellectual. Everyone spoke optimistically of the Negro Renaissance, and The New Negro, as if, somehow, the old Negro wasn't good enough. Harlem sparkled then, at least externally, and it took the depression to dull that sparkle, and the long lines of unemployed

Negroes and the longer lines at the soup kitchens and bread queues brought reality down hard on old and New Negroes alike. So the tourist trade diminished, and colorful Harlem became just a social liability for the white man, and an open air jail for the black.

The cold depression thirties, coupled with the decay 14 of old buildings and ancient neighborhoods, and, of course, the seeming inability of the "free enterprise" system to provide either jobs or hope for a great many black people in the city of Harlem, have served to make this city another kind of symbol. For many Negroes, whether they live in Harlem or not, the city is simply a symbol of naked oppression. You can walk along 125th Street any evening and meet about one hundred uniformed policemen, who are there, someone will tell you, to protect the people from themselves.

For many Negroes Harlem is a place one escapes 15 from, and lives in shame about for the rest of his life. But this is one of the weirdest things about the American experience, that it can oppress a man, almost suck his life away, and then make him so ashamed that he was among the oppressed, rather than the oppressors, that he will never offer any protest.

The legitimate cultural tradition of the Negro in 16 Harlem (and America) is one of wild happiness, usually at some black man's own invention—of speech, of dress, of gait, the sudden twist of a musical phrase, the warmness or hurt of someone's voice. But that culture is also one of hatred and despair. Harlem must contain all of this and be capable of producing all of these emotions.

People line the streets in summer—on the corners 17 or hanging out the windows—or head for other streets in winter. Vendors go by slowly . . . and crowds of people from movies or church. (Saturday afternoons, warm or cold, 125th is jammed with shoppers and walkers, and the record stores scream through loudspeakers at the street.) Young girls, doctors, pimps, detectives, preachers, drummers, accountants, gamblers, labor organizers, postmen, wives, Muslims, junkies, the employed, and the unemployed: all going someplace—an endless stream of Americans, whose singularity in America is that they are black and can never honestly enter into the lunatic asylum of white America.

Harlem for this reason is a community of noncon- 18 formists, since any black American, simply by virtue of his blackness, is weird, a nonconformist in this society. A community of nonconformists, not an artist's colony—though blind "ministers" still wander sometimes along 137th Street, whispering along the strings of their guitars—but a colony of old-line Americans who can hold out, even if it is a great deal of the time in misery and ignorance, but still hold out, against the hypocrisy and sterility of big-time America, and still try to make their own lives, simply because of their color, but by now, not so simply, because that color now does serve to identify people in America whose feelings about it are not broadcast every day on television.

BUILDING VOCABULARY

1. Explain the connotations (see page 381) conveyed by the italicized words in these phrases.

    a. "every *crippling* human vice" (par. 2)
    b. "a *teeming* branch office" (par. 5)
    c. "their new *Jordans*" (par. 11)
    d. "the *mecca* of the good time" (par. 12)
    e. "the old *darkies* of the plantation" (par. 12)
    f. "a symbol of *naked* oppression (par. 14)

2. Rewrite paragraph 7, finding substitutes for the following words: *actual; factors; catalysts; extremely; swelled; influx; notorious; squalor; autonomous.*

UNDERSTANDING THE WRITER'S IDEAS

1. What does Jones mean when he writes, "America has been divided into black and white, and the substance of the division is social, economic, and cultural"?

2. According to the author, does Harlem have one meaning or several meanings? Describe the meaning or meanings.

3. Trace in your own words the historic and geographic movement of black Americans in New York City.

4. What were some of the causes of the actual movement of black Americans into Harlem?

5. Explain the effect of the First World War on the population in Harlem.

6. Why are the 1920s important in terms of the history of Harlem?

7. How does Jones define the "legitimate cultural tradition" of black Americans?

8. Why does Jones state that the black American is a nonconformist?

9. Consult an encyclopedia or other reference source and obtain information on the following references in Jones's essay: *British Hondouras; New Amsterdam; Civil War Draft Riots; Spanish-American War; Stanford White; Jazz Age; Negro Renaissance; The American Depression.*

UNDERSTANDING THE WRITER'S TECHNIQUES

1. How does the first paragraph serve as an effective introduction for this essay?

2. Analyze paragraphs 2 and 3. What main rhetorical technique does Jones use to develop these paragraphs? What are some of the transition words (see page 391) that Jones employs from sentence to sentence? What is their effect?

3. What is the connection between narration and process analysis in this essay?

4. How many steps were involved in the process leading to the movement of black Americans into Harlem? Identify the steps in this process. Which paragraphs are devoted to this part of the process?

5. From the turn of the century to the present, what steps does Jones trace in the development of Harlem as "the capital of Black America"?

6. Where does Jones use causal analysis in the essay? definition? classification? comparison and contrast?

7. Explain the *tone* (see page 391) of Jones's essay.

Locate specific passages that provide clues to the author's tone, and discuss them. Where does Jones use *irony* (see page 386)? Is he ever sarcastic? How would you distinguish between irony and sarcasm?

8.   Compare historical narration in this essay with that in Maunsell's "Mau Mau" (see page 386). What are the similarities? differences?

EXPLORING THE WRITER'S IDEAS

1.   "Harlem" is a word that most Americans can identify. Prior to reading Jones's essay, what was your understanding of the term? What feelings and attitudes did you associate with it? How have your attitudes changed now that you have read the essay?

2.   Why are parts of most American cities composed of specific racial or ethnic groups? What are the advantages and disadvantages of this situation? Do cities around you have special names for areas composed of specific racial or ethnic groups? Do people in your city draw special connotations from the names of these areas?

3.   Jones speaks of the "lunatic asylum of white America." Are there "crazy" aspects to American life? What are they? If you think that there is something insane about America, is it an exclusively white phenomenon?

IDEAS FOR WRITING

Guided Writing

Select any subject that lends itself to that variety of process analysis that is based on the passage of time, and write a 500 to 750 word essay on it.

1.   The topic may be personal or impersonal. For instance, an analysis of the development of a problem in your life, and possibly its resolution, would be personal. On the other hand, analysis of a purely historical topic—Westward Expansion, the rise of the Roman Empire, the Civil War—would be impersonal (and probably would require

considerable narrowing and preliminary research). The point is to show how something happened through time.

2. Introduce your topic by explaining possible definitions or approaches to it. Consult paragraphs 1 to 3 of Jones' essay for ideas.

3. In the body of the essay, trace the development of your subject through a series of clear stages. Proceed from start to finish in the process. Identify each important step clearly, and connect it with a particular time; use dates whenever appropriate. Each step must be an identifiable stage in the development of your chronological or historical process.

4. Provide sufficient details and examples for each important step in the process.

5. Use other writing techniques that you have learned—for instance, comparison and contrast, causal analysis, description—to reinforce the process analysis.

6. State your opinion about the process, in detail, in the conclusion of your essay. Make certain that the *tone* comes through to the reader.

More Writing Projects

1. In class, select a single historical movement that all members will research. At the end of the week, each class member should list the steps, with dates, that he or she has found in the historical process under consideration. Then, write your own essay analyzing the process that is central to your subject.

2. Take a famous personality from television, sports, or entertainment, and analyze the steps in the process through which he or she established and developed a career. Use dates to identify all important steps in the process.

eight

Cause-and-Effect Analysis

The analysis of cause and effect—often called *causal analysis*—seeks to explain why events occur, or what the outcome or *expected* results of a chain of happenings might be. Basically, cause-and-effect analysis looks for connections between things and reasons behind them. It involves a way of thinking that identifies conditions (the causes) and establishes results or consequences (the effects). In order to discuss an idea intelligently a writer needs to explore causes and effects. The strength of an explanation may lie simply in his or her ability to point out *why* something is so.

Like all the other writing patterns discussed in this text, cause-and-effect analysis reflects a kind of thinking we do every day. If someone were to ask you why you selected the college that you are now attending, you would offer reasons to explain your choice: the cost, the geographic location, the reputation of the institution, and so forth. These would be the *causes* that you have identified. On the other hand, someone might ask you if and why you like the college now that you are there. You could discuss your satisfaction (or lack of it) with the teachers, the course offerings, the opportunity to work part time, the availability of scholarship money and loans, the beauty of the campus, the variety in your social life. Those are the consequences or results—in other words, the *effects*—of your decision. Of course, basic reasoning and common sense are involved in the way that you identify causes and effects.

When writers use causal analysis as a pattern, they can concentrate either on causes or effects, or they can attempt to balance the two. Moreover, in longer and more complicated papers, a writer can show how one cause produces an effect that, in turn, creates *another* set of causes leading to a second effect. Wherever the pattern takes you, remember to be thorough in presenting all links in your chain of analysis; to consider all possible factors; to avoid oversimplification; and to emphasize all important major and minor causes and effects. The more details and evidence you can offer the better your cause-and-effect paper will be.

Selma H. Fraiberg

WHY DOES THE BABY SMILE?

Selma Fraiberg, a professor of child psychoanalysis, discusses in this chapter from her book, *The Magic Years*, her views on the reasons behind an infant's first real smile. Notice how the author traces more than just a single cause and effect; interrelationships between causes and results help her explain the question she raises in the title. Notice, too, how she offers details as evidence to support parts of her theories.

Words to Watch

milestone (par. 1): important event; major step
solemnly (par. 4): seriously
crudely (par. 4): roughly; without knowledge or skill
evokes (par. 4): calls forth
discriminate (par. 5): tell the difference
crowing (par. 8): making sounds of pleasure or well-being
commonplace (par. 8): ordinary

    The response smile which occurs around two months 1
is a significant milestone in the baby's development. Scientists have been much slower to grasp the significance of this

event than a baby's parents. This is the occasion for great
excitement. The news is transmitted to grandparents and
all interested relatives. No trumpets are blown, no formal
holidays proclaimed, but everyone concerned seems to understand that this smile is very special.

Now no parent cares in the least *why* the baby 2
smiles, or why the psychologists think he smiles, and you
might wish to skip the next few paragraphs except that I
hope you don't. Why the baby smiles is a matter of some
significance in understanding the early phases of human
attachment in the infant.

First of all, let's remember that this response smile 3
has had antecedents. Even in the early weeks we will notice
that satisfaction in the course of nursing or at the end of the
nursing period will cause the mouth to relax in a little smile
of contentment. This early smile of satisfaction is an instinctive reaction and is not yet a response to a human face.

Now let's watch this baby as he nurses. If he is not 4
too sleepy his eyes fix solemnly on the face of his mother.
We have learned experimentally that he does not take in
the whole face before him, only the upper part of the face,
the eyes and forehead. Through repetition of the experience
of nursing and its regular accompaniment, the human face,
an association between nursing and the human face will be
established. But more than this, the pleasure, the satisfactions of nursing become associated with the human face.
Repetition of this pleasurable experience gradually traces
an image of the face on the surface of the memory apparatus
and the foundations of memory are established. When the
mental image is firmly established the visual image of the
human face is "recognized" (very crudely), that is, the sight
of the human face evokes the mental image and it is
"remembered." Now comes the turning point. This is not
just a memory based on pictures, but a memory derived from
image plus pleasure, the association established through
nursing. The baby's response to the sight of the human face
is now seen as a response of pleasure. He smiles at the sight
of the human face. The little smile which had originated as
an instinctive reaction to satisfaction in nursing is now

produced occasionally, then more and more, at the sight of the face, as if the face evokes the memory of satisfaction and pleasure. The baby has made his first human connections.

We should not be disappointed to learn that the baby does not yet discriminate his mother's face from other human faces. "How can they prove *that?*" we'd like to know. "That smile certainly *looks* very special." We know this from two sets of observations. For many weeks after the response smile has been established, almost any human face that presents itself to the baby can elicit the smile. (Ironically, a mask representing the eyes and forehead of the human face can be presented to the baby of this age and this, too, will bring forth a pleasure response.) We may not find this so convincing a proof. How do we know this isn't just a sociable little guy who likes his mother *and* the rest of the human race? And maybe his response to the mask only proves that he has a sense of humor. Perhaps the second set of observations will be more convincing. Psychologists place the positive identification and differentiation of the mother's face around eight months because of certain responses of the infant which are familiar to all of us. He no longer smiles at any face that swims into view. On the contrary, let your jolliest uncle approach with beaming face and twenty keys on a chain to dangle before his eyes and he may be greeted by a quizzical look, an uncomprehending stare or—worse for family relations—a howl! Now let mother or father come over to offer reassurances to the baby and apologies to the uncle, and upon seeing these two faces, the baby relaxes, wriggles and smiles. He may study these three sets of faces for a few minutes and, finally satisfied that the familiar faces are re-established, he turns to the unfamiliar face and permits his uncle to jingle keys and make comical faces for which he may later be rewarded with a smile. Or let grandma who is a frequent, but not constant visitor, offer to take over a bottle feeding. He is hungry, shows eagerness for the bottle, but when he takes in the face that is not mother's he looks dismayed, the face puckers and he howls in protest. "He never did *that* before!" says his grandmother. And it is true that several weeks ago when grandma had taken over a feeding he had polished off his bottle with as much zest as when his mother fed him.

This reaction to the strange face, the not-mother 6 face, is the first positive evidence that he differentiates his mother's face from others. (We should not fail to mention that if father has had close contact with the baby and if there are sisters and brothers, these faces will be differentiated, too. We use "mother" as a convenient reference point and with the understanding that for the period of infancy she will be the primary love object.) The reaction to being fed by grandma shows us, too, that pleasure in eating is no longer simply a matter of biological need and satisfaction, but is bound to the person of his mother. He has finally linked this face, this person, with the satisfaction of his needs and regards her as the source of satisfaction. The pleasure and satisfaction given him through feeding and caring for him are now transferred to her image, and the sight of her face, her presence, will bring forth such crowing and joyful noises, and the disappearance of her face such disappointment that we can say that he loves his mother as a person.

That has a curious sound! "Loves his mother as a 7 person." Obviously, since she is a person how else could he love her? And if we say that we mean "loves her as a person outside himself," that sounds just as foolish to our adult ears. Of course, she is a person outside himself. We know that! But the baby did not. He learned this slowly, awkwardly, in the course of the first months of life. For during the early months the infant doesn't differentiate between his body and other bodies, or between mental images and perceptions, between inner and outer. Everything is undifferentiated oneness, the oneness being centered in the baby himself.

At the time that the baby discovers that his mother 8 is a person outside himself a tremendous amount of learning has taken place. In order to achieve something that seems commonplace to us he had to engage in hundreds of experiments over a period of months. He had to assemble hundreds of pieces in a vast and intricate jig-saw puzzle in order to establish a crude picture of the person-mother and a crude image of his own body. We can reconstruct these experiments largely through observation.

BUILDING VOCABULARY

1.   Look up each word below in a dictionary. Write a definition in your own words. Then, explain how the underlined part(s) of the word contributes to its meaning. Finally, write a sentence that uses the word correctly.

    a. proclaimed (par. 1)
    b. antecedent (par. 3)
    c. accompaniment (par. 4)
    d. uncomprehending (par. 5)
    e. reassurances (par. 5)
    f. differentiate (par. 6)

2.   After you check in a dictionary for meanings of the words in italics, explain the meaning of each word group below:

    a. a smile of *contentment* (par. 3)
    b. *instinctive* reaction (par. 3)
    c. *quizzical* look (par. 5)
    d. face *puckers* (par. 5)
    e. *intricate* puzzle (par. 8)

UNDERSTANDING THE WRITER'S IDEAS

1.   How do parents usually react to the baby's first smile?

2.   Why does the author think we should know why the baby smiles even though we might think it unimportant?

3.   What antecedent for the baby's response smile does the author mention?

4.   How much of the mother do the baby's eyes take in as he nurses?

5.   What important associations develop as the child nurses?

6.   What does Fraiberg mean when she talks of "memory derived from image plus pleasure"?

7.   How do we know that the child, when he first begins to smile, is not discriminating his mother's face from other human faces? What is the first positive evidence that the child differentiates his mother's face from others?

8.   Why does the baby not know the mother as a person outside himself?

UNDERSTANDING THE WRITER'S TECHNIQUES

1.   How does the title almost predict for the reader that the writer's main technique of development will be cause and effect?

2.   In attempting to explain why babies smile, Fraiberg first explores the infant's responses during nursing. How does the writer use cause and effect to explain her point in paragraphs 3 and 4?

3.   What single sentence in paragraph 4 best explains the causes for the baby's smile as a response of pleasure?

4.   What kind of evidence does Fraiberg offer to support her idea that the baby at first does not discriminate his mother's face from other human faces? You notice that she mentions no specific psychologists who performed the experiments nor does she give exact details about the experiments themselves. Why does she not do so? How can she expect readers to accept her evidence?

5.   What kind of evidence does the writer give to show that at about eight months, the baby can differentiate his mother's face? Do you think the evidence convincing? Why? Might the evidence in paragraph 5 be considered oversimplified? Why or why not?

6.   How does the introduction (paragraph 1, perhaps 2) serve to involve the reader immediately in the topic? Which sentence states Fraiberg's main point in writing the essay?

7. Why does the writer state the title as a question? Is it effective? Why do you think so? Where else do you find questions asked by the writer in this essay? Do you find them effective? Why?

8. For what kind of audience do you think Fraiberg is writing: uneducated parents? future teachers? fellow psychiatrists? general magazine readers? children? some other audience? Which of those groups would the author probably not be aiming at? How can you tell? What qualities of Fraiberg's style help you guess at the readers she would like to have?

9. Which paragraphs show these prose techniques: description; narration; illustration; comparison?

10. Does paragraph 8 serve as a strong conclusion? What does Fraiberg try to do there? Does she succeed? This essay is a chapter from a book. What, therefore, do you think is the purpose of the last sentence? If this were an essay for a journal, do you think the writer would have written the last sentence in this way? How might she have changed her conclusion?

EXPLORING THE WRITER'S IDEAS

1. Do you agree that the baby's first smile is usually an occasion for great excitement? Why is this so? Fraiberg suggests that *parents* (more so than scientists) have grasped the significance of this event. Do you agree? How does the rest of Fraiberg's essay serve in some ways to *deny* that parents have grasped the significance?

2. Do you find the writer's idea of "memory derived from image plus pleasure" believable? What other reasons might there be for a baby's smiling? Fraiberg stresses the visual image the child has of the parent. Might senses other than sight be involved here, perhaps sound or smell?

3. Scientific evidence now shows that between seven and eight weeks after the human egg is fertilized, parts of the brain are already recognizable. An eight-week-old *fetus* already shows brain use and the start of a behavior pattern. Does the possibility of a well-developed brain suggests other

reasons than memory for a baby's abilities to respond to external stimuli?

4. If, as Fraiberg suggests, the memory factor is so important, what other kinds of responses based upon memory could we expect from an infant? Psychologists like Carl Jung talk about racial and cultural "memories" with which a child is born, memories he inherits and which contribute to his psychology. Do you think it is possible for a child to be *born* with memories he inherits because of his particular race or culture? You might want to read about Jungian psychology and to report on some of his ideas in regard to racial and cultural inheritance.

IDEAS FOR WRITING

Guided Writing

Using cause-and-effect analysis as your main technique, write a 500-word essay with the following title, after you fill in the blanks:

"Why does the _____ _____?"

You might choose a scientific topic: "Why does the lemming march to the sea?"; a social one, "Why does a woman get less pay than a man when they both perform the same management job?"; a topic based on your own experience or those of your friends, "Why does a child steal?" or "Why do teenagers drink excessively?" These are only guidelines, so feel free to select a topic of your choice.

1. Limit your topic sufficiently so that you concentrate your attention on the causes of the single situation or event you are explaining.

2. In the introduction, show the importance of the situation whose causes you aim to analyze. Somewhere in your introduction, write a sentence that says just what effect you are trying to discuss.

3. Discuss the causes of any earlier situation that might influence the effect you are trying to explain. See paragraph 3 in Fraiberg's essay.

4. In the course of your essay cite evidence that

supports your explanations. This evidence may be statistical detail, quotations from reliable sources, concrete sensory detail, or cases that illustrate your point. If you can use experimental evidence in the way Fraiberg does in paragraph 5, you should name your sources.

5. In your conclusion, show the significance of the effect whose causes you have explained.

More Writing Projects

1. Write a short essay in which, after some research, you try to explain the causes of some very specific behavior in a child. Fraiberg chose to explain the smile of response; you might show the causes of crying, or tantrums, or fantasy play.

2. Write an essay in which you discuss what you believe are some causes that would explain why a child is happy (or unhappy).

3. In an essay of 500 to 750 words, show why the parent plays such an important part in the development of the child's personality.

Diane Narek

A WOMAN SCIENTIST SPEAKS

As a chemist and physicist, Diane Narek understands the unique problems that women must overcome in order to succeed in science in America. Her essay explores both the causes behind the relative absence of women in technical areas, and the consequences a woman faces once she does succeed in a scientific career.

Words to Watch

actuarial (par. 2): relating to the calculation of risks and premiums in insurance
prospective (par. 5): future; expected
alienated (par. 5): separated; removed from
belittling (par. 6): the act of making something seem unimportant or trivial
wiles (par. 7): sly tricks
laud (par. 9): praise

On July 22, 1969, several of my friends and I were   1 watching the astronauts land on the moon. We watched and asked the same question. "Why aren't there any women astronauts on the moon?" "Why aren't there any women technicians?" "How are we kept from these fields?"

As a woman scientist and someone who wanted to 2
be an astronaut, I feel that I know some of these answers.
I have worked as an actuarial trainee, an engineer, a solid
state physicist, and a college teacher of mathematics, chemistry, and physics. From these experiences I would like to
tell you some of the reasons for the lack of women in
technical fields.

As a child I liked to make and build objects. My 3
parents encouraged this interest and my desire to pursue a
scientific career. I was also encouraged in school, especially
by a woman mathematics teacher in junior high school. This
teacher continued to encourage me after I had completed
her class. Both my parents and teachers helped me in my
personal projects such as breeding fish and plants. This
encouragement continued in high school. Several teachers
helped me to obtain a National Science Foundation research
grant. Following this outside recognition from the NSF, the
mathematics department chairman added his help. He
coached me in college level mathematics so that I could skip
freshmen courses and he also helped me to get research
grants. I used one of these grants to study electricity and to
build my own radio set. The school where I took this course
was normally attended only by men and did not even have
a ladies' bathroom. At the time I thought nothing of this,
but it was the beginning of the discouragement I was to
receive in pursuing my interests. Up to this point I had
received only encouragement and help from school and home
in learning about science. I wanted to study science because
I enjoyed the subject and while I was encouraged I did quite
well in this pursuit. Until I graduated from high school,
nobody ever questioned my motives or my interest in the
subject.

When I began to apply to college I suddenly discov- 4
ered resistance. I knew that I had to be twice as good as a
man to get into college and even better for a scholarship. So
I was. I worked hard to graduate first in my class and get
700–800 on the College Boards. In addition I participated in
as many school activities as possible. Yet when I applied to
college I was told not to indicate my interest in science. I

was told that I would not be able to compete with men once I entered college. It was not that I could not, but that I was not allowed. I had already shown that I could. When the scholarships and admissions were given out, I watched as men with poorer grades than my own were awarded the prizes. When I complained I was told that companies and colleges did not want to invest in a woman because she would eventually get married. This was the first time that I learned what it meant to be a woman. But since I did receive offers and was able to go to college I let it slide and the anger passed.

Once I entered college though, I couldn't let the anger pass because I was constantly being reminded that I was a woman and women shouldn't study science and mathematics. Professors told us women that we were not serious enough and we had to prove ourselves. In many science courses the requirements for women were much higher than for men. In my school the course which prospective mathematics majors were required to pass was taught by just such a professor. Many women were denied entrance into the major because he felt they were not serious enough. Once again a woman had to be twice as good to get by. An average man is encouraged to study these subjects but an average woman is denied the same opportunity. I was able to major in mathematics because a visiting woman professor taught the required course one semester. Instead of having to prove myself, I was encouraged to continue. I later switched my major to physics and the pressures on me as a woman became much greater. I was constantly reminded that physics was a man's domain and in order to earn equality and respect for my work I would have to give up my "female privileges." What this meant was that I had to carry my own equipment and open doors for myself. I also had to learn to use tools and although the men knew how they would not give me any of the help they gave to each other. Naturally when a woman learns these things she is laughed at. I was told that I was no longer feminine and ridiculed for this. Many women envy another woman who pursues a scientific career. It is often felt that she will meet many men. The men who are her fellow students do not agree. They do not consider her a woman, but a queer and a threat to themselves. In this way a woman scientist becomes alienated from others very early. Other women are awed by her, men treat her as a freak.

Despite the discouragement I had received, I contin- 6 ued to study. I kept pursuing my interest in science partly to prove that I could do it and partly because I enjoyed it. However, that enjoyment had decreased very much during my college years. The constant discouragement and pressures that I received as a woman had their result. I became less interested and my work suffered. All the energy that I had put into fighting these pressures distracted me from my work. Eventually I believed the belittling, and the quality of my work was lowered. However I managed to finish school and then attempted to apply my skills.

A woman who seeks to continue in her scientific 7 work finds that she has obtained one of the following titles: "the first woman physics graduate in the school's history," "the woman in the mathematics department," "our prettiest engineer," or "the bird-brained scientist." A big fuss is made over her when she gets a job and she is publicly pointed out. However, like every other woman she receives lower salary, lower rank, and less interesting positions than men with the same qualifications. After obtaining the same skills as a man, spending the same time at the same schools, a woman is still treated as an inferior person. On my first job I was not even afforded the common courtesy of being invited to lunch by my co-workers. It is usual to take a new person to lunch. Well, on my first day all my colleagues marched out to lunch leaving me to sit alone in my office. When I was first hired I was told not to expect any favors because I was a woman. Yet every time I turned around my co-workers made a fuss. I cramped the style of the laboratory because they felt they couldn't use curse words in my presence. At the same time every man I worked with expected favors of me because I was a woman. I was told not to use my feminine wiles, but any time I participated in discussions or arguments I was put down as a flighty woman. The men did not respond to my logic but only to my feminine wiles. I wanted to be treated equally in my work but my male co-workers would not allow it. They did not want to follow my logic. They forced me to use my sex "privileges" to get attention for my work and then ridiculed me for it.

There is set up a constant conflict between a woman 8 as a woman and her abilities as a scientist. This conflict is caused by those around her. She is told not to act like a woman but she is always treated like a woman. Her work is belittled and she is constantly asked to prove herself in both her work and her intentions. It is never thought that she is interested in her work. Every man thinks she is interested in him. I was constantly asked why I was wasting my time and told to get married. I was told that their wives preferred homemaking and since I was a woman I wouldn't be happy unless I did the same. My work was considered to be a waste of time, while my co-workers who were doing the same thing were considered to be conducting important research. Even after several years of teaching I find that male students find it necessary to criticize my work as a mathematics teacher.

In addition to being an outcast among my male 9 colleagues I was shunned by other women because I was different. Other women are in awe of the female member of the technical staff and they do not become friends. They also resent any superiority that is held over them and a woman scientist acts superior. The woman scientist feels that she has proven that she is a skilled and accomplished person. She does not receive any recognition from men so she seeks to gain it from the women who are under her. In this way we women are kept divided. The secretaries resent the woman scientist's slight authority, while the woman scientist resents the lack of recognition. At present we are venting these hostilities on each other instead of on the cause, which is men. It is the men who treat us all unequally and do not recognize our individual achievements. As my awareness developed in Women's Liberation, I became less interested in gaining recognition from men and it was no longer necessary to laud my position over other women.

When my position was not used this way I became friends with the secretary and we helped and supported each other in our work. I helped her do the mimeographing and she gave me useful information. I used to feel put down when my colleagues suggested that I eat with the secretaries. I not only felt slighted but resentful because I was kept from many fruitful discussions about work. Many ideas and experiments are suggested as a result of social meetings. I felt that I was being deprived of scientific opportunities and did not want to waste this time discussing subjects which I considered to be less important with the secretaries. Since Women's Liberation I actively seek out the secretaries for social company. There is a pleasant atmosphere rather than the competitive hostility I found with men. There is no competition among us for we treat each other equally as women, not as inferiors, while the men treat all women equally, as inferiors.

The only reason that there aren't any more women 10 scientists and technicians is because the men don't allow it. They tell us women that we are not good at mechanical skills. If we disprove their theory by learning these skills, they accuse us of being unfeminine. As a youngster I was encouraged in my scientific pursuits, yet when I tried to achieve these goals I was harassed. I had the confidence in my ability and the desire to study science. The constant pressures that I received caused me to lose both. No wonder a woman who as a child did not receive this encouragement does not enter science. No matter when we feel them, the pressures and discouragement keep us women from becoming scientists. Having the early encouragement I went further but eventually I too lost interest. It was only after my involvement in Women's Liberation that I again found enjoyment in science. I now teach mostly women students who encourage me in my work. In return I encourage them to study mathematics. They are not put down as women and I am not overly criticized and harassed by male students. In this atmosphere, where I am not ill-treated as a woman, I have rediscovered my enjoyment of science.

BUILDING VOCABULARY

1. Rewrite the following sentences, substituting appropriate synonyms for the words in italics.

a. "When I began to apply to college, I suddenly discovered *resistance*." (par. 2)

b. "I was constantly reminded that physics was a men's *domain*." (par. 5)

c. "Many women *envy* another woman who *pursues* a scientific career." (par. 5)

d. "I was told not to use my feminine *wiles*." (par. 7)

e. "At present we are *venting* our *hostilities* at each other." (par. 9)

2. Use the following words in sentences of your own:

a. motives (par. 3)
b. prospective (par. 5)
c. ridiculed (par. 5)
d. flighty (par. 7)
e. resent (par. 9)

UNDERSTANDING THE WRITER'S IDEAS

1. Why was the first landing of astronauts on the moon significant for the author?

2. Explain the attitude of the author's mathematics teachers in junior high and high school.

3. Why did the author complain about college scholarships and admissions when she was about to graduate from high school?

4. What does the author mean by "female privileges"? How do these "privileges" relate to her college experiences?

5. According to Narek, what do other women think about a woman scientist?

6. What was the attitude of Narek's co-workers on her first job?

7. Explain the following sentence: "There is a constant conflict between a woman as a woman and her abilities as a scientist."

8. Why was women's liberation important to the author?

9. According to Narek, what is the main reason for the absence of women in scientific and technical fields?

10. How do male scientists regard a woman scientist's research and work?

UNDERSTANDING THE WRITER'S TECHNIQUES

1. One strategy for developing an introductory paragraph is to ask a question. What is the purpose of the questions that the author asks in the opening paragraph? What is the relationship among the questions? How do the questions themselves dictate a cause-effect pattern of development?

2. What is the function of paragraph 2? Why does the author refer to her background?

3. How does the author employ causal analysis to build paragraphs 3, 4, 5, and 6? How does cause-effect analysis operate in paragraphs 6 to 9?

4. Is the author's use of herself as a personal example effective? Does it permit her to support the generalizations that she makes in this essay? How, for example, could she have used statistics to prove her main point?

5. What is the thesis of this essay? Where is it stated most clearly?

6. The author uses colloquial language (see page 381) on several occasions. Locate examples. Why does she use such language? Is it appropriate in terms of the purpose of the essay? How does point of view (see page 388) relate to this technique?

7. Analyze the concluding paragraphs carefully. How does the author develop it? What are some connections

between the concluding paragraph and earlier parts of the essay?

EXPLORING THE WRITER'S IDEAS

1. Why might you accept Narek's thesis that women are deliberately kept out of certain fields today? Which fields are they? Why do you think women are not found in those fields?

2. When you were in high school, was it boys or girls (or both) who demonstrated an interest and talent for math and science? Do your experiences match Narek's or contradict them? How do you explain the fact that, statistically, female students do poorer than males in science and math today?

3. Do you think it is true that a woman "receives lower salary, lower rank, and less interesting positions than men with the same qualifications"? How could you support your opinion? Do you think women should receive the same salary as men with similar qualifications? Why? Are women ever given jobs for which they are not as highly qualified as men simply because of their sex?

4. The women's liberation movement clearly had an effect on Narek's attitudes and behavior. Do you think that she would have succeeded without the impact of women's liberation? Do you admire her decision to work closely with women students who are interested in science and mathematics? Why or why not?

5. What steps would you urge schools to take in order to involve women more in scientific careers?

IDEAS FOR WRITING

Guided Writing

Write a cause-effect essay of 500 to 750 words on the reasons why or why not women or people from other minority groups require special consideration in job recruitment or in college admissions.

1.   In your introduction, ask a series of questions that you plan to answer in the body of the essay. Use the "why" technique in framing these questions.

2.   Be sure to explain each reason you give.

3.   Feel free to use personal experience if you can. Were you or one of your friends denied a job or a place in an educational institution because majority privileges prevented you?

4.   If you have no personal experience, check resources in your library: newspapers, journals, books. Discuss at length the idea of preferred treatment for certain groups of people.

5.   Toward the conclusion of the essay, name certain trends or movements that have encouraged job and educational opportunities for minority groups.

6.   In the concluding paragraph, try to answer specifically the questions you raised in the introduction. Also provide a short summary of the main points raised in the body of the essay.

More Writing Projects

1.   Write an extended paragraph on the causes and effects of "competitive hostility" (the battle between the sexes) between men and women.

2.   Write a short essay on the reasons why there is so much resistance to women in one of these fields: sports, police, fire fighting, science, or banking.

3.   Bring to class examples of advertisements that show men in certain career roles and women in others. Try also to find advertisements that deliberately place women in "new" career roles. Write a short paper analyzing your findings.

C effect

Sloan Wilson

WHY JESSIE HATES ENGLISH

Sloan Wilson is an American author best known for his novel, _The Man in the Gray Flannel Suit_ (1955). As a former English teacher, he was disturbed when he discovered his daughter's dislike of the subject. In this essay, Wilson begins with a clear effect, and then seeks the causes of widespread unhappiness with English as it is taught in the public schools.

Words to Watch

progenitors (par. 2): ancestors; forefathers
aborigines (par. 3): natives; first inhabitants of a region
ogre (par. 4): monster
deposed (par. 12): removed from a position
facade (par. 20): a "front" that conceals something that is wrong
gaudy (par. 20): bright and showy, but lacking taste
euphemism (par. 22): a word or phrase for an unpleasant or
　　　distasteful word that is less direct than another word
compulsory (par. 27): required
codify (par. 32): to arrange in an orderly way
devoid (par. 32): empty; completely lacking
conducive (par. 35): helpful; contributive to
predecessors (par. 36): a person or thing that comes before
　　　another
proliferation (par. 37): rapid growth or spreading

Not long ago, my youngest daughter, Jessica, who 1
is twelve years old, came home from school, dropped her
book bag in the middle of our living room, and yelled, "I
hate English!"

In some families this might not cause much of a stir, 2
but I am an old English teacher, as well as a writer. My
father was an English teacher and so was *his* father. As a
matter of fact, my father, who enjoyed exaggeration, used
to claim that all his progenitors had been English teachers,
going clear back to a lone Wilson aboard the *Santa María,*
who died horribly while attempting to give a lesson in
English grammar to the Indians. They skinned him alive,
Dad said, and boiled him.

When Jessie came home with her shocking an- 3
nouncement, my first impulse was to find the teacher who
had made her hate English and give her the same treatment
that the aborigines had given my ancestor. I should add
here my objective, impartial view that my youngest daughter
is extremely bright, especially gifted in English, and a
surprisingly dedicated scholar. All right, the opinion of a
father concerning his youngest daughter has to be discounted
at least 50 percent. Even so, Jessie is a child who reads far
more than most adults do at home, and she writes well
enough to get the highest marks whenever she pens a report
for a course other than English. In her English course she
never has had to write much of anything. In many modern
sixth-grade English courses, I had already discovered, writing does not occupy a large part of the curriculum, if any.

But what had the teacher been doing to make Jessie 4
hate English? She was not, Jessie hastened to tell me, the
kind of classroom ogre who can make a student hate
anything.

"It's not the teacher, Daddy," she said with some 5
exasperation, as though I were a very slow pupil, "it's just
English."

"Don't you enjoy all the stories and poems you get 6
in English?"

"We hardly ever get stories and poems. All we get, 7

Daddy, is grammar. That's all we're supposed to study, right through high school. I'll show you my books."

That night I spent several hours poring over my 8 daughter's textbooks after she had finished her homework.

"What do you think?" my wife asked, poking her 9 head into my study when it was time for bed.

"I hate English!" I replied. "These books have con- 10 verted me from a lifelong lover of the language to a truant."

"What's the matter with them?" 11

I showed her two books. They were the official kind 12 of modern textbook that apparently is contrived to look as little like a textbook as possible. The layout looks as though it is the brainstorm of the art director of a struggling new advertising agency after a three-martini lunch. Much of the copy was apparently supplied by a deposed editor of the New York *Daily News*. Headlines scream. There are eye-catching photographs of football players and full-page reproductions of old advertisements for expensive coats, cosmetics, and automobiles. In one book, my favorite horror, there is an entire section on the grammar of Madison Avenue, which the authors obviously admire.

For a long time I have been aware that we all live 13 in a nightmare world, but I had not realized that the schools have substituted advertising copy for the prose and poetry of the masters, which students in my antique day used to study and occasionally enjoy. Why are they doing this sort of thing?

To find out, I telephoned my *oldest* daughter, Lisa, 14 who followed the family trade and is or, rather, was an English teacher. Unlike me, she has recent knowledge of what goes on in the public schools.

"A lot of advertising copy is used to teach English 15 nowadays," she said. "The words are short and the sentences simple—"

"I'm not talking about a class for retarded children," 16 I objected.

"Neither am I. That's the depressing part of it. Even 17 in classes for the brightest children, the advertising copy is sometimes useful, just to keep the kids awake."

"I hate the whole system!" I exploded. "Jessie spends 18 hours at home looking at television, and when she finally goes to school, they teach her advertisements as though they were gems of English prose! Pretty soon she's going to think and talk like a deodorant commercial!"

"Do I ?" Lisa asked with a laugh. "What do you think 19 I had to study? The lucky thing is that most kids ignore school."

Perhaps in an effort to preserve some façade of 20 respectability, Jessie's English textbooks also included some brief snippets of good books by recognizable authors. A few paragraphs by the masters, from Mark Twain to Ray Bradbury, were sandwiched between the gaudy photographs and the advertising copy, free samples of a product that many of the students may never see in its entirety.

The jazzy layout, which made a textbook look like 21 a sales brochure, and the snippets of real writing were all sugarcoating for the main subject of Jessie's English books, which was, of course, grammar. Page after page was devoted to this dismal exercise, chapter after chapter. Many little tests in grammar were offered. Most of them I could not pass despite a lifetime of making a living by writing English.

What are "derivational suffixes"? How about a "sub- 22 jective completion"? While I puzzled over "subjective completion," I thought it might be some sort of euphemism for "premature ejaculation," but the textbook tells me that it is "a word which completes the verb and refers back to the subject." Understand now?

I have here a whole bagful of nuggets of information 23 mined from Jessie's textbook. Here is one sentence: "Just as there are determiners to signal the presence of nouns in a sentence, so too are there signal words which point to the presence of verbs—structure words called *auxiliaries*."

That is the kind of sentence that I cannot understand 24 and do not want to understand. People who understand sentences like that are thrown out of the Authors League and the Roma Bar, my favorite hangout.

Do you have "terminal clusters"? They are not a 25 form of cancer, but something that adds to the descriptive power of prose, the book assures me. Are you a master of the "multi-level sentence"? Apparently it has nothing to do with the critics' favorite, the multi-level novel. Are you good at "parallel repetition" and "chain linking"? We are still talking about English prose, mind you, not wire fences. Are you a master of that new addition to marlinespike scholarship, the "comma splice"?

26   My twelve-year-old daughter has to be able to interpret all this nonsense. If she can't, she will fail her examinations in English, no matter how much she reads at home, no matter how well she writes for other classes.

27   Who invented all this hideous jargon used by grammarians? I don't know, but my quotations are from that favorite horror book of Jessie's, *Grammar Lives*. The title becomes more nonsensical the more one thinks about it. This mercifully slender volume, which presumably has been sold to many school systems, was published in 1975 by McDougal, Littell & Company. The names of the people responsible for this reverse masterpiece go on like the "crawl" preceding a pornographic movie, constituting a list of individuals eagerly seeking credit for the discreditable. The "consultant" is Karen J. Kuehner. The "authors" are Ronald T. Shephard and John MacDonald. The "editorial direction," which must have been remarkable, was supplied by Claudia Norlin. These people presumably all got together, invented or borrowed phrases like "terminal clusters," reprinted some old advertisements and snippets of legitimate prose, and then really demonstrated their talents by finding a way to make this stuff compulsory reading for hundreds of thousands, if not millions, of innocent children. They should not, however, feel alone in their guilt. Plenty of other "educators" are helping them to make children hate English and to be illiterate.

28   I could quote many more examples of the grammarian's art, but I have to take it easy on my blood pressure.

29   "Why does grammar make you so angry?" my wife asked. "Doesn't everybody have to study it?"

30   The answer, of course, is that for the last few thousand years nobody was asked to study grammar any-

where near as much as the pupils in most American public schools, where it often occupies most of the English curriculum. In my own youth I studied formal grammar briefly in the fifth grade. I remember it because it seemed so silly. Who but a schoolteacher would diagram sentences and make simple prose so complex? Fortunately my teacher hated grammar as much as I did. Soon she returned to assigning us themes and correcting them in detail, a much better way to teach the mechanics of the language. She also asked us to read good books—*whole books,* not snippets. When we wrote book reports, the teacher got another shot at correcting our English. I often wonder what she would have said if someone had asked her to give us advertisements for study.

31   I have heard it said that the students of my generation and of prior ones did not need to learn grammar because we studied so much Latin. I believe that this contradicts everything that has been learned about learning, part of which can be summed up with the astonishing news that when a boy studies Latin, he just learns Latin. My own case provides only one correction to that. For eight years I studied Latin, but I didn't acquire any lasting knowledge of Latin. I just learned to hate school, except for English, which made sense. I do not owe my knowledge of English to Latin, except for the fact that Latin made everything else appear easy.

32   Those who are in charge of planning English courses in the public schools do not seem to be aware of the fact that those who study grammar do not learn English—they just learn the crazy jargon of the grammarians and all their rules and regulations for English when studied as a dead language. Grammar is an attempt to codify the English language, reduce it to abstractions devoid of meaning or beauty, break it into "rules," "laws," and pseudomathematical "rights" and "wrongs." The fact that it is necessary to learn to speak and write grammatically does not mean that one must devote much time to the abstract study of grammar. One should, instead, study, of all things, speaking and writing.

33   Some youngsters can find real joy in writing a good

theme and welcome a teacher's attempts to show them how to improve it, even if the corrections involve the use of a few basic rules of grammar. In a properly run English composition class, grammar has specific applications and is not taught as an abstract "science." As it should be, it is always subordinate to the basic urge to communicate, not an end in itself.

I think I know how the public schools came to rely 34 more and more heavily on the teaching of grammar as an abstract science. As the children of parents who themselves spoke broken English flooded the public schools, something had to be done to help countless students learn whole new speech patterns. The study of grammar is not good remedial English, as the performance of so many high school graduates sadly proves, but it must have seemed a good solution at first and a much cheaper one than the complex programs necessary for helping a person change speech patterns acquired in infancy.

Although classes in grammar didn't teach children 35 anything but how to pass examinations devised by the grammarians, they offered certain practical advantages. Tests in grammar can be graded by machines. A teacher who asks his class to write themes every day may be deluged with papers that have to be corrected line after line by a human hand. It is also true that almost any adult, after a few months of specialized instruction, can teach grammar. To be a good teacher of English composition, one has to be able to write good English oneself. As has been often remarked, English has rarely been a strong point of the teachers colleges and departments of education, which have produced most of our public school teachers. The jargon of the educators is not conducive to teaching good, clear English.

The current discovery that high school graduates on 36 the whole read and write with more difficulty than even their recent predecessors hits educators hard. The public schools have been supported and defended as an act of faith by most Americans all during their periods of rapid growth, especially since World War II. Criticisms have been shrugged off as the work of crackpots or intellectual snobs. When the book *Why Johnny Can't Read* came out, more than twenty years ago, it sold a lot of copies, but it was never quite respectable among people who were seriously concerned with the schools. If the schools were not teaching reading well at the moment, the feeling was, the difficulties would soon be overcome.

Now decades have passed, and there is evidence that 37 the schools are teaching reading worse than they have in the past and that writing among recent high school graduates is almost a lost art. There have been loud cries for "a return to the fundamentals." And what are the fundamentals? Reading? Writing? Of course not! In the minds of the educators, *grammar* is the real fundamental. If the proliferation of courses in grammar has resulted in the graduation of countless youngsters who can hardly read or write, the obvious answer is to give the youngsters even more grammar. If one aspirin doesn't stop your headache, take two.

Apparently no one puts himself in the position of 38 the student who sits squirming while the teacher drills him in grammar day after day, year after year. It's easy to see why such a student doesn't want to read anything—he is taught to regard the text as a boneyard of grammar problems on which he will probably be quizzed. Writing, too, becomes a test of fitting together words and phrases in a way that is *grammatical,* not interesting, funny, or meaningful. My youngest daughter is not the only pupil in her school who hates English, and as a result, she gives it as little time as possible.

Like many other parents, I have tried to do some- 39 thing about this situation for my child. I wrote a long letter to my old friend David S. Siegel, the superintendent of schools in Ticonderoga, N.Y., the upstate village where we live. Dave really wanted to help. He referred the matter to the "language arts coordinator," a title that apparently means "head English teacher" in the language of contemporary public schools. He turned out to be a pleasant, intelligent young chap who is alarmingly well versed in the theories of modern public schools, but ambitious and idealistic concerning the English courses nonetheless. He organized a class for students from three grades who are especially gifted in English and invited my youngest daughter to join it. The class is known as a speed group, and now, poor Jessie reports, she is being fed about three times as much grammar as before. Her new ambition is to be a veterinarian. With animals, after all, she will be asked neither to write, to read, nor even to talk.

BUILDING VOCABULARY

1. For each italicized word in Column A, write the correct *antonym* (a word of opposite meaning) from Column B. Look up unfamiliar words in a dictionary.

Column A	Column B
a. *impartial* view	1. general
b. *dedicated* scholar	2. unjustified
c. apparently *contrived*	3. loathe
d. obviously *admire*	4. biased
e. *antique* day	5. undevout
f. *jazzy* layout	6. modern
g. this *dismal* exercise	7. attractive
h. *hideous* jargon	8. unplanned
i. *legitimate* prose	9. dull
j. *specific* applications	10. pleasant

2. A word from which other words are derived is called a *root*. For instance, in the first sentence of the essay, "youngest" is a derivative of the root "young." Write as many derivatives as possible for the following root words taken from the essay.

a. impulse (par. 3)
b. modern (par. 12)
c. enjoy (par. 13)
d. ignore (par. 19)
e. horror (par. 27)

UNDERSTANDING THE WRITER'S IDEAS

1. Why is Jessie's announcement so "shocking" to her father?

2. Why does Wilson turn from a "lifelong lover of language to a truant"?

3. Explain in your own words Wilson's description of the two English textbooks in paragraphs 12 and 13.

4. What is the connection between advertising copy and grammar in the textbooks that Wilson is analyzing?

5. Does Wilson think that an ability to understand grammar helps someone to write well? Point to specific statements to support your answer.

6. Did Wilson study grammar as a child? With respect to the teaching of grammar, did Wilson's education differ from his daughter's? Why or why not?

7. Explain Wilson's statement that the students of today "just learn the crazy jargon of the grammarians and all their rules and regulations for English when studied as a dead language."

8. When the author refers to "the abstract study of grammar," what does he mean?

9. What are some of the reasons that "the teaching of grammar as an abstract science" is so popular in today's schools?

10. What was the effect of the author's protest to the superintendent of schools?

UNDERSTANDING THE WRITER'S TECHNIQUES

1. How does the author arrange the cause-and-effect pattern in this essay? Does he start with a cause or an effect? Does he establish a dominant cause throughout the essay, and if so, how?

2. Explain the cause-effect relationship in paragraphs 1 to 10. Are the causes clearly stated?

3. *Paradox* is a special variety of irony (see page 387) in which there is a clear contradiction in a situation. A paradox is a statement which, on the surface, seems

unlikely, and yet, on analysis, can indeed be true. For instance, it is paradoxical that Wilson's daughter should dislike English. Why? Which paragraphs in the essay utilize paradox as a means of development? What paradoxes are involved?

    4. The author also employs *satire* throughout the essay. Satire is humorous or comic criticism of a subject in order to encourage a change in some situation. List the various objects of satire in this essay, and the paragraphs devoted to them.

    5. Would you describe the tone of this essay as subjective or objective? Why? Find examples to support your point.

    6. Explain the author's use of narration in this essay. Explain his use of illustrations, of comparison and contrast.

    7. Analyze the pattern of cause and effect in paragraphs 34 to 38.

    8. Why is paragraph 39 an especially effective conclusion? How does the author develop it?

    9. Does Wilson explain successfully the effect he names in his title?

EXPLORING THE WRITER'S IDEAS

    1. Wilson seems almost totally negative in his attitude toward grammar. Do you agree or disagree with his position? Do you think that he is reasonably objective, or is he stacking the cards against his subject? Can you think of any beneficial reasons for studying grammar? Recall some of your experiences with English grammar.

    2. The author traces the cause of Jessie's dislike of English specifically to the teaching of grammar. What other causes might be involved in a student's dislike of English? Make a list of these causes.

    3. Using Wilson's last paragraph as a starting point, discuss other examples of a school's failure to correct major academic problems that you know about through personal experience.

4. Do you agree or disagree with the idea that schools today must return to the "basics"—sound reading, writing, and mathematical skills? Should colleges also deal with these fundamentals? In what ways?

IDEAS FOR WRITING

Guided Writing

Write an essay of at least 500 words in which you examine the causes of the decline in writing ability among today's students.

    1. Begin with a personal anecdote involving you and/or another individual. Develop the anecdote fully, and permit it to reveal your thesis.

    2. Decide to make this a humorous, perhaps even a satirical treatment of the subject. Although the subject itself is serious, try to follow Wilson's many humorous methods designed to expose faults in the school system.

    3. Decide on the order in which you want to present the causes, and develop each cause fully. For instance, if you think that television is a cause of the decline in writing ability, present enough illustrations (or one long, extended example) to support your generalization. Again, if you believe that schools too frequently pass students who cannot write well, try to provide vivid examples of this point, and investigate causes behind it.

    4. Save one short anecdote for the end, and include it in a well-developed final paragraph.

More Writing Projects

    1. Write an essay in which you discuss the reasons why college students should be *required* to take courses in writing.

    2. Write an essay which you title (after filling in the blank) "Why I Hate _____." Whatever it is that you hate, explain the causes and/or effects of your hatred.

Mitchell Lazarus

RX FOR MATHOPHOBIA

Dr. Mitchell Lazarus is a senior staff associate at the Education Development Center, Newton, Massachusetts. In this essay, he examines the fear inspired in many people by mathematics. He outlines causes, and suggests different effects if a new strategy for teaching mathematics can be established.

Words to Watch

converse (par. 1): hold a conversation
vehemence (par. 3): intense feeling or violent action
etiology (par. 4): the science of causes or origins
aversion (par. 6): intense dislike
province (par. 13): territory or place
inadvertently (par. 14): unintentionally
rote (par. 14): by memory alone
set theory and number base (par. 15): set theory is that branch of mathematics dealing with collections of objects or elements classed together; number base is the number with reference to which a mathematical table is constructed
axiomatic (par. 16): accepted as true
obsolete (par. 17): no longer in use or practice
prescribed (par. 18): originally set down or planned
alcoves (par. 18): recessed sections of a room
constraining (par. 20): confining; forcing into
intimidating (par. 20): making afraid; forcing with threats
contrived (par. 24): planned; designed; schemed
pertinence (par. 24): appropriateness; relevance

theoretical (par. 25): based on ideas or theories
pedagogy (par. 25): the art or science of teaching
valid (par. 26): sound; effective; well grounded and based on
  evidence.

Most people dislike—or fear—mathematics. Some- 1
how, a vast majority of the population has come to believe
that mathematics must be difficult, unpleasant, and mysterious. Even people who are good at mathematics and use
it every day are comfortable only to a point. I hold a graduate
degree in engineering, and my own mathematics is pretty
good, but I still feel uneasy listening to arguments based on
mathematics more advanced than I can understand. Yet, I
can converse among historians, musicians, philosophers,
and others, understanding just as little but feeling much
less uncomfortable about it.

Now, my work involves designing new approaches 2
to the teaching of elementary mathematics. And whenever
I talk about this work, about sensible ways of handling
mathematics education that will appeal to children, the
reaction is nearly always the same: "I wish there had been
something like that when I was a kid. I always hated math
in school!"

Jerrold Zacharias, noted physicist and educator, 3
calls the problem *mathophobia*: a fear of mathematics. Most
people will indeed try to avoid mathematical problems,
sometimes with the vehemence of an acrophobe avoiding a
high place. Both the acrophobe and the mathophobe deny
themselves fascinating views and vistas, unnecessarily narrowing their horizons.

Curiously, there has been virtually no formal re- 4
search concerning this very widespread—nearly universal—
problem. In the absence of organized data, my colleagues
and I have had to fall back on anecdotal evidence. Over the
past few years we have discussed mathematics experiences

with people in all walks of life. These were not formal interviews; we have no coded data. Instead, they were casual conversations with friends, acquaintances, and people met in passing. With their help we have tried to construct an etiology of mathophobia and to indicate strategies for its prevention.

For example, many adults say that they liked mathematics "until we did so-and-so in school"—until they were exposed to some topic that seemed particularly difficult. But did the enjoyment of mathematics ever return after the hard topic was past? Almost never. The dislike is usually irreversible. 5

If one looks at the curricula in use at most schools, this aversion is not surprising. The mathematics taught in each grade depends strongly on most of the work done in preceding years: trouble in any year, for any reason, is nearly certain to spell trouble in all the years to come. 6

A second factor in the curriculum is the frequent lack of any meaningful connection between school mathematics and the rest of the student's life. Thus the mathematics people *do* learn in school is quickly forgotten; most of us have little use for it after graduation. 7

Perhaps another element is mathophobia's social acceptability. Even those who are otherwise proud of their education tend to speak up freely about their mathematical ignorance. They can say, "I'm terrible at math," almost with a hint of pride, as if being poor at mathematics somehow is a mark of good taste in failure. 8

This attitude affects our treatment of children in school. Parents often seem unconcerned about a child's failure in mathematics, as if to say, "Well, I was never good at math in school; so I shouldn't be too upset if Johnny isn't, either." Unfortunately, Johnny is likely to sense this attitude and react accordingly. 9

Moreover, many teachers are themselves affected by mathophobia, sometimes admitting that they feel uncomfortable when they teach mathematics. If the teacher is tense and ill at ease with mathematics, such feelings infect the class with the idea that mathematics is hard or unpleasant. 10

When people withdraw from mathematics, exactly 11
what are they avoiding?

From conversations with many mathophobes, two 12
distinct impressions emerge of what mathematics is like.
One view equates mathematics with the tedious, boring,
exacting routines of school arithmetic. Yet, if total exposure
to music over several years were limited to just scales and
mechanical exercises, music would be unpleasant, too.

The other popular view of mathematics sees it as 13
the arcane province of a select few geniuses. Someone who
feels that mathematics must forever be beyond his or her
ken will quite naturally shy away from it and need not
hesitate to admit—or even boast of—a distaste for the
subject.

In reality arithmetic is always a means to an end, 14
never an end in itself—except in school. Indeed, very few
activities call for actual skill in arithmetic nowadays. With
computers, elaborate cash registers, and now the small
electronic calculators, the mechanics of arithmetic take
second place, in practice, to choosing the necessary calcu-
lations and the right numbers to work with. Thus, we ask
children to spend several years learning difficult, tedious
skills that are rapidly coming to be of limited value. In doing
so, we inadvertently teach that mathematics is not only
hard but also not very useful. Rote arithmetic is a difficult
and tedious branch of mathematics—a poor starting point
for most students.

The "new math" tried to help by showing why 15
arithmetic results come out the way they do, starting from
"basic principles" that typically included set theory and
number base. But for a great many students (and their
parents), these special topics were at least as confusing as
the arithmetic had been.

Parts of the "new math" tried to deemphasize pure 16
arithmetic or at least to set arithmetic in a wider mathematical context. But the "new math" context is that of the
professional mathematician: abstract, definitional, axiomatic, and supposedly rigorous. The result is to pull mathematics even farther from its actual uses.

Mathematics does not belong to the professional 17

mathematician alone. It cuts across many other fields of endeavor and touches upon many people's lives. This perspective—mathematics that is useful to people—should be the starting point for a new approach to mathematics education. This alternative builds upon usefulness as a basic ingredient of elementary mathematics. Choice of topics and ways of teaching should center on mathematics as a helpful force in day-to-day life and should take into account the fact that the technology has made longhand arithmetic all but obsolete. Such a program has a twofold aim: to provide the mathematical tools and skills children will find useful and enlightening now and in later life and to make them comfortable with, and appreciative of, mathematical subject matter. The two aims are very closely related.

18   The new approach will find its place in the vast middle ground between rote arithmetic and the work of the professional mathematician. It includes, for example, the mathematics of cooking, carpentry, engineering, wallpaper hanging, dressmaking, magazine editing, bartending, store-keeping, and a vast array of other occupations and pastimes. It is the kind of mathematics that grows from real problems and returns in real solutions. It adapts recipes to serve more than the prescribed number of guests, fits bookshelves neatly into alcoves, purchases the right amount of shelf paper, carries the driver from one gasoline pump to the next, and in general helps people through a multitude of ordinary tasks. It also develops the kind of understanding that children will find most useful in their ongoing activities—the kind that will apply to many of their current interests.

19   The topics stressed should be those with the most direct link between mathematics and the real world—the topics most helpful to people who use mathematics for practical reasons. These include, for example, measurement and estimation, making rough maps and sketching simple graphs, and the performance of quick, approximate arithmetic in our heads—skills that will not get rusty because they will be used constantly by people of all ages.

20   One important development not covered by conventional curricula would be an appreciation of inexact answers.

"Mathematics is an exact science," many teachers say, "and there is only one right answer." Often that statement is worse than wrong. It is constraining and intimidating. Estimation, approximation, rough calculation—all part of mathematics—are often very useful, need not be exact, and can have many "right answers," if a right answer is one to meet our needs. Most of us tried to learn in school how to find that 49 × 319 works out to be 15,631. Few of us learned to see the problem quickly and roughly as 50 × 300, which mentally becomes 15,000—close enough for most practical purposes.

A widescale approach to mathematics that stems 21 from realistic situations which children find interesting and which gives them new power to cope with situations outside of school would go a long way toward preventing mathophobia. Mathematics can be a part of everyday life; it need not be special and apart. Most people can read street maps, for example, which involves a lot of mathematics that ordinarily we do not recognize. We understand how an "average family" can have 1.9 children, even though we may joke about it. The concept of odds in betting is clear to most of us, although it is based on quite sophisticated concepts. People who cook know that it is safe to triple recipes for soup, but not for cake.

As an educational issue, reading street maps, for 22 example, is unimportant in itself. But maps involve a number of mathematical ideas that *are* important and general: ratio, proportion, scaling, measuring and estimating length and distance, estimating time, and some geometry. In most curricula nowadays these ideas appear in the abstract if they appear at all. A proportion problem, for example, might appear as: $20/5 = ?/2$. The new approach would stay with the street map—or even better, a student-made map of the classroom—and ask: according to the map, how far is it from the door to the chalkboard? The mathematical issue of proportion is the same, but the map puts the idea in a much more concrete and realistic context. Thus the student can better understand the idea of proportion and how it applies in real situations. Moreover, the "hands-on" experience of making the measurements, sketching the map, and checking the results is a valuable aid in acquiring the concept and contributes to a good "feel" for what proportion is about.

Symbols and abstraction for their own sakes, now 23 very common in mathematics curricula, often strike students as pointless and confusing. As far as possible, all of the concepts presented to students should appear in realistic, familiar contexts. Symbols and abstraction are still important—indeed, are the essence of mathematics—but should serve ends that students can understand. Presentations ought to begin and end with reality in order that students can make sense of the mathematics in between.

Applications have always been a part of mathematics 24 education, but until now they have played a very minor role. The applications in most textbooks were contrived—transparent excuses for more calculation. Use of applications of primary function, so that calculation serves as the means (rather than the other way around), will impart to school mathematics the pertinence, meaning, and impact that it presently lacks. Children will understand why mathematics is important and worth knowing.

Some students do very well in the "new math," and 25 some even seem to enjoy rote calculation. Students with a knack and a flair for mathematics will find as much in this approach that captures their interest as there was in earlier curricula, for here there is a great deal of room for exploring theoretical relationships and plenty of opportunity for calculation. The topics are rich and the pedagogy open-ended. Just as important, however, is the fact that many students who have *not* liked mathematics until now—and these are a majority—will begin to see a place for mathematics in their own lives and will start feeling comfortable with mathematical ideas.

Eventually, a curriculum reform on the scale of the 26 "new math" will probably be necessary. The "new math" is not working out well, and there is a strong national trend away from it. Most educators seem disinclined to go back to the "old math," seeing that the arguments against it are still valid. In contrast, the approach outlined here will appeal directly to students' interests and needs and will provide a strong foundation for more advanced work.

The key to preventing mathophobia is letting math- 27 ematics take root in the student's daily life. Reality-based teaching will go a long way toward solving the national mathematics problem because it will put elementary mathematics into a form that will make sense to children.

BUILDING VOCABULARY

1. Develop definitions of your own for the italicized words by relying on context clues. Then check your definition against a dictionary definition.

a. "Most people will indeed try to avoid mathematical problems, sometimes with the vehemence of an *acrophobe* avoiding a high place." (par. 3)

b. "The mathematics taught in each grade depends strongly on most of the work done in *preceding* years; trouble in any year, for any reason, is nearly certain to spell trouble in all the years to come." (par. 6)

c. "One view equates mathematics with the *tedious*, boring, exacting routines of school arithmetic." (par. 12)

d. "The other popular view of mathematics sees it as the *arcane* province of a select few geniuses." (par. 13)

e. "It includes, for example, the mathematics of cooking, carpentry, engineering, wallpaper hanging, dressmaking, magazine editing, bartending, storekeeping, and a vast *array* of other occupations and pastimes." (par. 18)

2. Suffixes often aid in establishing the meaning of a word. They are like prefixes (see page 388), except that they come at the ends of words. Explain how the underlined suffixes help to establish the meanings of the following words from the essay. If needed, consult a dictionary for definitions of the suffixes themselves:

a. comfort<u>able</u> (par. 1)
b. mathemat<u>ics</u> (par. 1)
c. anecdo<u>tal</u> (par. 4)

d. teacher (par. 10)
e. tedious (par. 12)
f. technology (par. 17)
g. useful (par. 17)

UNDERSTANDING THE WRITER'S IDEAS

1. Who or what is a "mathophobe"?
2. What is the author's attitude toward mathematics? How does this attitude bear upon his job?
3. Why must the author rely on "anecdotal evidence" in discussing the causes of mathophobia?
4. What are four causes of mathophobia?
5. Describe the two general impressions that people have about mathematics. What examples does the author provide to demonstrate these impressions?
6. What should be "the starting point for a new approach to mathematical education"?
7. Explain the author's "new approach" to mathematics. What results would it bring about?
8. How can mathematics relate to the ordinary world?
9. Why does the author think that we need "an appreciation of inexact answers"?
10. How does the author's approach make use of the best of the "old math" and the "new math"? Will his method be easy to implement? Why or why not?

UNDERSTANDING THE WRITER'S TECHNIQUES

1. Although the tone of this essay is fairly objective, the author chooses to introduce the subjective "I" in the introductory paragraph. Why does he do this?
2. Which paragraphs in the essay deal with the causes of mathophobia? How do transitions aid the reader in moving from one cause to the next? Identify and evaluate the transitions used.
3. Explain the pattern of the cause-effect relationship in paragraphs 11 to 15.

4. What effects does Dr. Lazarus analyze in paragraph 16? What is the overall function of this paragraph? Why is it one of the most important paragraphs in the essay? Has it been placed in the right spot?

5. Paragraph 17 relies on a pattern of examples in series. Is this an effective strategy? Why or why not?

6. Explain the importance of careful use of examples in paragraphs 18 to 22. Why does the author not rely on simply one example to illustrate his new approach to mathematics? What ways does he use to develop examples?

7. What underlying pattern of effect do you notice in the second half of this essay? How do the last four paragraphs reinforce this pattern?

EXPLORING THE WRITER'S IDEAS

1. Do you agree with the author's statement that most of us have a negative attitude toward mathematics? Which of the causes that he lists is closest to your personal experience? Can you think of other causes that relate to your dislike—or like—of mathematics?

2. What does Lazarus mean by "new math"? Did you ever learn it? What is your attitude toward it? If you have not had the new math, what have you heard about it? What do you think the causes of its failure have been?

3. Does the author's new approach to mathematics make sense to you? What examples in your own experience show how mathematics relates to everyday life?

4. As a general principle, do you think that "reality-based teaching" is the best approach to providing instruction?

IDEAS FOR WRITING

Guided Writing

Select any *phobia* (fear) you are familiar with and write a well-developed essay of 500 to 750 words in which you discuss its causes and the steps to take in order to overcome it. You might select familiar phobias such as fear of heights, water, or animals. Or, you might wish to discuss some very special fear and to coin a phrase for it as Lazarus did (jobophobia? loveophobia? sportsophobia?)

1. In the first few paragraphs explain the phobia you are writing about. Define it, quoting some noted authority if you can.

2. Explain how a person might develop the phobia you are discussing. Give several illustrations.

3. Discuss some of the things a person misses out on because of his or her phobia.

4. Offer some possible outcomes to the person who overcomes this fear.

5. At the end of your essay, give one or two keys to preventing the phobia you chose to explore.

More Writing Projects

1. If you liked mathematics throughout your school years, write an essay discussing the reasons for your positive attitude; if you disliked it, write an essay explaining your negative attitude.

2. Write a humorous essay in which you explain the possible results if children were no longer required to learn or to study mathematics, English, or some other key subject in the school curriculum.

nine

Argumentation and Persuasion

Argumentation in prose is an attempt to convince the reader to have the opinion *you* have on a subject; frequently, it also involves an effort to persuade the reader to act in a particular manner. In many ways, argumentation is a good end point for a course in writing. In a formal argument, you can use, according to your purpose, all the prose strategies and principles of sound composition practiced until now.

You can see how important it is to state your thesis very clearly in argumentation, and to support your main point with convincing minor points. You have to make these points according to reason, and you need to arrange them so they have the greatest effect on your reader. Moreover, as in any prose, writers of argument must offer the reader particulars of details, whether sensory, quoted, statistical, or based upon historical evidence. Finally, techniques of comparison, process analysis, description, narration, cause and effect, definition, all can help strengthen an argument.

Although argumentation reflects all these earlier prose techniques, it is important for you to understand the special characteristics of this method. To begin with, although argumentation as a written prose form is often emotional, it differs sharply from those little battles and major disagreements with friends over coffee or in hallways outside class. Perhaps that last shouting match between you and your friend about who would win the World Series is, no doubt, one that you would call an argument: There is a disagreement there for which each of you tries to make your own point of view stick. Yet often these argumentative conversations deteriorate into loss of temper, angry personal comments about your friend's judgment or character, departures from the argument itself, and inability to reason.

In written arguments, writers always should keep very clearly in mind the point they wish to make, and not lose sight of it. They may try to convince readers that some issue requires action ("Colleges and businesses should follow special admissions procedures for minority applicants"). Or, they may try to convince readers that something is true ("Gun control laws do not work"). Whatever the point, writers always offer their reasons for their beliefs in a logical way, without losing command of their subject and without attacking anyone personally; they may, though, attack someone's ideas or attitudes.

The main point in an argument—often called a *proposition*—is an idea which is debatable, or which can be disputed. As such, it differs from the thesis in ordinary essays, which explains a main idea without necessarily taking sides. This "argumentative edge" in an essay is frequently reflected in the title, and is reinforced from the beginning to the end of the piece in various ways. In short, you must attempt to prove your argument through an extended series of major and minor points relating to your proposition. You must also recognize and deal with opposing arguments, a process called *refutation*. You will make your own point stronger if you show what others think about the issue, explaining why you believe they are wrong. By learning how to write convincing argumentative essays, you will also learn how to analyze and deal with those arguments, many of which are important, that occur in your daily life.

Judy Syfers

I WANT A WIFE

Judy Syfers, a wife, and mother of two children, argues in this essay for a wife of her own. Although her argument might seem strange, her position will become apparent once you move into the essay. She presents many points to support her position, so you want to keep in mind those you think are the strongest.

Words to Watch

nurturant (par. 3): someone who feeds and takes care of children as they grow up
hors d'oeuvres (par. 6): food served before the regular courses of the meal
monogamy (par. 8): the habit of having only one mate; the practice of marrying only once during life

I belong to that classification of people known as 1 wives. I am A Wife. And, not altogether incidentally, I am a mother.

Not too long ago a male friend of mine appeared on 2 the scene fresh from a recent divorce. He had one child, who is, of course, with his ex-wife. He is obviously looking for another wife. As I thought about him while I was ironing one evening, it suddenly occurred to me that I, too, would like to have a wife. Why do I want a wife?

I would like to go back to school so that I can become 3 economically independent, support myself, and, if need be, support those dependent upon me. I want a wife who will work and send me to school. And while I am going to school I want a wife to keep track of the children's doctor and dentist appointments. And to keep track of mine, too. I want a wife to make sure my children eat properly and are kept clean. I want a wife who will wash the children's clothes and keep them mended. I want a wife who is a good nurturant attendant to my children, who arranges for their schooling, makes sure that they have an adequate social life with their peers, takes them to the park, the zoo, etc. I want a wife who takes care of the children when they are sick, a wife who arranges to be around when the children need special care, because, of course, I cannot miss classes at school. My wife must arrange to lose time at work and not lose the job. It may mean a small cut in my wife's income from time to time, but I guess I can tolerate that. Needless to say, my wife will arrange and pay for the care of the children while my wife is working.

I want a wife who will take care of *my* physical 4 needs. I want a wife who will keep my house clean. A wife who will pick up after me. I want a wife who will keep my clothes clean, ironed, mended, replaced when need be, and who will see to it that my personal things are kept in their proper place so that I can find what I need the minute I need it. I want a wife who cooks the meals, a wife who is a *good* cook. I want a wife who will plan the menus, do the necessary grocery shopping, prepare the meals, serve them pleasantly, and then do the cleaning up while I do my studying. I want a wife who will care for me when I am sick and sympathize with my pain and loss of time from school. I want a wife to go along when our family takes a vacation so that someone can continue to care for me and my children when I need a rest and change of scene.

I want a wife who will not bother me with rambling 5 complaints about a wife's duties. But I want a wife who will listen to me when I feel the need to explain a rather difficult point I have come across in my course of studies. And I want a wife who will type my papers for me when I have written them.

I want a wife who will take care of the details of my 6 social life. When my wife and I are invited out by my friends, I want a wife who will take care of the babysitting arrangements. When I meet people at school that I like and want to entertain, I want a wife who will have the house clean, will prepare a special meal, serve it to me and my friends, and not interrupt when I talk about the things that interest me and my friends. I want a wife who will have arranged that the children are fed and ready for bed before my guests arrive so that the children do not bother us. I want a wife who takes care of the needs of my guests so that they feel comfortable, who makes sure that they have an ashtray, that they are passed the hors d'oeuvres, that they are offered a second helping of the food, that their wine glasses are replenished when necessary, that their coffee is served to them as they like it.

And I want a wife who knows that sometimes I need 7 a night out by myself.

I want a wife who is sensitive to my sexual needs, 8 a wife who makes love passionately and eagerly when I feel like it, a wife who makes sure that I am satisfied. And, of course, I want a wife who will not demand sexual attention when I am not in the mood for it. I want a wife who assumes the complete responsibility for birth control, because I do not want more children. I want a wife who will remain sexually faithful to me so that I do not have to clutter up my intellectual life with jealousies. And I want a wife who understands that *my* sexual needs may entail more than strict adherence to monogamy. I must, after all, be able to relate to people as fully as possible.

If, by chance, I find another person more suitable as 9 a wife than the wife I already have, I want the liberty to replace my present wife with another one. Naturally, I will expect a fresh, new life; my wife will take the children and be solely-responsible for them so that I am left free.

When I am through with school and have a job, I want my wife to quit working and remain at home so that my wife can more fully and completely take care of a wife's duties. 10

My God, who *wouldn't* want a wife? 11

BUILDING VOCABULARY

1.   After checking a dictionary write definitions of each of these words:

    a. attendant (par. 3)
    b. adequate (par. 3)
    c. peers (par. 3)
    d. tolerate (par. 3)
    e. rambling (par. 5)
    f. replenished (par. 6)
    g. adherence (par. 8)

2.   Write an original sentence for each word above.

UNDERSTANDING THE WRITER'S IDEAS

1.   What incident made Syfers think about wanting a wife?

2.   How would a wife help the writer achieve economic independence?

3.   In what ways would a wife take care of the writer's children? Why would the writer like someone to assume those responsibilities?

4.   What physical needs would Syfers's "wife" take care of?

5.   How would a wife deal with the writer's social life? Her sex life?

UNDERSTANDING THE WRITER'S TECHNIQUES

1.   In formal argumentation, we often call the writer's main point the *major* or *main proposition*. What is Syfers's major proposition? Is it simply what she says in

paragraph 2, or is the proposition more complex than that? State it in your own words.

2. What is the value of the question Syfers asks in paragraph 2? Where else does she ask a question? What value does this other question have in its place in the essay? What impact does it have on the reader?

3. The points a writer offers to support the major proposition are called *minor propositions*. What minor propositions does Syfers present to show why she wants a wife? In which instance do they serve as topic sentences within paragraphs? What details does she offer to illustrate those minor propositions?

4. What order has the writer chosen to arrange the minor propositions? Why has she chosen such an order? Do you think she builds from the least to the most important reasons for having a wife? What changes would you urge in the order of the minor propositions?

5. Most of the paragraphs here develop through illustration. Where has Syfers used a *simple listing* of details? Why has she chosen that format?

6. Syfers's style is obviously straightforward, her sentences for the most part simple and often brief. Why has she chosen such a style? What is the effect of the repetition of "I want" at the start of so many sentences? Why has Syfers used several short paragraphs (5, 7, 9, 10,11) in addition to longer ones?

7. What is the author's *tone* (see page 391)? Point out the uses of *irony* (see page 386) in the essay. How does irony contribute to Syfers's main intent in this essay? How does the fact that Syfers is a woman contribute to this sense of irony?

EXPLORING THE WRITER'S IDEAS

1. By claiming she wants a wife, Syfers is showing us all the duties and responsibilities of the woman in a contemporary household. Has Syfers represented these duties fairly? Do husbands generally expect their wives to do all these things?

2. To what degree do wives today fit Syfers' description? How could a wife avoid many of the responsibilities spelled out in the essay? How does the "modern husband" figure in the way many couples meet household responsibilities now?

3. Syfers has characterized all the traditional and stereotyped roles usually assigned to wives. What "wifely responsibilities" has she left out?

4. Has Syfers presented a balanced picture of the issues or is her argument one-sided? Support your opinion with specific references to the essay. Could the author have dealt effectively with opposing arguments? Why or why not? What might these opposing arguments be?

5. Answer the question in the last line of the essay.

IDEAS FOR WRITING

Guided Writing

Write an essay of 750 to 1,000 words, which you call, "I Want a Husband."

1. Write the essay from the point of view of a *man*. As Syfers wrote as a woman who wanted a wife, you write this essay as a man who wants a *husband*.

2. Start your essay with a brief personal story as in paragraph 2 in "I Want a Wife."

3. Support your main point with a number of minor points. Expand each minor point with details that explain your premises.

4. Arrange your minor premises carefully so that you build to the most convincing point at the end.

5. Use a simple and straightforward style. Connect your points with transitions; use repetition as one transitional device.

6. Balance your longer paragraphs with occasional shorter ones.

7. End your essay with a crisp, one-sentence question of your own.

More Writing Projects

    1.   Write an essay in which you argue *for* or *against* this issue: "A married woman belongs at home."

    2.   Write an essay in which you argue about whose role you think harder to play effectively in today's society: the role of the mother or the role of the father.

Barry Goldwater

WHY GUN CONTROL LAWS DON'T WORK

Barry Goldwater, conservative Republican senator for Arizona, ran for President of the United States against Lyndon Johnson in 1964. Here he argues, in a 1975 essay, an issue that finds strong and loud supporters on both sides.

Words to Watch

uncertified (par. 2): without guarantee
plea bargaining (par. 4): agreeing to a lesser offense than the one committed in order to speed action in the courts.
extrapolation (par. 6): an estimation made about a broad area on the basis of statistics which apply to a narrower range of information
felony (par. 11): serious crime
adjunct (par. 14): something added or connected but not a full part of

Let me say immediately that if I thought more gun- 1 control laws would help diminish the tragic incidence of robberies, muggings, rapes and murders in the United States, I would be the first to vote for them. But I am convinced that making more such laws approaches the problem from the wrong direction.

It is clear, I think, that gun legislation simply doesn't 2 work. There are already some 20,000 state and local gun laws on the books, and they are no more effective than was the prohibition of alcoholic beverages in the 1920s. Our most recent attempt at federal gun legislation was the Gun Control Act of 1968, intended to control the interstate sale and transportation of firearms and the importation of uncertified firearms; it has done nothing to check the availability of weapons. It has been bolstered in every nook and cranny of the nation by local gun-control laws, yet the number of shooting homicides per year has climbed steadily since its enactment, while armed robberies have increased 60 percent.

Some people, even some law-enforcement officials, 3 contend that "crimes of passion" occur because a gun just happens to be present at the scene. I don't buy that. I can't equate guns with the murder rate, because if a person is angry enough to kill, he will kill with the first thing that comes to hand—a gun, a knife, an ice pick, a baseball bat.

I believe our *only* hope of reducing crime in this 4 country is to control not the weapon but the user. We must reverse the trend toward leniency and permissiveness in our courts—the plea bargaining, the pardons, the suspended sentences and unwarranted paroles—and make the lawbreaker pay for what he has done by spending time in jail. We have plenty of statutes against killing and maiming and threatening people with weapons. These can be made effective by strong enforcement and firm decisions from the bench. When a man knows that if he uses a potentially deadly object to rob or do harm to another person he is letting himself in for a mandatory, unparolable stretch behind bars, he will think twice about it.

Of course, no matter what gun-control laws are 5 enacted—including national registration—the dedicated crook can always get a weapon. So, some people ask, even if national registration of guns isn't completely airtight, isn't it worth trying? Sure, it would cause a little inconvenience to law-abiding gun owners. And it certainly wouldn't stop all criminals from obtaining guns. But it might stop a few, maybe quite a few. What's wrong with that?

There are several answers. The first concerns en- 6 forcement. How are we going to persuade the bank robber or the street-corner stickup artist to register his means of criminal livelihood? Then there is the matter of expense. A study conducted eight years ago showed a cost to New York City of $72.87 to investigate and process one application for a pistol license. In mid-1970 dollars, the same procedure probably costs over $100. By extrapolation to the national scale, the cost to American taxpayers of investigating and registering the 40 to 50 million handguns might reach $4 billion or $5 billion. On top of that, keeping the process in operation year after year would require taxpayer financing of another sizable federal bureau. We ought to have far better prospects of success before we hobble ourselves with such appalling expenditures.

Finally, there are legal aspects based on the much- 7 discussed Second Amendment to the Bill of Rights, which proclaims that "A well regulated Militia, being necessary to the security of a free State, the right of the people to keep and bear Arms, shall not be infringed." The anti-gun faction argues that this right made sense in the days of British oppression but that it has no application today. I contend, on the other hand, that the Founding Fathers conceived of an armed citizenry as a necessary hedge against tyranny from within as well as from without, that they saw the right to keep and bear arms as basic and perpetual, the one thing that could spell the difference between freedom and servitude. Thus I deem most forms of gun control unconstitutional in intent.

Well, then, I'm often asked, what kind of gun laws 8 *are* you for? I reply that I am for laws of common sense. I am for laws that prohibit citizen access to machine guns, bazookas and other military devices. I am for laws that are educational in nature. I believe that before a person is permitted to buy a weapon he should be required to take a course that will teach him how to use it, to handle it safely and keep it safely about the house.

Gun education, in fact, can actually reduce lawless- 9
ness in a community, as was demonstrated in an experiment
conducted in Highland Park, Mich. City police launched a
program to instruct merchants in the use of handguns. The
idea was to help them protect themselves and their businesses from robbers, and it was given wide publicity. The
store-robbery rate dropped from an average of 1.5 a day to
none in four months.

Where do we go from here? My answer to this is 10
based on the firm belief that we have a crime problem in
this country, not a gun problem, and that we must meet the
enemy on his own terms. We must start by making crime
as unprofitable for him as we can. And we have to do this,
I believe, by getting tough in the courts and corrections
systems.

A recent news story in Washington, D.C., reports 11
that, of 184 persons convicted of gun possession in a six-
month period, only 14 received a jail sentence. Forty-six
other cases involved persons who had previously been convicted of a felony or possession of a gun. Although the
maximum penalty for such repeaters in the District of
Columbia is ten years in prison, half of these were not jailed
at all. A study last year revealed that in New York City,
which has about the most prohibitive gun legislation in the
country, only one out of six people convicted of crimes
involving weapons went to jail.

This sorry state of affairs exists because too many 12
judges and magistrates either don't know the law or are
unwilling to apply it with appropriate vigor. It's time to
demand either that they crack down on these criminals or
be removed from office. It may even be time to review the
whole system of judicial appointments, to stop weakening
the cause of justice by putting men on the bench who may
happen to be golfing partners of Congressmen and too often
lack the brains and ability for the job. In Arizona today we
elect our judges, and the system is working well, in part
because we ask the American and local bar associations to
consider candidates and make recommendations. In this
way, over the last few years, we have replaced many
weaklings with good jurists.

We have long had all the criminal statutes we need 13
to turn the tide against the crime wave. There is, however,
one piece of proposed legislation that I am watching with
particular interest. Introduced by Sen. James McClure (R.,
Idaho), it requires that any person convicted of a federal
crime in which a gun is used serve five to ten years in jail
automatically on top of whatever penalty he receives for the
crime itself. A second conviction would result in an extra
ten-year-to-life sentence. These sentences would be mandatory and could not be suspended. It is, in short, a "tough"
bill. I think that this bill would serve as an excellent model
for state legislation.

And so it has in California which, last September, 14
signed into law a similar bill requiring a mandatory jail
sentence for any gun-related felony.

Finally, it's important to remember that this is an 15
area of great confusion; an area in which statistics can be
juggled and distorted to support legislation that is liable to
be expensive, counter-productive or useless. The issue
touches upon the freedom and safety of all of us, whether we
own firearms or not. The debate over gun control is an
adjunct to the war against crime, and that war must be
fought with all the intelligence and tenacity we can bring
to it.

BUILDING VOCABULARY

1. For each word in Column A, select from Column
B a word or words whose meaning is most similar.

Column A	Column B
a. diminish (par. 1)	1. slavery
b. incidence (par. 1)	2. continuing forever
c. bolstered (par. 2)	3. firmness
d. enactment (par. 2)	4. supported
e. unwarranted (par. 4)	5. occurrence
f. mandatory (par. 4)	6. energy
g. perpetual (par. 7)	7. that which is made into law
h. servitude (par. 7)	8. without justification

i. vigor (par. 14)
j. tenacity (par. 15)

9. make less
10. required

2. Explain the meaning of these figurative expressions (see page 383–384). Why has the author used them?

    a. Hobble ourselves (par. 6)
    b. Turn the tide against the crime wave (par. 13)
    c. Statistics can be juggled (par. 15)

UNDERSTANDING THE WRITER'S IDEAS

1. Why, according to Goldwater, does gun legislation not work?
2. Why does he not agree that crimes of passion occur because guns happen to be present at the scene?
3. How does Goldwater propose that we reduce crime?
4. How do problems with *enforcement* and *expense* contribute to his view that national gun registration would not be worth a try?
5. How does the Second Amendment, according to Goldwater, make gun control unconstitutional?
6. What kinds of gun laws does Goldwater support? What does he mean by "gun education"?
7. What is the point Goldwater tries to make in his discussion of events in Washington D. C. and in New York City?
8. How does Goldwater explain the fact that criminals do not receive what he believes should be severer punishment?
9. What legislation has McClure introduced? Check outside resources, if you can, to see whether or not that legislation ever passed.

UNDERSTANDING THE WRITER'S TECHNIQUES

1. What is Goldwater's thesis in this essay? What sentence in the first two paragraphs most clearly states his

purpose in writing this piece? How is the thesis sentence related to the title of the essay?

2. His first minor premise is that gun legislation does not work. What evidence does he offer to support that idea? Has he provided specific facts to show that gun laws are ineffective? Why?

3. Where in this essay does Goldwater use statistics or cases effectively? Why does he offer such details in an essay of this sort?

4. Where in the essay does Goldwater introduce the point of view of those who favor gun legislation? How does the author respond to them? Do you think that it is important to deal with the arguments of the opposition? Why?

5. Paragraph 6 makes its point through illustration. What two examples does it offer? How does paragraph 7 continue the illustration? Could paragraphs 6 and 7 be combined into one?

6. The title with its question beginning with "why" suggests that the writer will explain *causes*. Has Goldwater discussed the reasons for the failure of gun control legislation? Would this essay stand as a good example of causal analysis?

7. The opening sentences of paragraphs 5, 6, 7, 8, and 9 all use transitional devices to help the writer and reader move from one idea to the next. What are those transitional devices? Are they effective? Why?

8. What is the effect of the question that opens paragraph 10?

9. What was the effect of gun education in Highland Park, Michigan? What cause-effect relationship is Goldwater suggesting?

10. In paragraph 12 Goldwater attacks judges and congressmen. Why? Is his attack logical? He has obviously not offered evidence to support the idea that judicial appointments put "men on the bench who may happen to be golfing partners of Congressmen and too often lack the brains and ability for the job." Why has he not supported this idea? Do you think he should be making such a statement without giving evidence?

11. Does the last paragraph serve as an effective conclusion? Why do you think so? Does that statement about juggling statistics make the reader careful even about the statistics Goldwater uses? How does this affect his total argument?

12. This essay first appeared in the *Reader's Digest,* a magazine that rewrites long essays to make them shorter and easier. How does Goldwater's style show that he knows he is writing for an audience that demands simple writing?

EXPLORING THE WRITER'S IDEAS

1. Do you agree that gun control laws do not work? Check statistics in your own city and see if you can find evidence to support your point.

2. What is a crime of passion? Do you agree that people angry enough to kill will kill with *any* available weapon? Why?

3. Goldwater argues that we should be stricter in our laws against criminals. Do you believe that strict laws against offenders discourage criminals? Have strict laws against drug users and suppliers worked in deterring crime? Has the death penalty worked reasonably well in preventing murders? Give evidence for your opinion.

4. Goldwater makes clear that gun licensing is very expensive and, therefore, an argument against gun control. How much should society consider financial matters in weighing laws on important social issues? Should welfare, for example, be eliminated because it is so costly?

5. Do you agree with Goldwater that the Second Amendment to the Bill of Rights makes gun control unconstitutional, or do you feel that the right to bear arms made sense during the American Revolution, but has no application today? Support your opinion.

6. Is Goldwater's proposal to elect judges a good one? What problems might exist in wholly elected judiciary?

7. How do you explain the shocking statistics in paragraph 6 on gun possession in Washington and New York? Is it only, as Goldwater seems to feel, because of weak

or ignorant judges that criminals who possess guns do not go to prison?

8. If you could vote on the McClure bill, what would you do? Why?

WRITING PROJECTS

Guided Writing

Write an essay in which you argue the opposite side of Goldwater's position (whether or not you agree with it). Try to convince your readers why gun control laws are necessary.

1. State your proposal carefully in the first or second paragraph. You might want to write an introduction like Goldwater's in which you briefly explain why you do *not* support the idea that gun control laws do not work.

2. Explain why you think gun legislation does work or might work. Try to gather impressive statistics to show how some community or state gun laws have seemed to work.

3. Try to *refute* the argument that what we need are stiffer laws against criminals. (When you refute something you argue against it.)

4. In your essay, refute the difficulties involved in enforcement, in expense, and/or in constitutionality. Point out how we might enforce gun laws; how or why we might pay the expenses; or why the Constitution would not be violated. Explain, further, why "gun education" might not work.

5. Whatever minor propositions you discuss, arrange them in an order that will help convince your reader.

6. As part of your refutation, make sure that you consider the arguments made by people who might disagree with you. After you explain what they say, you can *deny* that their point is right or true; or you can *admit* that what they say is true, but that they have left out important ideas; or you can try to find a *shortcoming* in the way they reason about the topic.

7. Write a conclusion that highlights an important

feature of the issue and summarizes the main point of your essay.

More Writing Projects

    1.   Write an essay in which you argue for or against capital punishment as a means of preventing the crime of murder.

    2.   Select any one of the amendments in the Bill of Rights and argue either that it *does* or *does not* serve the needs of twentieth-century Americans.

Jane Doe

I WISH THEY'D DO IT RIGHT

In this essay from the *New York Times,* a mother who wishes not to be identified (hence, the name Jane Doe, a pseudonym) argues against a feature of her son's life-style. As you read this selection, notice how the author attempts to understand her son's position, while maintaining and supporting her own.

Words to Watch

appraised (par. 2): told the value
Leboyer (par. 2): a physician whose ideas on birth without violence have drawn many followers to his method
legitimacy (par. 2): fact of being legal
surfeited (par. 7): filled with excess amount
executing (par. 7): carrying out
wedlock (par. 8): state of marriage
facetious (par. 8): amusing; humorous
bypassing (par. 9): avoiding
sanctuary (par. 12): holy place
assiduously (par. 12): constantly
foibles (par. 13): weaknesses of character
mandated (par. 13): commanded
adamancy (par. 14): stubbornness
harassment (par. 15): attacks; disturbances

My son and his wife are not married. They have lived together for seven years without benefit of license. Though occasionally marriage has been a subject of conjecture, it did not seem important until the day they announced, jubilantly, that they were going to have a child. It was happy news. I was ready and eager to become a grandmother. Now, I thought, they will take the final step and make their relationship legal.

I was appraised of the Lamaze method of natural childbirth. I was prepared by Leboyer for birth without violence. I admired the expectant mother's discipline. She ate only organic foods, abstained from alcohol, avoided insecticides, smog and trauma. Every precaution was taken to insure the arrival of a healthy, happy infant. No royal birth had been prepared for more auspiciously. All that was lacking was legitimacy.

Finally, when my grandson was two weeks old, I dared to question their intentions.

"We don't believe in marriage," was all that was volunteered.

"Not even for your son's sake?" I asked. "Maybe he will."

Their eyes were impenetrable, their faces stiffened to masks. "You wouldn't understand," I was told.

And I don't. Surely they cannot believe they are pioneering, making revolutionary changes in society. That frontier has long been tamed. Today marriage offers all the options. Books and talk shows have surfeited us with the freedom offered in open marriage. Lawyers, psychologists and marriage counselors are growing rich executing marriage contracts. And divorce, should it come to that, is in most states easy and inexpensive.

On the other hand, living together out of wedlock can be economically impractical as well as socially awkward. How do I present her—as my son's roommate? his spouse? his spice, as one facetious friend suggested? Even my son flounders in these waters. Recently, I heard him refer to her as his girl friend. I cannot believe that that description will be endearing to their son when he is able to understand.

I have resolved that problem for myself, bypassing ⑨
their omission, introducing her as she is, as my daughter-
in-law. But my son, in militant support of his ideology,
refutes any assumption, however casual, that they have
taken vows.

There are economic benefits which they are denying 10
themselves. When they applied for housing in the married-
students dormitory of the university where he is seeking his
doctorate, they were asked for their marriage certificate.
Not having one, they were forced to find other, more
expensive quarters off campus. Her medical insurance,
provided by the company where she was employed, was
denied him. He is not her husband. There have been and
will be other inconveniences they have elected to endure.

Their son will not enjoy the luxury of choice about 11
the inconveniences and scurrility to which he will be subject
from those of his peers and elders who dislike and fear
society's nonconformists.

And if in the future, his parents should decide to 12
separate, will he not suffer greater damage than the child
of divorce, who may find comfort in the knowledge that his
parents once believed they could live happily ever after, and
committed themselves to that idea? The child of unwed
parents has no sanctuary. His mother and father have
assiduously avoided a pledge of permanency, leaving him
drifting and insecure.

I know my son is motivated by idealism and honesty 13
in his reluctance to concede to what he considers mere
ceremony. But is he wise enough to know that no one
individual can fight all of society's foibles and frauds. Why
does he persist in this, a battle already lost? Because though
he rejects marriage, California, his residence, has declared
that while couples living together in imitation of marriage
are no longer under the jurisdiction of the family court, their
relationship is viewed by the state as an implicit contract
somewhat like a business agreement. This position was
mandated when equal property rights were granted a woman
who had been abandoned by the man she had lived with for
a number of years.

Finally, the couple's adamancy has been depriving 14
to all the rest of the family. There has been no celebration
of wedding or anniversaries. There has been concealment
from certain family elders who could not cope with the
situation. Its irregularity has put constraint on the grandparents, who are stifled by one another's possible embar-
rassment or hurt.

I hope that one day very soon my son and his wife 15
will acknowledge their cohabitation with a license. The rest
of us will not love them any more for it. We love and support
them as much as possible now. But it will be easier and
happier for us knowing that our grandson will be spared the
continued explanation and harassment, the doubts and
anxieties of being a child of unmarried parents.

BUILDING VOCABULARY

1. Check the definitions of each of these words.
Then explain how its prefix and/or suffix, named alongside,
contributes to its meaning.

Prefix or Suffix

a. conjecture (par. 1)	con	
b. impenetrable (par. 3)	im	able
c. concede (par. 13)	con	
d. concealment (par. 14)	con	ment
e. constraint (par. 14)	con	
f. cohabitation (par. 15)	co	tion

2. You know that by changing the form of a word
(and, as a result, usually its grammatical function) you can
change its meaning. Determine the definition of each word
in Column A below. Then, write a definition of the word
related to it in Column B.

Column A	Column B
jubilantly (par. 1)	jubilation

abstained (par. 2)	abstention
trauma (par. 2)	traumatic
auspiciously (par. 2)	inauspicious
endearing (par. 8)	endearment
militant (par. 10)	militancy
endure (par. 10)	endurable
scurrility (par. 11)	scurrilous
implicit (par. 13)	implied
stifled (par. 14)	stifling

3. Write original sentences for any five words defined in the Words to Watch section.

UNDERSTANDING THE WRITER'S IDEAS

1. Why did the writer think her son should get married?

2. Why does she compare the coming birth of her son's child to a "royal birth"?

3. Why does she not understand when her son and his woman say that they do not believe in marriage?

4. Why does the writer believe that marriage offers all the options? What is "open marriage"?

5. Why does the writer have problems in introducing her son's girlfriend? Why does she think that living together without being married is impractical?

6. What problems does she forsee for her grandchild if his parents do not marry?

7. What law did the state of California pass in regard to couples who live together? How, according to the writer, has this affected her son's decision.

8. How has the rest of the family been deprived, according to the writer?

UNDERSTANDING THE WRITER'S TECHNIQUES

1. What is Doe's major premise in this essay? One sentence about a third of the way through could be called the *thesis sentence*. Which do you think it is?

2. It is not until paragraph 7 that the writer actually begins arguing her point. What is the purpose of paragraphs 1 and 2? Are they necessary to the essay? Why?

3. What minor premise does she make and develop in paragraph 7?

4. In paragraph 8 she takes up the problems that she sees for people who do not agree with her point; in the rest of the essay she offers several minor premises to explain what those problems would be. What minor premise do paragraphs 8 and 9 develop? paragraph 10? 11 and 12? 14?

5. Paragraph 13 attempts to set up a *causal* relationship. What is it? Does the writer convince you of the reason for her son's behavior?

6. What is the *tone* of this essay (see page 391)? Would you say the writing shows *anger, indifference, control, distance, coolness, passion,* or *resignation*? Support your response.

7. In this essay the writer uses the *passive voice* in a number of places. (A sentence like "I was told" is passive: The subject of the sentence is acted upon; it does not itself carry out some action.) A passive construction helps a writer stress an action that is performed, and helps avoid a stress on the person or thing performing that action. Usually too many passives weaken a writer's style. What examples of passive voice do you find here? Has the writer used passive effectively, or has she overused it? Does the passive voice contribute anything to the tone?

8. Comment on the writer's use of transitions in the first sentence of each of these paragraphs: 3, 7, 8, 9, 12, 14.

9. How do the closing paragraphs serve as a summary of the writer's position? Why does she focus on the unborn child at the end? Is this reference sentimental (see p. 389)? Does Doe rely on other emotional appeals throughout her essay? List examples.

10. Where in the essay does the writer deal with the opposition—the reasons why her son and his woman might *not* want to marry? Should she have offered any other opposing arguments to strengthen her own position? Or, do

you think she was wise in avoiding too much discussion of the opposition's point of view?

EXPLORING THE WRITER'S IDEAS

1. Why do you think many young people in our current times often decide not to marry, despite the fact that they live together and have children? What benefits do you see in such arrangements? What problems, other than those Doe spells out, do you see?

2. The writer says she cannot understand the lifestyle her son and his woman have chosen. Is this simply a reflection of the "generation gap"? Or, do you think there are more basic, philosophical differences here that transcend age?

3. Do you agree with the writer's view of the problems for the child if it is born illegitimate? Why? Are people today more willing than in the past to accept socially a child born to unwed parents? Why?

4. Several of the writer's points focus on the problems unmarried couples cause their families. Should young people consider the effects of their decisions on their parents? Why or why not?

5. The writer suggests that her son's idealism is an important factor in his behavior. What is "idealism"? Do you agree that "no one individual can fight all of society's foibles and frauds"? Why? Is it possible to be an idealist and to live happily in today's world?

6. By the title the author suggests that there is a "right" and a "wrong" way. Is it possible that these are merely *alternative* ways, the traditional view of marriage and the more contemporary concept of "living together"? Should there be room in this society (politically, legally, economically, socially) for alternative life-styles? Why?

7. Many people say that in a "living together" relationship, the woman suffers most because the man, if he leaves, avoids all responsibilities for woman, child, and home. Do you agree? Why?

8. What is a "common law marriage"? Does your state recognize such marriages as legal?

WRITING PROJECTS

Guided Writing

Write an essay in which you explain the advantages of a young man and woman living together unmarried. (You might even write this from the point of view of Jane Doe's son or daughter-in-law.)

1. Decide on the main thrust of your essay and write a thesis statement which makes clear your major premise.

2. In two or three paragraphs describe briefly the most convincing reasons for life together without marriage. Give specific illustrations to support your point.

3. In the rest of the essay discuss the problems for a young man and woman who *do* get married, problems which living together without marriage does not bring up. (These are your *minor premises*.) Again, be specific in offering reasons to explain why marriage is *not* an attractive alternative for two people who love each other.

4. Connect your ideas with carefully chosen transitions.

5. Save your most convincing minor premise for last.

6. Write a conclusion summarizing your main argument.

More Writing Projects

1. Write an essay in which you defend or oppose some other "alternative life-style" available in today's culture. You might wish to argue for or against communal living, open marriage, or homosexuality, for example.

2. Write an essay in which you argue about the responsibilities an adult should (or should not) have to his parents.

James Baldwin

MY DUNGEON SHOOK

In this letter, James Baldwin (1924–   ) tries to persuade his nephew of the ways a black can survive in a white world. This is the first time in this text that you will consider a prose letter. While reading it, try to determine the letter's usefulness in advancing the argument that Baldwin develops.

Words to Watch

vulnerable (par. 1): easily hurt
truculent (par. 1): fierce and cruel
E. Franklin Frazier (par. 1): a noted contemporary black sociologist
devastation (par. 2): ruin

Dear James:

I have begun this letter five times and torn it up 1
five times. I keep seeing your face, which is also the face of your father and my brother. Like him, you are tough, dark, vulnerable, moody—with a very definite tendency to sound truculent because you want no one to think you are soft. You may be like your grandfather in this, I don't know, but certainly both you and your father resemble him very much

physically. Well, he is dead, he never saw you, and he had a terrible life; he was defeated long before he died because, at the bottom of his heart, he really believed what white people said about him. This is one of the reasons that he became so holy. I am sure that your father has told you something about all that. Neither you nor your father exhibit any tendency towards holiness: you really *are* of another era, part of what happened when the Negro left the land and came into what the late E. Franklin Frazier called "the cities of destruction." You can only be destroyed by believing that you really are what the white world calls a *nigger*. I tell you this because I love you, and please don't you ever forget it.

I have known both of you all your lives, have carried 2 your Daddy in my arms and on my shoulders, kissed and spanked him and watched him learn to walk. I don't know if you've known anybody from that far back; if you've loved anybody that long, first as an infant, then as a child, then as a man, you gain a strange perspective on time and human pain and effort. Other people cannot see what I see whenever I look into your father's face, for behind your father's face as it is today are all those other faces which were his. Let him laugh and I see a cellar your father does not remember and a house he does not remember and I hear in his present laughter his laughter as a child. Let him curse and I remember him falling down the cellar steps, and howling, and I remember, with pain, his tears, which my hand or your grandmother's so easily wiped away. But no one's hand can wipe away those tears he sheds invisibly today, which one hears in his laughter and in his speech and in his songs. I know what the world has done to my brother and how narrowly he has survived it. And I know, which is much worse, and this is the crime of which I accuse my country and my countrymen, and for which neither I nor time nor history will ever forgive them, that they have destroyed and are destroying hundreds of thousands of lives and do not know it and do not want to know it. One can be, indeed one must strive to become, tough and philosophical concerning destruction and death, for this is what most of mankind has been best at since we have heard of man. (But remember: *most* of mankind is not *all* of mankind.) But it is not permissible that the authors of devastation should also be innocent. It is the innocence which constitutes the crime.

Now, my dear namesake, these innocent and well- 3 meaning people, your countrymen, have caused you to be born under conditions not very far removed from those described for us by Charles Dickens in the London of more than a hundred years ago. (I hear the chorus of the innocents screaming, "No! This is not true! How *bitter* you are!"—but I am writing this letter to *you,* to try to tell you something about how to handle *them,* for most of them do not yet really know that you exist. I *know* the conditions under which you were born, for I was there. Your countrymen were *not* there, and haven't made it yet. Your grandmother was also there, and no one has ever accused her of being bitter. I suggest that the innocents check with her. She isn't hard to find. Your countrymen don't know that *she* exists, either, though she has been working for them all their lives.)

Well, you were born, here you came, something like 4 fifteen years ago; and though your father and mother and grandmother, looking about the streets through which they were carrying you, staring at the walls into which they brought you, had every reason to be heavyhearted, yet they were not. For here you were, Big James, named for me— you were a big baby, I was not—here you were: to be loved. To be loved, baby, hard, at once, and forever, to strengthen you against the loveless world. Remember that: I know how black it looks today, for you. It looked bad that day, too, yes, we were trembling. We have not stopped trembling yet, but if we had not loved each other none of us would have survived. And now you must survive because we love you, and for the sake of your children and your children's children.

This innocent country set you down in a ghetto in 5 which, in fact, it intended that you should perish. Let me spell out precisely what I mean by that, for the heart of the matter is here, and the root of my dispute with my country. You were born where you were born and faced the future that you faced because you were black and *for no other reason*. The limits of your ambition were, thus, expected to be set forever. You were born into a society which spelled out with brutal clarity, and in as many ways as possible, that you were a worthless human being. You were not expected to aspire to excellence: you were expected to make peace with mediocrity. Wherever you have turned, James, in your short time on this earth, you have been told where you could go and what you could do (and *how* you could do it) and where you could live and whom you could marry. I know your countrymen do not agree with me about this, and I hear them saying, "You exaggerate." They do not know Harlem, and I do. So do you. Take no one's word for anything, including mine—but trust your experience. Know whence you came. If you know whence you came, there is really no limit to where you can go. The details and symbols of your life have been deliberately constructed to make you believe what white people say about you. Please try to remember that what they believe, as well as what they do and cause you to endure, does not testify to your inferiority but to their inhumanity and fear. Please try to be clear, dear James, through the storm which rages about your youthful head today, about the reality which lies behind the words *acceptance* and *integration*. There is no reason for you to try to become like white people and there is no basis whatever for their impertinent assumption that *they* must accept *you*. The really terrible thing, old buddy, is that *you* must accept *them*. And I mean that very seriously. You must accept them and accept them with love. For these innocent people have no other hope. They are, in effect, still trapped in a history which they do not understand; and until they understand it, they cannot be released from it. They have had to believe for many years, and for innumerable reasons, that black men are inferior to white men. Many of them, indeed, know better, but, as you will discover, people find it very difficult to act on what they know. To act is to be committed, and to be committed is to be in danger. In this case, the danger, in the minds of most white Americans, is the loss of their identity. Try to imagine how you would feel if you woke up one morning to find the sun shining and all

JAMES BALDWIN 323

the stars aflame. You would be frightened because it is out of the order of nature. Any upheaval in the universe is terrifying because it so profoundly attacks one's sense of one's own reality. Well, the black man has functioned in the white man's world as a fixed star, as an immovable pillar: and as he moves out of his place, heaven and earth are shaken to their foundations. You, don't be afraid. I said that it was intended that you should perish in the ghetto, perish by never being allowed to go behind the white man's definitions, by never being allowed to spell your proper name. You have, and many of us have, defeated this intention; and, by a terrible law, a terrible paradox, those innocents who believed that your imprisonment made them safe are losing their grasp of reality. But these men are your brothers—your lost, younger brothers. And if the word *integration* means anything, this is what it means: that we, with love, shall force our brothers to see themselves as they are, to cease fleeing from reality and begin to change it. For this is your home, my friend, do not be driven from it; great men have done great things here, and will again, and we can make America what America must become. It will be hard, James, but you come from sturdy, peasant stock, men who picked cotton and dammed rivers and built railroads, and, in the teeth of the most terrifying odds, achieved an unassailable and monumental dignity. You come from a long line of great poets, some of the greatest poets since Homer. One of them said, *The very time I thought I was lost, My dungeon shook and my chains fell off.*

You know, and I know, that the country is cele- 6 brating one hundred years of freedom one hundred years too soon. We cannot be free until they are free. God bless you, James, and Godspeed.

Your uncle,
James

BUILDING VOCABULARY

1. Select the word or phrase which best defines the word in italics.

a. *tendency* (par. 1)

1. dwelling   2. laughter   3. choice
4. leaning toward some action   5. tender
  b. *era* (par. 1)
1. mistake   2. period of time   3. weak   4. family
5. hope
  c. *perspective* (par. 2)
1. mental views   2. prejudice   3. behavior   4. attitude
5. persecution
  d. *aspire* (par. 5)
1. sweat   2. pray   3. aim for   4. avoid
5. take aim against
  e. *mediocrity* (par. 5)
1. physicians   2. boredom   3. being weak
4. being average   5. the enemy
  f. *impertinent* (par. 5)
1. rude   2. ridiculous   3. immediate   4. timely
5. unfortunate
  g. *aflame* (par. 5)
1. colorful   2. interesting   3. unmatched   4. weak
5. on fire
  h. *upheaval* (par. 5)
1. digging   2. radical change   3. speech   4. action
5. weariness
  i. *profoundly* (par. 5)
1. deeply   2. weakly   3. happily   4. methodically
5. worriedly
  j. *unassailable* (par. 5)
1. unloved   2. cannot be feared   3. unhealthy
4. cannot be attacked   5. tired

UNDERSTANDING THE WRITER'S IDEAS

  1. How is Baldwin's nephew like the boy's father, the author's brother? How are boy and father like the boy's grandfather (Baldwin's father)?
  2. Why, according to the author, did his father have a terrible life? In what way do the boy and his father *not* resemble the boy's grandfather?

3. Why, according to Baldwin, does he have a "strange perspective on time and human pain and effort"? What is that perspective?

4. Of what crime does he accuse his countrymen? What does he mean when he says "*most* of mankind is not *all* of mankind"?

5. What conditions about growing up in London a hundred years ago did Charles Dickens describe (check *David Copperfield, Great Expectations,* or *Martin Chuzzlewit,* Dickens' novels about youth growing up)? Why does Baldwin say that his nephew was born under similar conditions in modern-day America?

6. Why, despite these bad conditions surrounding Big James' birth, were the child's parents not heavy-hearted?

7. What is at the root of Baldwin's dispute with America?

8. What is the only hope Baldwin sees for white people? Why?

9. Why, according to the author, do more people who know that blacks are not inferior to whites not act on what they know?

10. What is "the reality which lies behind the words *acceptance* and *integration,*" as Baldwin sees it?

11. What does Baldwin mean when he says that it was intended that his nephew should perish "by never being allowed to go beyond the white man's definitions, by never being allowed to spell [his] proper name"?

12. How, according to Baldwin, will whites be forced to see themselves as they are? What is the "terrible paradox" he mentions near the end of paragraph 5?

UNDERSTANDING THE WRITER'S TECHNIQUES

1. What was Baldwin's main purpose in writing this letter to his nephew? Where in the piece do you find one or two sentences that might be called the "major premise" in Baldwin's argument? What recommendation for action does Baldwin's main premise include?

2.   Usually a writer lets the reader know early in the essay what the main point will be. Why does Baldwin offer his main premise more than halfway through this piece?

3.   What are the minor premises in Baldwin's argument? Make a list of them. Which does he support with *specific* details? Why for the point "my country and my countrymen . . . have destroyed and are destroying hundreds of thousands of lives and do not know it and do not want to know it" does Baldwin not offer any specific support? Would you call that lack of detail a weakness in the essay? Why? For what other points does Baldwin offer no specific details (see paragraph 3)?

4.   The *personal letter* as a prose form allows for much more flexibility and informality than a bona fide "essay." Why? How does Baldwin's language reflect that informality? How does the letter form influence the position of the major premise (see paragraph 2)? of the quantity and quality of detail to support minor points?

5.   What point does Baldwin set out early in paragraph 5? Does he support that point or does he rephrase and expand it, assuming that his reader will know the details? If this were an essay instead of a letter, would readers expect specific examples to prove this point, or would they, too, simply agree to the point because it is obvious?

6.   How does Baldwin's introduction lay the groundwork for the points he wishes to develop in his piece? What is the significance of the word "love" in the last line of the introductory paragraph? How is that word related to the major premise of the piece? How does the discussion of love in paragraph 2 contribute to the argument?

7.   Near the end of paragraph 5, Baldwin offers an *analogy* between the black man's condition and the sun and stars. (An analogy is a comparison based on some similarities in particular circumstances.) What is the basis of the comparison? Explain it in your own words. Why does Baldwin use an analogy? What effect does it have on the visual quality of the writing? How does it affect your understanding of the point he is trying to make?

8. What is your sense of the meaning of the statement in italics at the end of paragraph 5? To what is it an *allusion* (see page 379)? How does the allusion contribute to the point Baldwin is making?

9. The conventions of the letter require certain features at the beginning ("Dear _____") and at the end. What conventional features appear at the close of Baldwin's letter? How does the last paragraph serve as a fit conclusion to the arguments the writer makes?

EXPLORING THE WRITER'S IDEAS

1. Baldwin mentions that his father became holy because he believed what white people said about him. What did they say? What does the white world mean by the word *nigger*? Do people today still say about blacks what Baldwin believes people said about his father?

2. Baldwin suggests that love gives a person a strange perspective. Do you agree? Why? How do you account for the special vision love creates?

3. What does the phrase "cities of destruction" mean to you? Does the term apply to urban centers today? How do they "destroy"?

4. Do you agree that your countrymen have destroyed and are destroying hundreds of thousands of lives and do not know it or want to know it? How? Why might a person in an American minority group believe it?

5. Do you agree that conditions for the young American black growing up today are similar to the conditions Dickens described? Why? What *differences* exist between the London city child and the black American city child?

6. Do you believe with Baldwin that a person faces his future based only on his race? Why? Why does Baldwin believe it? Why would his nephew not find it difficult to believe?

7. Do you agree that whites do not have to accept blacks but that blacks have to accept whites? Why?

8.   Why does Baldwin recommend love as the only way to get people to see themselves as they are? Do you agree with that recommendation? Why? How does it compare with recommendations made by militant members of ethnic groups? Why does Baldwin make his recommendation in light of the more passionate (and more popular) modern alternative of violence?

9.   What does Baldwin mean that the country is celebrating freedom one hundred years too soon? Why might you agree or disagree? Who is enslaved?

IDEAS FOR WRITING

Guided Writing

Write a letter to a relative or friend who has a serious problem or problems. In your letter argue how your friend might deal with or solve these problems.

1.   Decide on your major premise: What, from your argument, is the single most significant action your relative or friend should follow in order to deal with his problem?

2.   Do not write your major premise early in the essay—save it for a point at least halfway through.

3.   Make a list of your minor premises, the points that will back up your main position. Arrange them in some reasonable order. Discuss and support with details these minor points first, as you build to the statement of your major premise.

4.   Write an introduction in which you discuss the personal background of the relative or friend to whom you are writing. Show how he or she represents qualities relating to an ethnic or racial group, to a social or economic group, to a religious group, or even to identification as a man or woman. (You might want to deal with several of these categories.) Mention personal anecdotes in the way that Baldwin does.

5.   Somewhere in your essay, offer an *analogy* to clarify one of your points.

6. Somewhere in your essay, make an *allusion* to some literary or historical fact.

7. Write a closing which clinches your whole argument.

8. Throughout the essay, use an informal style appropriate to a letter.

More Writing Projects

1. Write an answer to Baldwin's letter from the point of view of his nephew.

2. Write a letter to the editor of the most important newspaper in your town or city, arguing for some course of action your local government should take in order to solve some pressing problem. You are not writing to a relative or friend here: Make sure your language, style, and content suit your audience.

ten

Prose for Further Reading

Santha Rama Rau
"DINNER IN INDIA"

Dinner was an entirely different meal. It was served late, about nine o'clock, and, we discovered, was the chief meal of the day. *Chota hasari*—the little breakfast—consists of a cup of tea at five-thirty or six in the morning, with possibly some fruit or toast served with it. At about eleven or at midday a heavier meal is eaten, *chapatis*—thin unleavened wheat cakes—and curry, with *dal*—a kind of lentil soup—and curds and sweets of some sort. But for dinner, I was to learn, there was always rice, several varieties of curry, pepper-water and *dal, chapatis,* curds, buttermilk, pickles of various sorts, cabbage spiced with bay leaves. Afterwards all kinds of sweets were served, some heavily spiced, tasting unfamiliar and strong, and some that seemed to be just sweetened milk. Fruit from the garden and from the bazaars was then brought on—mangoes, guavas, pomegranates, nectarines—they all had exotic, story-book names.

This meal was eaten on the wide veranda opening off the living room. An enormous cloth was spread on the stone floor. By the light of the oil lamps which were used on the veranda (though the rest of the house had electricity) the silver and the brassware on the "table" looked bright and foreign. The food was placed on flat, round silver *thalis,* like small trays, and the curries and other dishes were contained in little matching bowls clustered round the *thalis;* even the water glasses were made of silver.

We sat on low wooden stools round the cloth and ate with our fingers. The technique of this was hard enough to master, particularly with liquids, but we had to remember as well the complicated and formal ritual of the rest of the meal. As the servants bring round fresh dishes, you serve yourself with the left hand. You must always use only your right hand in the actual eating of your food. You must wait until the men have begun their meal before you may begin on your own food. And even then, you must wait till the older women start to eat. This grading system we were told, was a concession to changing times and relaxing manners and formalities. In the old days, the women would not even sit down to their meal until the men had entirely finished. They would wait in the kitchen and help the servants in serving the food, or in the more well-to-do homes they would wait in their rooms. I noticed that my grandmother still maintained this custom, and although she would sit with us she would eat nothing until her husband had finished his meal. I think she would have liked to compel all the women in her household to behave in the traditional way, but this was one of the few instances in which she had found that social progress had got out of hand.

Richard Selzer

THE DISCUS THROWER

I spy on my patients. Ought not a doctor to observe his patients by any means and from any stance, that he might the more fully assemble evidence? So I stand in the doorways of hospital rooms and gaze. Oh, it is not all that furtive an act. Those in bed need only look up to discover me. But they never do.

From the doorway of Room 542 the man in the bed seems deeply tanned. Blue eyes and close-cropped white hair give him the appearance of vigor and good health. But I know that his skin is not brown from the sun. It is rusted, rather, in the last stage of containing the vile repose within. And the blue eyes are frosted, looking inward like the windows of a snowbound cottage. This man is blind. This man is also legless—the right leg missing from midthigh down, the left from just below the knee. It gives him the look of a bonsai, roots and branches pruned into the dwarfed facsimile of a great tree.

Propped on pillows, he cups his right thigh in both hands. Now and then he shakes his head as though acknowledging the intensity of his suffering. In all of this he makes no sound. Is he mute as well as blind?

The room in which he dwells is empty of all possessions—no get-well cards, small, private caches of food, day-old flowers, slippers, all the usual kick-shaws of the sickroom.

There is only the bed, a chair, a nightstand, and a tray on wheels that can be swung across his lap for meals.

"What time is it?" he asks.

"Three o'clock."

"Morning or afternoon?"

"Afternoon."

He is silent. There is nothing else he wants to know.

"How are you?" I say.

"Who is it?" he asks.

"It's the doctor. How do you feel?"

He does not answer right away.

"Feel?" he says.

"I hope you feel better," I say.

I press the button at the side of the bed.

"Down you go," I say.

"Yes, down, " he says.

He falls back upon the bed awkwardly. His stumps, unweighted by legs and feet, rise in the air, presenting themselves. I unwrap the bandages from the stumps, and begin to cut away the black scabs and the dead, glazed fat with scissors and forceps. A shard of white bone comes loose. I pick it away. I wash the wounds with disinfectant and redress the stumps. All this while, he does not speak. What is he thinking behind those lids that do not blink? Is he remembering a time when he was whole? Does he dream of feet? Of when his body was not a rotting log?

He lies solid and inert. In spite of everything, he remains impressive, as though he were a sailor standing athwart a slanting deck.

"Anything more I can do for you?" I ask.

For a long moment he is silent.

"Yes," he says at last and without the least irony. "You can bring me a pair of shoes."

In the corridor, the head nurse is waiting for me.

"We have to do something about him," she says. "Every morning he orders scrambled eggs for breakfast, and, instead of eating them, he picks up the plate and throws it against the wall."

"Throws his plate?"

"Nasty. That's what he is. No wonder his family doesn't come to visit. They probably can't stand him any more than we can."

She is waiting for me to do something.

"Well?"

"We'll see," I say.

The next morning I am waiting in the corridor when the kitchen delivers his breakfast. I watch the aide place the tray on the stand and swing it across his lap. She presses the button to raise the head of the bed. Then she leaves.

In time the man reaches to find the rim of the tray, then on to find the dome of the covered dish. He lifts off the cover and places it on the stand. He fingers across the plate until he probes the eggs. He lifts the plate in both hands, sets it on the palm of his right hand, centers it, balances it. He hefts it up and down slightly, getting the feel of it. Abruptly, he draws back his right arm as far as he can.

There is the crack of the plate breaking against the wall at the foot of his bed and the small wet sound of the scrambled eggs dropping to the floor.

And then he laughs. It is a sound you have never heard. It is something new under the sun. It could cure cancer.

Out in the corridor, the eyes of the head nurse narrow.

"Laughed, did he?"

She writes something down on her clipboard.

A second aide arrives, brings a second breakfast tray, puts it on the nightstand, out of his reach. She looks over at me shaking her head and making her mouth go. I see that we are to be accomplices.

"I've got to feed you," she says to the man.

"Oh, no you don't," the man says.

"Oh, yes I do," the aide says, "after the way you just did. Nurse says so."

"Get me my shoes," the man says.

"Here's oatmeal," the aide says. "Open." And she touches the spoon to his lower lip.

"I ordered scrambled eggs," says the man.

"That's right," the aide says.

I step forward.

"Is there anything I can do?" I say.

"Who are you?" the man asks.

In the evening I go once more to that ward to make my rounds. The head nurse reports to me that Room 542 is deceased. She has discovered this quite by accident, she says. No, there had been no sound. Nothing. It's a blessing, she says.

I go into his room, a spy looking for secrets. He is still there in his bed. His face is relaxed, grave, dignified. After a while, I turn to leave. My gaze sweeps the wall at the foot of the bed, and I see the place where it has been repeatedly washed, where the wall looks very clean and very white.

Suzanne Britt Jordan

'I WANTS TO GO TO THE PROSE'

I'm tired—and have been for quite a while. In fact, I think I can pinpoint the exact minute at which I first felt the weariness begin. I had been teaching for three years at a community college. I had, for quite a while, overlooked ignorance, dismissed arrogance, championed fairness, emphasized motivation, boosted egos and tolerated laziness. I was, in short, the classic modern educator.

One day a student, Marylou Simmons, dropped by my office. She had not completed a single assignment and had missed perhaps 50 per cent of her classes. Her writing, what little I saw of it, was illogical, grammatically incorrect and sloppy. "Can I help you, Marylou?" I said cheerily, ever the understanding and forgiving teacher. Her lip began to tremble; her eyes grew teary. It seemed she had been having trouble with her boyfriend. "I'm sorry, but what can *I* do?" I asked. Suddenly all business, Marylou said, "Since I've been so unhappy, I thought you might want to just give me a D or an Incomplete on the course." She smiled encouragingly, even confidently. That's when the weariness set in, the moment at which I turned into a flaming conservative in matters education. Whatever Marylou's troubles, I suddenly saw that I was not the cause, nor was I about to be the solution.

When I read about declining SAT scores, the "functional illiteracy" of our students, the namby-pamby courses, the army of child psychologists, reading aides, educational liaisons, starry-eyed administrators and bungling fools who people our school systems, my heart sinks. Public schools abide mediocre students; put 18-year-olds, who can't decide what to wear in the morning, into independent study programs; excuse every absence under the sun, and counsel, counsel, counsel. A youngster in my own school system got into a knife fight and was expelled—for one week. I noticed in the paper that bus drivers regularly see riders smoking marijuana and drinking wine on the bus at, for God's sake, 8 in the morning. I could go on, but the public knows well enough the effects of a system of education gone awry.

Consider for a moment what caused the mess. A few years ago people began demanding their rights. Fair enough. They wanted equal education under the law. I'm for it. Social consciousness was born. Right on. Now, enter the big wrong turn, the one that sent our schools into never-never land. We suddenly, naïvely, believed that by offering equal opportunities we could (1) make everybody happy, (2) make everybody well-adjusted, (3) forgive everybody who failed, and (4) expect gratitude to boot. When students were surly, uncooperative, whiny and apathetic, educators decided they themselves didn't know how to teach. So they made it easier on the poor, disadvantaged victims of broken homes, the misfits, the unloved. Well and good. But the catch to such lofty theories is evident. Poverty, ignorance and just plain orneriness will always abound. We look for every reason in the world for the declining test scores of our children, except for stupidity and laziness.

I'm perfectly aware that I sound like an old curmudgeon and it frightens me more than it offends you. But I have accepted what educators can't seem to face. The function of schools, their first and primary obligation, is not to probe tender psyches, to feed and clothe the homeless, nor to be the papa and mama a kid never had. The job is to teach.

The teacher's job is to know his subject, inside out, backward, forward and every which way. Nothing unnerves a student more than to have a teacher who doesn't know his or her stuff. Incompetence they cannot abide. Neither can I.

Before educators lost their way and tried to diversify by getting into the business of molding human beings, a teacher was, ideally, someone who knew a certain body of information and conveyed it. Period. Remember crochety old Miss Dinwiddie, who could recite 40 lines of the "Aeneid" at a clip? Picture Mr. Wassleheimer, who could give a zero to a cheating student without pausing in his lecture on frog dissection. Every student knew that it wasn't wise to mess around with a teacher who had the subject down cold. They were the teachers we once despised and later admired.

I want them back, those fearsome, awe-inspiring experts. I want them back because they knew what a school was for and didn't waste any time getting on with the task at hand. They were hard, even at times unjust, but when they were through, we knew those multiplication tables blindfolded with both trembling hands tied behind our backs.

Before the schoolmasters and the administrators change, they will have to shake off the guilt, the simpering, apologetic smiles and the Freudian theories. Which is crueler? Flunking a kid who has flunked or passing a kid who has flunked? Which teaches more about the realities of life? Which, in fact, shows more respect for the child as a human being?

Just today I talked to a big blond bruiser of a football player who wants to learn the basics of grammar. I didn't tell him it was too late. You see, he was a very, very good football player, so good that he never failed a course in high school. He had written on a weekly theme, "I wants to go to the prose and come fames." He may become a pro, may even become famous, but he will probably never read a good book, write a coherent letter or read a story to his children. I will, however, flunk him if he does not learn the material in the course. My job means too much to me to sacrifice my standards and turn soft. Suppose that every time my student played football badly, the coach said it was "just a game." Suppose the coach allowed him to drink booze, stay up all night, eat poorly and play sloppily. My student would be summarily dismissed from the team or the team would lose the game. So it goes with academic courses.

The young people are interested, I think, in taking their knocks, just as adults must take theirs. Students deserve a fair chance, and, failing to take advantage of that chance, a straightforward dismissal. It has been said that government must guarantee equal opportunity, not equal results. I like that. Through the theoretical fog that has clouded our perceptions and blanketed our minds, we know what is equitable and right. Mother put it another way. She always said, "Life is real; life is earnest." Incidentally, she taught me Latin and never gave me air in a jug. I had to breathe on my own. So do we all.

William Saroyan

MEDITATIONS ON THE LETTER Z

Zzz in the American comic strips both ancient and modern signifies sleep: it is supposed to represent the sound of breathing, the sound of snoring. The sound might be spelled zuzz, but zzz or zuzz, the sound does not seem to accurately or even unimportantly inaccurately represent the sound of a sleeper's breathing.

Can it be that it has always meant to represent something else? Something like unconsciousness?

If so, why should being asleep be approximated by zzz or zuzz?

Let that rest; it is important, but it is not crucial.

My summing up of zzz in American comic strips is incomplete, for zzz is also the sign of sawing, actual sawing with a saw, through a branch of a tree or through a piece of lumber, but this also connects to sleep, for the breathing of some sleepers sounds like the action of certain saws—inhale, exhale, back and forth, zzz in, zzz out, and so on. Let that also rest.

It is still not important, although sleep itself, to which we move steadily through all of our time, is as important as anything else we have, and it has engaged the thought and speculation of everybody since the beginning of dreams and the remembering of them.

We come out of sleep when we come out of the womb.

The mother's mystic body is constant, and all of her tides and tie-ins with everything everywhere are constant in the womb, which is itself the equivalent of the universe and everything unknown about everything, and the first arena of human connection with private and racial sleep.

Coming out of there suggests that we go into something like it again when we stop being out, when we stop breathing, when we put it all away, or permit it all to be put away, and remember nothing, and have no way of guessing what happens after we are gone. We don't even know if the word *gone* is the proper word, for it clearly may not be at all, leaving one's private life in one's private body and one's private adjuncts of the body, mind, memory, soul, leaving the marvelous mechanics of ebb and flow, of breathing, of cellular death and birth, of intake of matter in the form of grass and its byproducts, including flesh of fish, fowl, and animal, leaving the constant chemical action of processing intake to outgo, bread and onion and wine to a light brown outgo, leaving all of it may not be leaving at all. Still, we think of death as a departure, at least from our survivors: anybody dies, he's gone from himself and from everybody else.

A man's relationship to where he has come from and to where he is going is close and intimate, although traditionally mainly ignored; everybody must sleep soon enough during the course of one turn of the apportionment of light and dark, one turn of twenty-four hours; some sleep for ten hours, some for eight, some for six, some for four, and a few for only two, and another two hours in naps.

But whatever the portion of sleep out of the full twenty-four hours may be, nobody goes for very long with his connection to sleep severed—not being able to sleep *does* seem to render the man mad, all his balances and procedures are impaired and he is literally a lunatic.

Birth is birth and death is death no matter how you look at them, most likely, but birth is also death, and consequently death may very well also be birth—the religions certainly must have picked up the hint soon after the picking up of hints became unavoidable.

Zaven Minasian was my mother Takoohi's sister Parrantzie's son, and he died in 1968 in El Paso, at the age of sixty. We were good friends from my eighth year to my twenty-eighth, when he sued *Vanity Fair* for publishing my story "Little Caruso," alleging that my comic view of his ambition to be a Metropolitan Opera star discouraged Eddie Arakelian from financing his singing lessons in New York. I told Frank Crowninshield at lunch that I would pay for any loss sustained by *Vanity Fair,* but the famous editor said such legal actions were commonplace, forget it. In the end the matter was settled out of court for something like $1,000, about half of which went to Zav's lawyer. We were friends because we were precisely the same age, had large ambitions, and shared a compulsion to take great risks and to gamble everything, without reservation—life itself.

I bet my life that if I was not a published writer by the age of thirty, I would be nothing—a full refuser, and for that reason alone likely not to be permitted to live. The story that ended my apprenticeship contains within its swift short form the title: "Application for Permission to Live."

I had good luck.

Zav had good luck, too, for he was never not his own man, at any rate. If he didn't sing in opera, he damned well did in life.

Zav and I also shared a quality of behavior which is described by the word, in the language of our families, *zavzak.* This word calls for a small portion of definition: to begin with, it is not an Armenian word, it is Turkish, but in our family it ceased being Turkish and not only became Armenian, it became Saroyan, it became Zav's word, and my word, and we used it and we knew what it meant, for it was placed *upon us* by our elders to describe the style with which we refused to take anything too seriously, all the while taking nothing at all less than totally seriously, if you can guess about that seeming contradiction.

The Turks pronounce the word nearer to *zevzek* than our *zaavzaak,* but that is also the way languages touch upon one another and stay alive and are given new vitality.

An example of *zavzak* behavior and style might be

this: the son of a pompous man of wealth has come to Emerson School in neat expensive shoes while the rest of us are barefooted.

One of us says to him, "Got your shoes on?"

That's all.

That constitutes the style of being *zavzak*.

The boy with the shoes on his feet, surely innocent enough, may not even suspect that he is being ridiculed, and he may smile shyly, whereupon the barefooted boy says, "Your father's got money, has he?"

If the boy also accepts this remark, he is told, "You live in a fine house?"

And then, "Among your ancestors are kings?"

And on and on until the son of the rich man begins to suspect that he is being slowly trussed and put over a fire for roasting.

But the range of *zavzak* behavior is great, and the game has unlimited variation and subtlety. It is never so amusing as when two experts, such as Zav and myself, belittle one another politely.

It is health-giving, of course, and if nothing else causes laughter, and prevents the need of the hired help of a psychiatrist—something no Saroyan would permit because it would seem a foolish bargain to pay money to somebody just to listen to an hour of comic talk. A Saroyan would say to the psychoanalyst, "Got your notebook?" The game would be on, and the racket would be shot.

The order of the kids of Armenak Saroyan and his bride, Takoohi Saroyan, was Cosette, 1899, named after the girl in *Les Miserables,* of course, read by my father, totally unknown to my mother; Zabel, from Isabelle, most likely, but called by all of us Zabe, 1902; Henry, 1905; and myself, 1908.

Siblings fight it out, and why shouldn't they, everybody is unique, and so impossible: thus, Zabe and I got along reasonably well, and Cosette and Henry seemed to understand one another.

Zabe certainly took my side in disputes. When the going was very bad for me and I was trying to improve matters by petty gambling on Third Street in San Francisco, at Breen's Rummy Parlor, and at the Kentucky Club, and at the Barrel House, and I was sweating out not making any sense at all, or having any luck worth a damn, I walked from 348 Carl Street in San Francisco one night to Zabe's house on Fourteenth Avenue in San Francisco, walked very slowly after a full day of gambling and not winning more than a quarter now and then, only to lose it back, and finally not having a nickel for carfare, to get home for a meal of bulgur pilaf with yogurt.

Zabe had heard from the rest of the family that I was gambling, and she had probably been instructed to use her good influence, to the end that I would find a job and start making sense.

Instead of giving me a bad time, however, Zabe placed a silver dollar in my hand, and then asked me to sit down at the kitchen table with her family and have some coffee and homemade apple pie.

That was a big event in my life at that time, and ever after.

Zevart is a word as well as a girl's name: the word means blithe, sunny, wholesome, and in a sense surely it may be said that it means rosy, for the Armenian word for rose is vart.

Not everybody is lucky enough to have a blithe nature, but whoever has it can also have all of the black rage that the soul knows and still somehow soon enough be equal to quiet acceptance, resignation, the will, and the ability to move along—in light rather than in darkness. Finally, zarmonk: it means wonder.

It is an important Armenian word, both in the church and out of it. One experiences zarmonk by both the unaccountably good and magnificent, and the unbelievably bad and destructive; the same astonishment, the same wonder, the same disbelief applies to all opposites. I like that. If you love the sun, you know zarmonk; if you hate evil, you experience zarmonk.

The sun is wonderful, but, in another way, so is evil.

Someday perhaps I will write about *zahlah,* a very special word, even to an illiterate of Armenian, Turkish, Kurdish, Arabic, Hebrew, and all languages excepting possibly English. It has to do with the pain that comes from being nagged.

Maya Angelou
"THE FIGHT"

The last inch of space was filled, yet people continued to wedge themselves along the walls of the Store. Uncle Willie had turned the radio up to its last notch so that youngsters on the porch wouldn't miss a word. Women sat on kitchen chairs, dining-room chairs, stools and upturned wooden boxes. Small children and babies perched on every lap available and men leaned on the shelves or on each other.

The apprehensive mood was shot through with shafts of gaiety, as a black sky is streaked with lightning.

"I ain't worried 'bout this fight. Joe's gonna whip that cracker like it's open season."

"He gone whip him till that white boy call him Momma."

At last the talking was finished and the string-along songs about razor blades were over and the fight began.

"A quick jab to the head." In the Store the crowd grunted. "A left to the head and a right and another left." One of the listeners cackled like a hen and was quieted.

"They're in a clench, Louis is trying to fight his way out."

Some bitter comedian on the porch said, "That white man don't mind hugging that niggah now, I betcha."

"The referee is moving in to break them up, but Louis finally pushed the contender away and it's an uppercut to the chin. The contender is hanging on, now he's backing away. Louis catches him with a short left to the jaw."

A tide of murmuring assent poured out the doors and into the yard.

"Another left and another left. Louis is saving that mighty right . . ." The mutter in the Store had grown into a baby roar and it was pierced by the clang of a bell and the announcer's "That's the bell for round three, ladies and gentlemen."

As I pushed my way into the Store I wondered if the announcer gave any thought to the fact that he was addressing as "ladies and gentlemen" all the Negroes around the world who sat sweating and praying, glued to their "master's voice."

There were only a few calls for R. C. Colas, Dr. Peppers, and Hire's root beer. The real festivities would begin after the fight. Then even the old Christian ladies who taught their children and tried themselves to practice turning the other cheek would buy soft drinks, and if the Brown Bomber's victory was a particularly bloody one they would order peanut patties and Baby Ruths also.

Bailey and I lay the coins on top of the cash register. Uncle Willie didn't allow us to ring up sales during a fight. It was too noisy and might shake up the atmosphere. When the gong rang for the next round we pushed through the near-sacred quiet to the herd of children outside.

"He's got Louis against the ropes and now it's a left to the body and a right to the ribs. Another right to the body, it looks like it was low . . . Yes, ladies and gentlemen, the referee is signaling but the contender keeps raining the blows on Louis. It's another to the body, and it looks like Louis is going down."

My race groaned. It was our people falling. It was another lynching, yet another Black man hanging on a tree. One more woman ambushed and raped. A Black boy whipped and maimed. It was hounds on the trail of a man running through slimy swamps. It was a white woman slapping her maid for being forgetful.

The men in the Store stood away from the walls and

at attention. Women greedily clutched the babes on their laps while on the porch the shufflings and smiles, flirtings and pinching of a few minutes before were gone. This might be the end of the world. If Joe lost we were back in slavery and beyond help. It would all be true, the accusations that we were lower types of human beings. Only a little higher than the apes. True that we were stupid and ugly and lazy and dirty and, unlucky and worst of all, that God Himself hated us and ordained us to be hewers of wood and drawers of water, forever and ever, world without end.

We didn't breathe. We didn't hope. We waited.

"He's off the ropes, ladies and gentlemen. He's moving towards the center of the ring." There was no time to be relieved. The worst might still happen.

"And now it looks like Joe is mad. He's caught Carnera with a left hook to the head and a right to the head. It's a left jab to the body and another left to the head. There's a left cross and a right to the head. The contender's right eye is bleeding and he can't seem to keep his block up. Louis is penetrating every block. The referee is moving in, but Louis sends a left to the body and it's the uppercut to the chin and the contender is dropping. He's on the canvas, ladies and gentlemen."

Babies slid to the floor as women stood up and men leaned toward the radio.

"Here's the referee. He's counting. One, two, three, four, five, six, seven . . . Is the contender trying to get up again?"

All the men in the store shouted, "NO."

"—eight, nine, ten." There were a few sounds from the audience, but they seemed to be holding themselves in against tremendous pressure.

"The fight is all over, ladies and gentlemen. Let's get the microphone over to the referee . . . Here he is. He's got the Brown Bomber's hand, he's holding it up . . . Here he is . . ."

Then the voice, husky and familiar, came to wash over us—"The winnah, and still heavyweight champeen of the world . . . Joe Louis."

Champion of the world. A Black boy. Some Black mother's son. He was the strongest man in the world. People drank Coca-Colas like ambrosia and ate candy bars like Christmas. Some of the men went behind the Store and poured white lightning in their soft-drink bottles, and a few of the bigger boys followed them. Those who were not chased away came back blowing their breath in front of themselves like proud smokers.

It would take an hour or more before the people would leave the Store and head for home. Those who lived too far had made arrangements to stay in town. It wouldn't do for a Black man and his family to be caught on a lonely country road on a night when Joe Louis had proved that we were the strongest people in the world.

Dick Gregory

"CHRISTMAS EVE"

It's a sad and beautiful feeling to walk home slow on Christmas Eve after you've been out hustling all day, shining shoes in the white taverns and going to the store for the neighbors and buying and stealing presents from the ten-cent store, and now it's dark and still along the street and your feet feel warm and sweaty inside your tennis sneakers even if the wind finds the holes in your mittens. The electric Santa Clauses wink at you from windows. You stop off at your best friend's house and look at his tree and give him a ball-point pen with his name on it. You reach into your shopping bag and give something to everybody there, even the ones you don't know. It doesn't matter that they don't have anything for you because it feels so good to be in a warm happy place where grownups are laughing. There are Daddies around. Your best friend's so happy and excited, standing there trying on all his new clothes. As you walk down the stairs you hear his mother say: "Boo, you forgot to say good-by to Richard, say good-by to Richard, Boo, and wish him a . . ."

Then you're out on the street again and some of the lights have gone out. You take the long way home, and Mister Ben, the grocer, says: "Merry Christmas, Richard," and you give him a present out of the shopping bag, and you smile at a wino and give him a nickel, and you even wave at Grimes, the mean cop. It's a good feeling. You don't want to get home too fast.

And then you hit North Taylor, your street, and something catches your eye and you lift your head up and it's there in your window. Can't believe it. You start running and the only thing in the whole world you're mad about is that you can't run fast enough. For the first time in a long while the cracked orange door says: "Come on in, little man, you're home now," and there's a wreath and lights in the window and a tree in the kitchen near the coal closet and you hug your Momma, her face hot from the stove. Oh, Momma, I'm so glad you did it like this because ours is new, just for us, everybody else's tree been up all week long for other people to see, and, Momma, ours is up just for us. Momma, oh, Momma, you did it again.

My beautiful Momma smiled at me like Miss America, and my brothers and sisters danced around that little kitchen with the round wooden table and the orange-crate chairs.

"Go get the vanilla, Richard," said Momma, "Presley, peel some sweet potatoes. Go get the bread out the oven, Dolores. You get away from that duckling, Garland. Ronald, oh, Ronald you be good now, stand over there with Pauline. Oh, Richard, my little man, did you see the ham Miz White from Eat Shop sent by, and the bag of nuts from Mister Myers and the turkey from Miz King, and wouldn't you know, Mister Ben, he . . ."

"Hey, Momma, I know some rich people don't got this much, a ham, and a turkey, Momma. . . ."

"The Lord, He's always looking out for my boys, Richard, and this ain't all, the white folks'll be by here tomorrow to bring us more things."

Momma was so happy that Christmas, all the food folks brought us and Mister Ben giving us more credit, and Momma even talked the electric man into turning the lights on again.

"Hey, Momma, look here, got a present for Daddy. A cigarette lighter, Momma, there's even a place to scratch a name on it."

"What you scratch on it, Richard, Big Pres or Daddy?"

"Nothing, Momma. Might have to give Daddy's present to old Mister White from the Eat Shop again."

She turned away and when she turned back her eyes were wet. Then she smiled her Miss America smile and grabbed my shoulder. "Richard, my little man, if I show you something, you won't tell nobody, will you?"

"What is it, Momma?"

"I got something for you."

"Oh, Momma, you forgot, everything's under the tree."

"This is something special, just for you, Richard."

"Thanks, Momma, oh, thanks, how'd you know I wanted a wallet, Momma, a real wallet like men have?"

Momma always gave each of us something special like that, something personal that wasn't under the tree, something we weren't supposed to tell the other kids about. It always came out, though. Garland and I'd be fighting and one of us would say, "Momma likes me better than you, look what she gave me," and we both found out the other got a secret present, too.

But I loved that wallet. First thing I did was fill out the address card. If I got hit by a car someone would know who I am. Then I put my dollars in it, just like men do. Ran outside that night and got on a streetcar and pulled out my wallet and handed the conductor a dollar.

"Got anything smaller, boy?"

"Sure, Mister," I said and I pulled out my wallet again and took a dime out of the coin purse and snapped it shut and put the dollar back in the long pocket and closed the wallet and slipped it into my back pocket. Did the same thing on the way back home.

Did we eat that night! It seemed like all the days we went without food, no bread for the baloney and no baloney for the bread, all the times in the summer when there was no sugar for the Kool-Aid and no lemon for the lemonade and no ice at all were wiped away. Man, we're all right.

After dinner I went out the back door and looked at the sky and told God how nobody ever ate like we ate that night, macaroni and cheese and ham and turkey and the old duckling's cooking in the oven for tomorrow. There's even whiskey, Momma said, for people who come by. Thanks, God, Momma's so happy and even the rats and roaches didn't come out tonight and the wind isn't blowing through the cracks.

How'd you know I wanted a wallet, God? I wonder if all the rich people who get mink coats and electric trains got that one little thing nobody knew they wanted. You know, God, I'm kinda glad you were born in a manger. I wonder, God, if they had let Mary in the first place she stopped at, would you have remembered tonight? Oh, God, I'm scared. I wish I could die right now with the feeling I have because I know Momma's going to make me mad and I'm going to make her mad, and me and Presley's gonna fight. . . .

"Richard, you get in here and put your coat on. Get in here or I'll whip you."

See what I mean, God, there she goes already and I'm not even cold, I'm all wrapped up in You.

"What's wrong, Richard? Why you look so strange?"

"You wouldn't understand, Momma."

"I would, Richard, you tell me."

"Well, I came out to pray, Momma, way out here so they wouldn't hear me and laugh at me and call me a sissy. God's a good God, ain't He, Momma?"

"Yes, Richard."

"Momma, if I tell you something, would you laugh at me, would you say I'm crazy, would you say I was lying? Momma?"

"What is it, Richard?"

"I heard Him talk to me, Momma."

She put her arm around my shoulders and pulled me against her. "He talks to people, Richard, some people that are real special and good like you. Do me a favor, Richard?"

"Sure, Momma."

"Next time you talk to Him, ask Him to send Daddy home."

Anonymous

DARKEN YOUR GRAYING HAIR, AND HIDE YOUR FRIGHT

I am male, white, 46. I have undergraduate and graduate degrees from two reasonably well-known Eastern institutions. My first job lasted for four years, my second for ten, my third for seven. I have a wife, three daughters, a mortgaged home and a 1972 "Beetle" for which I paid cash.

Whereas I once earned over $400 a week, New York State now provides me with $95 a week in unemployment benefits.

I am smoking almost two packs a day. I try not to drink before 5 o'clock.

The other day I encountered the man who fired me. He is an affable, bright man, and on the eve of retirement. Many months ago he told me I had outlived my usefulness, and he wished me well. The other day he said he knew what I have been going through. When I said he didn't, he looked just a little startled. He does not, never did, like to be contradicted. But I knew he had never been without work. I told him that physically, fiscally and spiritually I and all members of my family had been wiped out. Then he asked why I was having such trouble finding a new job.

The easiest, possibly even the only truthful answer would have been this: "No one wants me." That is the way I feel, of course. (Paranoia. Depression. I used to think these were modern conveniences that only others could afford.) But I told him what I know: My age, sex, and salary needs work against me. So, of course, does the shortage of jobs. Then he turned to talk with another passer-by; he meant well, though.

I have discovered there is an entire literature on the art of job-hunting. One book—I think it was the same one that said if you are over 35 and out of work, you're in great trouble—offered a few how-to's on rejuvenation:

If you have too much gray hair, darken it. If you look younger than you are, revise your birth date in your résumé. Be relaxed during interviews, avoid personnel managers (go right to the top!).

I have been told I look younger than 46, but if I change the year of my birth from 1931 to, say, 1934, then I have to change graduate dates, military-service dates, previous-employment dates. Barring a gin-induced stupor, how can anyone be relaxed during an interview. (And why that noun? Why not "interrogation"?) My hair is too gray now. A dye, I think, would be conspicuous.

Unemployment is a leveler. The lines and the people in them—I report to the New York State Employment Service's local office every Thursday between 3 and 3:30 P.M.—remind me of my basic training at Fort Dix. Then and now there was, and is, little in common except shared misfortune. Just why the lines move so slowly, I don't know. It should be a fairly mechanical, effortless process.

I went to Washington for an interview in early April. It was raining, and Newark, Philadelphia, Wilmington and Baltimore looked uglier than ever. The interview lasted only 15 minutes because the salary was $10,000 less than what I had been making. In Washington, that salary would translate into about $95 a week.

The snack car on the Metroliner on the way back to New York was crowded with men in double-knit suits, carefully cut hair. Some held computer sheets. There was talk about budgets and personnel. I hated them all. They had jobs.

I used to ridicule lesser beings who drank martinis

with their dinners. No longer. In fact, I usually continue after dinner. Vodka martinis. I know what I'm inviting (or may already have), but they do help me sleep. I should say get to sleep. Because it seldom lasts. I have nightmares, and I scream and I awaken others. Usually, I seem to be in pursuit of an object of one kind or another; just as I'm within reach it moves beyond my touch. Then I scream.

Among our neighbors is a young psychiatrist. My wife has suggested that I talk to him, friend-to-friend (we *are* friends) about my problems, paranoia, depression, nightmares. Perhaps he would know of a pill that would dilute my anxieties, my problems. But I know the bare root of all of them, and unless he can provide me with a job, why bother with a pill? So I drink in lieu of a pill.

One interviewer eventually turned me down because, he said, I lack eyeball contact. When I called him to say I didn't understand, he told me that because of my courage in asking such a question, he would reopen "the discussions." We had dinner at the Yale Club, in New York (he had one beer, I had nothing), and he said we had misread each other's "signals." We would start afresh, and he would be back in touch with me. A month later, he wrote to tell me that he had decided not to fill the position after all. (I heard shortly afterward that he had lost *his* job.)

The help-wanted ads are the first things I look at in Sunday's paper. But they're strange. Box numbers and employment agencies. My résumés go out on Monday, but there's seldom an acknowledgment.

The corporate display ads are a little different. Most of the time an answer is forthcoming. The final sentence, often enough, is, "I wish you well in your future endeavors." Earlier in the form letter are references to the numbers of applicants, all good, but a few better suited for "our needs" than others. But the résumés of the rejects, of course, will remain in "our active files."

A vice president of an organization asked me to meet him for breakfast at a Park Avenue hotel. Two days later, I received a note from him saying he was impressed by my credentials, liked my answers to his questions and would probably invite me to his base for additional interviews. I was skeptical—he wasn't the first vice president with whom I had had breakfast in New York—but two days later his assistant ushered me from one vice president to another, and finally to the president.

A week later, I was told that everything had gone well and that I could expect a decision within two weeks. I received the decision—from the assistant—three months later. It was formal, brief and negative. The job went to a young woman. The organization is the defendant in a number of affirmative-action cases in the courts.

A friend of mine, a president, once told me that whenever he advertises a vacancy, it's an easy matter to skim off the four or five most outstanding candidates. After their interviews, he compares not their experience, but their statistics—their total compensation packages, retirement and medical benefits in particular. If you're not young, he said, it sure helps to be single. I, as he knows, am neither.

I'm never sure just how the children are taking it. I think they see it all in very different ways, for they are not at all alike. One is a sphinx, one seems almost (though not intentionally) removed, and one sees it all. But they all know my countenance and can interpret it. They know I spend most of the week in my chair. Only one of them has said that I no longer talk, and I frown when others are talking.

There are times when I wonder not whether I will ever have a job again, but whether if I do, I will be able to function. For almost a year, I have not done what I was trained to do. I have, as they say, vegetated.

The invitations for interviews never come by mail, always by telephone. So I stay home and wait for the phone to ring. It's not that I have nothing else to do, but it is a matter of how I spend that waiting time. After the newspaper there is coffee, and junk mail, and boredom. I eat too much for lunch because there's nothing else to do. Lately a friend has supplied me with Irish novels and short stories, all new and none published in this country. I am Irish and know something of earlier Irish literature, but my friend's books offer little release, less escape.

At dusk, in those unearthly hours between sleep and wakefulness, I have visions. I see pictures of small-bore pistols. Lethal, but, I hope, quick and comparatively painless. Not heroic, certainly, but not cowardly either. But, then, there's my wife and our daughters. Because I love—and I do—all four, I have to ask whether my death is preferable to my (mere) despair. I do not know. Would they be better off without me? I do not know. When I first lost my job, the real pain derived from the (eventual) realization that I had failed not only myself but four others.

I recently read about a White House deputy press secretary, I think he was not quite 30, whose new salary is $39,500. No, maybe it was $49,500. I had never heard of him before, but I hate the son of a b - - - -.

I knew that life isn't fair long before J.F.K. went on television to tell us as much. But fair isn't the right word. It's not fairness that's lacking; it's balance. Proportion maybe.

When the phone does ring, it's usually someone asking for one of our daughters to babysit. "We have to go out tonight, and I was just wondering if . . ."

We never go out anymore. It's not just the money— our hearts aren't in it. We are obsessed and can talk only to each other. But only about our obsession.

I weep when I write my mother, my brother, my sister. I tell them that we're all well, that the family fabric is intact, that I have a half-dozen irons in the fire. But they've heard all that too many times now, so I seldom write.

I have nothing to say.

Paul Jacobs
TWO CITY SCHOOLS

She has been an elementary school principal since 1939. Her school, in the heart of the Negro ghetto, has fifteen hundred kids in it, almost all of them Negro, and fifty teachers, nearly 60 percent of whom are Negro. She describes her pupils: "They don't come with a rich background. I knew how to read when I was in the first grade and there was a time sense in my home that isn't here. They don't have as many clocks, you know, as we do. I probably have a clock in every room of the house, but if they've got one clock, they're lucky. They don't care about time—time doesn't mean anything to them." Then she adds, her voice becoming patronizing, "So we come in carelessly, we have to learn about that, we have to learn to be punctual, we have to learn to finish a thing we start, and all of those other things that are so important."

She walks through the hallways of her very new and modern school. She spots a piece of paper on the corridor floor and calls out, "You there, little boy, pick up that paper from the floor!" As the child reaches down she says with pursed lips, in his hearing, "That's one of our problems. We just drop whatever is in our hand whenever we want to because we don't learn about neatness at home. So we must learn it here."

On the second floor she looks out over a wall toward the schoolyard where some of the children are eating lunch and others are playing; three children are sitting on the edge of a concrete box in which a tree is planted. "Those boys don't belong there," she says angrily, trying to catch the eye of a teenage teacher's aide supervising the children eating at the tables in the yard. But he does not see her and she turns away, repeating "Those children shouldn't be sitting there," just as a whistle sounds and the playing children are shepherded into lines, ready to be marched back to their classes.

She walks through the corridors again, stopping occasionally to knock at one of the locked classroom doors. Inside the classrooms the teachers are nervous at her entrance, the pupils unaware of who she is or hostile. In one room the children are seated around a Negro teacher, frozen—hands clasped in front of them, backs stiff—as he makes them repeat, over and over, the lesson he is trying to teach them.

"I think he's probably just a little too strict with the children," she says after leaving the classroom, "but you see, he'd worked up to being a teacher from a custodian's job. But I do think he's probably too strict.

"We have school trips and we have a very lovely library, an A-one library," she explains in her office. "We teach the children to take books from here, out from the library; in the summer, they take them home and we have an enriched program. For example, we have a garden with animals to bring up the language and environment; all the time it's enrichment, because, you see, they have to have a rich environment to make up for what they have missed.

"Last year, we had two groups who went to the art museum on scholarships, studied art with the other children and were praised by the artists out there, who said, 'Where did you find such fine children?' Oh, that did so much for them. Now we have a sculpturing class going out, so we give them all this environment to get out where they see things wherever possible.

"And now when we take some students, if they have a good IQ to start with and have had some help and have gone through our schools, they'll measure up all right. They need a lot of extra help. By that, they need to know they can go into a library and be accepted, they have to have this barrier down; so we're working continuously at that, and our teachers are all the time, so they will know: you are important, finish your job, this is the thing to do. So I think if they have the ability at all, they'll measure up all right:"

Thirty miles away another principal walks through a corridor. This elementary school in the Mexican-American barrio is also new; it has 1350 pupils, mostly Mexican-Americans. Its teaching staff has four Mexican-Americans, including one who had been a student of the principal when he was a teacher in another school in the barrio, forty-one whites, and twelve Negroes. As the principal steps out into the schoolyard, he spots a piece of paper on the floor. He reaches down to get it, but before he has even straightened up a little boy darts up to him, grabs the scrap from his hand, and walks off with a grin as the principal calls out, "Thank you, Tiger, you're a real sport."

In this schoolyard, too, the children are playing and eating. As the principal strolls around, the children run up to him, shouting his name, grabbing at him; when the whistle blows to send them back into the classes, they simply walk back inside by themselves. And when he walks into the unlocked classrooms, the kids pay very little attention to him, except to acknowledge his presence—it is obvious that he is a familiar figure, one of whom they have no fear. The teachers also seem happy to see him and joke with him when he teases them about how they look. It is clear, too, both from their attitude toward him and the willingness with which they work from early morning to late afternoon, that they are committed to him as much as to teaching.

When they come to his school for a job interview, he asks them, "Can you talk 'nigger'?" In their shocked silence he continues with, "We get two kinds of kids in this school, those that speak Spanish and those that talk 'nigger,' and if you want to teach here, you'll have to learn one of these languages. And you'll have to learn not to be shocked by the common language of the streets. If you're not acquainted with those words, or if you're going to be shocked by them, you'd better start saying them over and over again, because we've got some awfully smart kids here in social adjustment class and they've shocked every little old lady teacher, male and female, they've run into. The teachers send them in to me and I say to those kids, 'What did you say to the teacher?' So the kid looks at me and he says, 'Well, I told her, "Go fuck yourself, you bitch," ' and he's waiting for me to drop dead. So I say, 'Well, what else did you say?' And you see then the kid begins to back off because he sees he can't shake this cat. Then after a while they quit talking that way because you begin to ask them, 'Well, do you really know what you said?'

"If he doesn't have the language, what you've got to do is get him to talk, bring up something ten thousand times and talk with him about it; and you don't have to make a big issue out of it by saying to the kid, 'Compare, listen to how I say it.' The kid's going to listen and get it by osmosis. He doesn't have the experience, and if you tell him that he's wrong, he'll be mute.

"In this school, the basic philosophy is 'Give these kids all they can take. But if they can't take it, ask yourself why they aren't getting it. Don't tell the kid he's stupid. Find out why you're not getting to him.'

"Now, if you still want to teach here, let's try it out."

These two principals represent the polar points of the educational system in the cities; neither is typical, although the one has been and the other ought to be, and between them are more than a thousand other principals and vice-principals in the six hundred schools that make up the Los Angeles School District. Most of these are probably more like the principal of another elementary school in the Negro area who stood uneasily watching a group of children in a prekindergarten class take water out of a big pot with measuring cups and pour the water into another pot—inevitably, some of the water slopped onto the floor. The teacher was explaining that for the first time these children were learning something about measuring volume, but her words were lost on the principal who kept watching the kids. Finally, no longer able to stand the sight of water spilling on the classroom floor, she took the pot and put it into the classroom sink, above the heads of the little children. They stood there then, eyes wide open, a little scared of the strange lady who took away their game because the floor had been getting wet. And if they didn't learn much more about the concept of measurement, they had learned how they were expected to behave. The teacher too had learned a lesson: she knew how she was expected to behave in that principal's school.

The principal's influence over a school's character is enormous, for the principal represents almost total authority over the entire school—pupils, teachers, clerks, and custodial personnel alike. The principal can substantively affect the teacher's future promotions, especially if the teachers want to become principals themselves. The principals can make the teachers' daily work life either a joy or a hell. A weak principal can weaken an entire school; a strong one can dominate it completely: the principal sets the style, establishes the mood, and creates a tone for the school.

Even more, the principals exercise real power over the school system through their own organization, one which few people want to antagonize. And naturally enough through their organization the principals protect what they see as their own interests.

Unfortunately, the environment of most cities' school systems was far more hospitable in the past to the kind of principal who believes that "they" are children who "don't care about time" than it was to the one who is convinced that the basic philosophy ought to be to "give the kids all they can take." And for the same reason the American school systems have fewer teachers of the kind who say of their principal, like the one in the Mexican-American school, "He's a maverick principal, and that's why I enjoy working for him," and more who believe incorrectly in the importance of "uniformity" in teaching methods—"The people who have written the books have worked on these techniques for years and years, and they have come up with most of the methods. And the teachers will find, after trying these methods, that one of them is going to work best for her."

These methods may have worked best for the teachers but they certainly haven't for the pupils; the American school system has failed its students, failed miserably. As the first agency of government with which children come into contact, it has been a negative rather than positive force in helping build the community. And while that charge can be leveled in varying degrees against the ways in which the school system has treated all its constituents, it has failed even more in its responsibilities toward the minority students. These are the truly tragic victims of a school system which accurately reflects what one school administrator describes as society's "twisted priorities."

S. I. Hayakawa

RED-EYE AND THE WOMAN PROBLEM: A SEMANTIC PARABLE

Once, long ago, tens of thousands of years before history began, people were worried, as they have often been since, about the chaotic condition of their lives. For in those days men took by force the women they desired. There was no way of stopping them.

If you wanted a woman but found that she was already the partner of another man, all you needed to do was to kill him and drag her home. Naturally, someone else might slug you a little later to get her away from you, but that was the chance you took if you wanted a woman at all.

Consequently, there wasn't much of what you could call family life. The men were too busy suspiciously watching each other. And time that might have been spent fishing or hunting or otherwise raising the general standard of living was wasted in constant and anxious measures to defend one's woman.

Many people saw that this was no way for human beings to live. As they said among themselves: "Truly we are strange creatures. In some ways we are highly civilized. We no longer eat raw flesh, as did our savage ancestors. Our technical men have perfected stone arrowheads and powerful bows so that we can slay the fastest deer that runs. Our medicine men can foretell the running of the fish in the streams, and our sorcerers drive away illnesses. At the Institute for Advanced Studies at Notecnirp, a group of bright young men are said to be working out a dance that will make the rain fall. Little by little, we are mastering the secrets of nature, so that we are able to live like civilized men and not like beasts.

"Yet," they continued, "we have not mastered ourselves. There are those among us who continue to snatch women away from each other by force, so that every man of necessity lives in fear of his fellows. People agree, of course, that all this killing ought to be stopped. But no one is stopping it. The most fundamental of human problems, that of securing a mate and bringing up one's children under some kind of decent, orderly system, remains unsolved. Unless we can find some way of placing the man-woman relationship on a decent and human basis, our pretensions to civilization are hollow."

For many generations the thoughtful men of the tribe pondered this problem. How could men and women, living peacefully together with their children, be protected from the lusts of the few, who went around killing other men in order to possess their women?

Slowly, and only after centuries of groping discussion, they evolved an answer. They proposed that men and women who have decided to live together permanently be bound by a "contract," by which they meant the uttering, before the priests of the tribe, of solemn promises binding on their future behavior. This contract was to be known as marriage. The man in the marriage was to be known as a husband, the woman as a wife.

They further proposed that this contract be observed and honored by all the people of the tribe. In other words, if a given woman, Slendershanks, was known to be the wife of a given man, Beetlebrow, everyone in the tribe was to agree not to molest their domestic arrangements. Furthermore, they proposed that if anyone failed to respect this contract and killed another man to possess that man's wife, he was to be punished by the collective force of tribal authority.

In order to put these proposals into effect, a great conference was called, and delegates arrived from all branches of the tribe. Some came with glad hearts, filled with the hope that humanity was about to enter a new era. Some came with faint hearts, not expecting much to come out of the conference, but feeling that it was at least worth a try. Some came simply because they had been elected delegates and were getting their expenses paid; they were willing to go along with whoever proved to be in the majority.

All the time the conference was going on, however, a big, backward savage called Red-Eye the Atavism, who was so loud-mouthed that he always had a following in spite of his unprepossessing personality, kept shouting scornful remarks from the sidelines. He called the delegates "visionaries," "eggheads," "impractical theorists," "starry-eyed dreamers," "crackpots," and "pantywaists." He gleefully pointed out that many of the delegates had themselves been, at an earlier date, women-snatchers. (This, unfortunately, was true.)

He shouted to Hairy Hands, who was one of the delegates, "You don't think Brawny Legs is going to leave your woman alone just because he makes an agreement, do you?" And he shouted to Brawny Legs, "You don't think Hairy Hands is going to leave your woman alone just because he makes an agreement, do you?" And he poured derision on all the delegates, referring to their discussion as "striped-pants kind of talk, like who ever heard of 'husband,' and 'wife,' and 'marriage' and all that double-dome Choctaw!"

Then Red-Eye the Atavism turned to his following, the crowd of timid and tiny-minded people who always found their self-assurance in the loudness of his voice, and he yelled, "Look at those fool delegates, will you? They think they can change human nature!"

Thereupon the crowd rolled over with laughter and repeated after him, "Haw, haw! They think they can change human nature!"

That broke up the conference. It was another two thousand years, therefore, before marriage was finally instituted in that tribe—two thousand years during which innumerable men were killed defending their women, two thousand years during which men who had no designs on their neighbors' women killed each other as a precaution against being killed themselves, two thousand years during which the arts of peace languished, two thousand years during which people despaired as they dreamed of a distant future time when a man might live with the woman of his choice without arming himself to the teeth and watching over her day and night.

What this illustrates is, of course, that all basic agreements by means of which human beings learn to live together amicably and harmoniously have grown out of prolonged thought, discussion, argumentation, and persuasion. Human institutions such as marriage, law, and government do not just happen somehow. They are social inventions, devised and developed in response to an urgently felt need for order in our lives.

Today many such institutions exist to make life orderly and livable. But as the world changes, new problems of social adjustment arise, and there seems constantly to be much more to do. Blacks and whites, Protestants and Catholics, Arabs and Israelis, French-speaking and Flemish-speaking Belgians, East and West Pakistanis, capitalists and communists, must somehow or other learn to live together.

As for instituting the social agreements to prevent international violence in a world of hydrogen bombs and guided missiles, we don't have two thousand years to find the solution. Indeed, we don't have two hundred years. Nor even twenty. Perhaps not even two.

And *that's* our problem.

Ingrid Bengis

LOVE, SEX, AND WOMEN

If Victorian society decreed that enjoying sex for women was taboo, and enlightened society decreed that women were entitled to as much pleasure in sex as men were, then "liberated" society decreed that sex and even exclusive love were oppressive to women. The seventies' interpretation of "women's place" made the emancipation I had struggled (and never succeeded) to achieve a symbol of sexism. The loves I'd committed myself to were part of a male-dominated, Hollywood plot. Sex between men and women was pure exploitation. I was a creation of Madison Avenue.

Suddenly I want to scream ... for God's sake just *stop*. Let me off this idiot merry-go-round. My psyche is not an ideological playground. My inner feelings, at their most genuine, are not ruled by social decree. You can have a thousand lovers if you want or have none. You can be a lesbian, a virgin, a career woman, a mother, or all four. But don't tell me who I am, or who it's best for me to be. You are right that A is true. But B and C and D are also true. Sandwiched in between three different mind sets, three different standards of "absolute right," I sometimes feel like a white rat being subjected to behavioral research with the data constantly being reevaluated. I recognize parts of myself when you speak of "women," but other parts don't fit the formula. I recognize parts of the males I know when you speak of men, but other parts defy categorization. I can't make the transitions required to fit the current theories of the age, especially since the ages are so telescoped that one barely has time to absorb one set of perspectives before another is all the rage. I don't know who women are. I scarcely even know who I am.

The rational mind is capable of making astounding leaps. I can espouse communism one evening and radical conservatism the next. I can theorize about the future of the family from dusk until dawn. I can create and destroy whole new systems of thought, systems of being, systems of living, all within the course of a dinner conversation. Similarly, I can create and re-create "new women" to suit the perspectives of the period. What I cannot do, however, is *become* the person each decade newly assumes I ought to be. I cannot be the completely feminine woman of the fifties, the emancipated, sexually free woman of the sixties, and the militant, antisexist woman of the seventies. I cannot ignore the fact that my own life has unfolded slowly, that it has been a part of all of those trends and none of them. I cannot ignore the fact that essentially the same me has persisted throughout the upheavals, throughout the analyses of historical circumstances and evaluations of what a woman's life ought to be.

The woman I've continued to be is a contradictory and uncertain human being. Believing in love, I am also terrified of it. Believing in stability, I live a thoroughly unstable life. Believing in marriage, I have never risked it. I am occasionally attracted to men exclusively on the basis of their sexuality, but am appalled when they are attracted to me on the basis of mine. I care about affection and doubt my capacities for it. I fantasize about conducting five love affairs simultaneously while living in sexless seclusion for long periods of time. I say friendship is superior to passion even as my throat is locking with the effort to suppress the effects of my latest passion. I long for liberation and don't know what it is. I hate when I would prefer to love and love when I would prefer to hate. The woman I am remembers a time in our not-so-remote history when American women (myself included) were objecting to the fact that American

men were not as virile or gallant as their European counterparts; remembers when no self-respecting Jewish girl
wanted to have anything to do with "nice Jewish boys." The
woman I am knows that when I meet a man who is kind but
sexless, my interest ebbs; that when I meet a man who is
less than kind but sexually attractive, there is a struggle;
that when I meet a man who is kind *and* sexually attractive,
I am afraid of falling in love. My needs, fears, and desires
remain as part of my daily life. The model of a liberated
woman often fades into obscurity. And I am forced instead
to confront a person . . . merely a person.

GLOSSARY

Abstract and concrete are ways of describing important qualities of language. Abstract words are not associated with real, material objects that are related directly to the five senses. Such words as "love," "wisdom," "patriotism," and "power" are abstract because they refer to ideas rather than to things. Concrete language, on the other hand, names things that can be perceived by the five senses. Words like "table," "smoke," "lemon," and "halfback" are concrete. Generally you should not be too abstract in writing. It is best to employ concrete words naming things that can be seen, touched, smelled, heard, or tasted in order to support your more abstract ideas.

Allusion is a reference to some literary, biographical, or historical event. It is a "figure of speech" (a fresh, useful comparison) used to illuminate an idea. For instance, if you want to state that a certain national ruler is insane, you might refer to him as a "Nero"—an allusion to the Emperor who burned Rome.

Alternating method in comparison and contrast involves a point-by-point treatment of the two subjects that you have selected to discuss. Assume that you have chosen five points to examine in a comparison of the Volkswagen "Rabbit" (subject A) and the Plymouth "Horizon" (subject B): cost, comfort, gas mileage, road handling, and frequency of repair. In applying the alternating method, you would begin by discussing cost in relation to A + B; then comfort in relation to A + B, and so on. The alternating method permits you to isolate points for a balanced discussion.

Ambiguity means uncertainty. A writer is ambiguous when using a word, phrase, or sentence that is not clear. Ambiguity usually results in misunderstanding, and should be avoided in essay writing. Always strive for clarity in your compositions.

Analogy is a form of figurative comparison that uses a clear illustration to explain a difficult idea or function. It is unlike a formal comparison in that its subjects of comparison are from different categories or areas. For example, an analogy likening "division of labor" to the activity of bees in a hive makes the first concept more concrete by showing it to the reader through the figurative comparison with the bees.

Antonym is a word that is opposite in meaning to that of another word: "hot" is an antonym of "cold"; "fat" is an antonym of "thin"; "large" is an antonym of "small."

Argumentation is a form of writing in which you offer reasons in favor of or against something. (See Chapter 9, pp. 293–294).

Block method in comparison and contrast involves the presentation of all information about your first subject (A), followed by all information about the second subject (B). Thus, using the objects of comparison explained in the discussion of the "alternating method" (see entry, p. 379), you would for the block method first present all five points about the Volkswagen. Then you would present all five points about the Plymouth. When using the block method, remember to present the same points for each subject, and to provide an effective transition in moving from subject A to subject B.

Causal analysis is a form of writing that examines causes and effects of events or conditions as they relate to a specific subject (See Chapter 8, pp. 249–250).

Characterization is the description of people. As a particular type of description in an essay, characterization attempts to capture as vividly as possible the features, qualities, traits, speech, and actions of individuals.

Chronological order is the arrangement of events in the order that they happened. You might use chronological order to trace the history of the Vietnam War, to explain a scientific process, or to present the biography of a close relative or friend. When you order an essay by chronology, you are moving from one step to the next in time.

Classification is a pattern of writing where the author divides a subject into categories and then groups elements in each of those categories according to their relationships to each other (See Chapter 6, pp. 175–176).

Clichés are expressions that were once fresh and vivid, but have become tired and worn from overuse. "I'm so hungry that

I could eat a horse" is a typical cliché. People use clichés in conversation, but writers should generally avoid them.

Closings or "conclusions" are endings for your essay. Without a closing, your essay is incomplete, leaving the reader with the feeling that something important has been left out. There are numerous closing possibilities available to writers: summarizing main points in the essay; restating the main idea; using an effective quotation to bring the essay to an end; offering the reader the climax to a series of events; returning to the conclusion and echoing it; offering a solution to a problem; emphasizing the topic's significance; or setting a new frame of reference by generalizing from the main thesis. Whatever type of closing you use, make certain that it ends the essay in a firm and emphatic way.

Coherence is a quality in effective writing that results from the careful ordering of each sentence in a paragraph, and each paragraph in the essay. If an essay is coherent, each part will grow naturally and logically from those parts that come before it. Coherence depends on the writer's ability to organize materials in a logical way, and to order segments so that the reader is carried along easily from start to finish. The main devices used in achieving coherence are *transitions,* which help to connect one thought with another.

Colloquial language is language used in conversation and in certain types of informal writing, but rarely in essays, business writing, or research papers. There is nothing wrong with colloquialisms like "cool," "I'm all right, Jack," or "pal" when used in conversational settings. However, they are often unacceptable in essay writing—except when used sparingly for special effects.

Comparison/contrast is a pattern of essay writing treating similarities and differences between two subjects. (See Chapter 4, pp. 107–108)

Composition is a term used for an essay or for any piece of writing that reveals a careful plan.

Concrete (See Abstract/Concrete)

Connotation/denotation are terms specifying the way a word has meaning. Connotation refers to the "shades of meaning" that a word might have because of various emotional associations it calls up for writers and readers alike. Words like "American," "physician," "mother," "pig," and "San Francisco" have strong connotative overtones to them. With denotation, however, we are concerned not with the suggestive meaning of a word but with its exact, literal meaning. Denotation refers to the "dictionary definition" of a word—its exact meaning. Writers must understand the connotative and denotative value of words, and must control the shades of meaning that many words possess.

Context clues are hints provided about the meaning of a word by another word or words, or by the sentence or sentences coming before or after it. Thus in the sentence, "Mr. Rome, a true *raconteur,* told a story that thrilled the guests," we should be able to guess at the meaning of the italicized word by the context clues coming both before and after it. (A "raconteur" is a person who tells good stories.)

Definition is a method of explaining a word so that the reader knows what you mean by it. (See Chapter 5, pp. 139–140.)

Derivation is how a word originated and where it came from. Knowing the origin of a word can make you more aware of its meaning, and more able to use it effectively in writing. Your dictionary normally lists abbreviations (for example, O.E. for Old English, G. for Greek) for word origins and sometimes explains fully how they came about.

Description is a type of writing that uses details of sight, color, sound, smell, and touch to create a word picture and to explain or illustrate an idea (See Chapter 1, pp. 1–2).

Dialogue is the exact duplication in writing of something people say to each other. Dialogue is the reproduction of speech or conversation; it can add concreteness and vividness to an essay, and can also help to reveal character. When using dialogue, writers must be careful to use correct punctuation. Moreover, to use dialogue effectively in essay writing, you must develop an ear for the way other people talk, and an ability to create it accurately.

Division is that aspect of classification (see Chapter 6, pp. 175–176) where the writer divides some large subject into categories. For example, you might divide "fish" into salt water and fresh water fish; or "sports" into team and individual sports. Division helps writers to split large and potentially complicated subjects into parts for orderly presentation and discussion.

Effect is a term used in causal analysis (see Chapter 8, pp. 249–250) to describe the outcome or expected result of a chain of happenings. When dealing with the analysis of effects, writers should determine whether they want to deal with immediate or final effects, or both. Thus, a writer analyzing the effects of an accidental nuclear explosion that happened in 1956 might choose to analyze effects immediately after the blast, as well as effects that still linger.

Emphasis suggests the placement of the most important ideas in key positions in the essay. Writers can emphasize ideas simply by placing important ones at the beginning or at the end of the paragraph or essay. But several other techniques help writers to emphasize important ideas: (1) key words and ideas can be stressed by repetition; (2) ideas can be presented in climactic order, by building from lesser ideas at the beginning to the main idea at the end; (3) figurative language (for instance, a vivid simile) can call attention to a main idea; (4) the relative proportion of detail offered to support an idea can emphasize its importance; (5) comparison and contrast of an idea with other ideas can emphasize its importance; and (6) mechanical devices like underlining, capitalizing, or using exclamation points (all of which should be used sparingly) can stress significance.

Essay is the name given to a short prose work on a limited topic. Essays take many forms, ranging from a familiar narrative account of an event in your life, to explanatory, argumentative, or critical investigations of a subject. Normally, in one way or the other, an essay will convey the writer's personal ideas about the subject.

Euphemism is the use of a word or phrase simply because it seems less distasteful or less offensive than another word. For instance, "mortician" is a euphemism for "undertaker"; "sanitation worker" for "garbage collector."

Fable is a narrative with a moral (see Chapter 4, p. 112). The story from which the writer draws the moral can be either true or imaginary. When writing a fable, it is important that a writer clearly presents the moral to be derived from the narrative, as Rachel Carson does in "A Fable for Tomorrow."

Figurative language, as opposed to *literal,* is a special approach to writing that departs from what is typically a concrete, straightforward style. It involves a vivid, imaginative comparison that goes beyond plain or ordinary statements. For instance, instead of saying that "Joan is wonderful," you could write that "Joan is like a summer's rose" (a *simile*); "Joan's hair is wheat, pale and soft and yellow" (a *metaphor*); "Joan is my Helen of Troy" (an *allusion*); or a number of other comparative approaches. Note that Joan is not a rose, her hair is not wheat, nor is she some other person named Helen. Figurative language is not logical; instead, it requires an ability on the part of the writer to create an imaginative comparison in order to make an idea more striking.

Flashback is a narrative technique in which the writer begins at some point in the action and then moves into the past in order to provide necessary background information. Flashback adds variety to the narrative method, enabling writers to approach a story not only in terms of straight chronology, but in terms of a back-and-forth movement. However, it is at best a very difficult technique and should be used with great care.

General/specific words are necessary in writing, although it is wise to keep your vocabulary as specific as possible. General words refer to broad categories and groups, while specific words capture with more force and clarity the nature of a term. The distinction between general and specific language is always a matter of degree. "A woman walked down the street" is more general than "Mrs. Walker walked down Fifth Avenue," while "Mrs. Webster, elegantly dressed in a muslin suit, strolled down Fifth Avenue" is more specific than the first two examples. Our ability to use specific language depends on the extent of our vocabulary. The more words we know, the more specific we can be in choosing words.

Illustration is the use of several examples to support our idea (see Chapter 3, pp. 67–68).

Imagery is clear, vivid description that appeals to our sense of sight, smell, touch, sound, or taste. Much imagery exists for its own sake, adding descriptive flavor to an essay, as when Scott Momaday in "The Way to Raining Mountain" writes: "The last time I saw her she prayed standing by the side of her bed at night, naked to the waist, the light of the kerosene lamp moving upon her dark skin." However, imagery can also add meaning to an essay. For example, in Kazin's essay, the pattern of imagery connected with the kitchen alerts the reader to the importance of that room in the author's life. Again, when Orwell writes at the start of "A Hanging," "It was in Burma, a sodden morning of the rains. A sickly light, like yellow tinfoil, was slanting over the high walls into the jail yard," we see that the author uses imagery to prepare us for the sombre and terrifying event to follow. Writers can use imagery to contribute to any type of wording, or they can rely on it to structure an entire essay. It is always difficult to invent fresh, vivid description, but it is an effort that writers should make if they wish to improve the quality of their prose.

Introductions are the beginning or openings of essays. Introductions should perform a number of functions. They should alert the reader to the subject, set the limits of the essay, and indicate what the thesis (or main idea) will be. Moreover, they should arouse the reader's interest in the subject, so that the reader will want to continue reading into the essay. There are several devices available to writers that will aid in the development of sound intro ductions.

1. Simply state the subject and establish the thesis. See the Jade Snow Wong essay (p. 3), and "Types of Propaganda" p. 203.

2. Open with a clear, vivid description of a setting that will become important as your essay advances. Save your thesis for a later stage, but indicate what your subject is. See the essay by Patricia Cayo Sexton (p. 9).

3. Ask a question or a series of questions, which you might answer in the introduction or in another part of the essay. See the Narek essay (p. 260) and the John Lame Deer essay (p. 123).

4. Refer to an historic event that serves to introduce your subject or to define it in a special way. See the Maunsell essay (p. 43).

5. Tell an anecdote (a short, self-contained story of an entertaining nature) that serves to illuminate your subject. See the Story essay (p. 148).

6. Use comparison or contrast to frame your subject and to present the thesis. See the Fulbright essay (p. 117).

7. Use several examples to reinforce your statement of the subject. See the Friedan essay (p. 98).

8. Begin by stating your personal attitude toward a controversial issue. See the Goldwater essay (p. 302).

These are only some of the devices that appear in the introductions to essays in this text. Writers can also ask questions, give definitions, or provide personal accounts—there are many techniques that can be used to develop introductions. The important thing to remember is that you *need* an introduction to an essay. It can be a single sentence or a much longer paragraph, but it must accomplish its purpose—to introduce readers to the subject, and to engage them so that they want to explore the essay further.

Irony is the use of language to suggest the opposite of what is stated. Writers use irony to reveal unpleasant or troublesome realities that exist in life, or to poke fun at human weaknesses and foolish attitudes. For instance, in "A Hanging," the men who are in charge of the execution engage in laughter and lighthearted conversation after the event. There is irony in the situation and in their speech because we sense that they are actually very tense—almost unnerved—by the hanging; their laughter is the opposite of what their true emotional state actually is. Many situations and conditions lend themselves to ironic treatment.

Jargon is the use of special words associated with a specific area of knowledge or a specific profession. It is similar to "shop talk" that members of a certain trade might know, but not necessarily people outside it. For example, in Bettleheim's essay there are several terms or applications of jargon relating to psychology. Use jargon sparingly in your writing, and be certain to define all specialized terms that you think your readers might not know.

Journalese is a level of writing associated with prose types normally found in newspapers and popular magazines. A typical newspaper article tends to present information factually or objectively; to use simple language and simple sentence structure; and to rely on relatively short paragraphs. It also stays close to the level of conversational English without becoming chatty or colloquial.

Metaphor is a type of figurative language in which an item from one category is compared briefly and imaginatively with an item from another area. Writers create metaphors to assign meaning to a word in an original way.

Narration is telling a story in order to illustrate an important idea (see Chapter 2, pp. 31–32).

Objective/subjective writing refers to the attitude that writers take toward their subject. When writers are objective, they try not to report their own personal feelings about their subject. They attempt to control, if not eliminate, their own attitude toward the topic. Thus in the essay by Agee (see pp. 177–182), we learn about forms of secret writing without knowing whether Agee approves of the practice or not; he merely has presented information in an objective way. Many essays, on the other hand, reveal the authors' personal attitudes and emotions. In Bradbury's essay (see pp. 79–83) the author's personal excitement over Halloween comes clear. He takes a highly subjective approach to the topic. For some kinds of college writing, such as business or laboratory reports, research papers, or literary analyses, it is best to be as objective as possible. But for many of the essays in composition courses, the subjective touch is fine.

Order is the manner in which you arrange information or materials in an essay. The most common ordering techniques are *chronological order* (involving time sequence); *spatial order* (involving the arrangement of descriptive details); *process order* (involving a step-by-step approach to an activity); *deductive order* (in which you offer a thesis and then the evidence to support it); and *inductive order* (in which you present evidence first and build toward the thesis). Some rhetorical patterns such as comparison and contrast, classification, and argumentation require other ordering techniques. Writers should select those ordering principles that permit them to present materials clearly.

Paradox is a statement that *seems* to be contradictory but actually contains an element of truth. Writers use it in order to call attention to their subject.

Parallelism is a variety of sentence structure in which there is "balance" or coordination in the presentation of elements.

"I came, I saw, I conquered" is a good example of parallelism, presenting both pronouns and verbs in a coordinated manner. Parallelism can also be applied to several sentences and to entire paragraphs (see the Fulbright essay, pp. 117–118). It can be an effective way to emphasize ideas.

Personification is giving an object, thing, or idea lifelike or human qualities. For instance, Ray Bradbury personifies Halloween when he writes that it "didn't just stroll into our yards" (see p. 80). Like all forms of figurative writing, personification adds freshness to description, and makes ideas vivid by setting up striking comparisons.

Point of view is the angle from which a writer tells a story. Many personal or informal essays take the *first-person* (or "I") point of view, as the essays by Wong, Momaday, Kazin, Hughes, Orwell, Williams, Bradbury, and others reveal. The first-person "I" point of view is natural and fitting for essays when the writer wants to speak in a familiar and intimate way to the writer. On the other hand, the *third-person* point of view ("he," "she," "it," "they") distances the reader somewhat from the writer. The third-person point of view is useful in essays where writers are not talking exclusively about themselves, but about other people, things, and events, as in the essays by Maunsell, Carson, and Story. Occasionally, the second-person ("you") point of view will appear in essays, notably in essays involving process analysis where the writer directs the reader to do something; part of Ernest Hemingway's essay (which also utilizes third-person point of view) uses this strategy. The position that you take as a writer depends largely on the type of essay that you write.

Prefix is one or more syllables attached to the front of another word in order to influence its meaning or to create a new word. A knowledge of prefixes and their meanings aids in establishing the meanings of words and in increasing the vocabulary that we use in writing. Common prefixes and their meanings include *bi-*(two), *ex-*(out, out of), *per-*(through), *pre-*(before), re-(back), *tele-*(distant), and *trans-*(across, beyond).

Process analysis is a pattern of writing that explains in a step-by-step way the methods for doing something or reaching a desired end (see Chapter 7, pp. 215–216).

Proposition is the main point in an argumentative essay. It is like a *thesis* except that it usually presents an idea that is debatable or can be disputed.

Refutation is a technique in argumentative writing where you recognize and deal effectively with the arguments of your opponents. Your own argument will be stronger if you can refute—prove false or wrong—all opposing arguments.

Root is the basic part of a word. It sometimes aids us in knowing what the larger word means. Thus if we know that the root *doc*-means "teach" we might be able to figure out a word like "doctrine." *Prefixes* and *suffixes* are attached to roots to create words.

Sarcasm is a sneering or taunting attitude in writing. It is designed to hurt by ridiculing or criticizing. Basically, sarcasm is a heavy-handed form of irony, as when an individual says, "Well, you're exactly on time, aren't you" to someone who is an hour late, and says it with a sharpness in the voice, a sharpness designed to hurt. Writers should try to avoid sarcastic writing and to use more acceptable varieties of irony and satire to criticize their subject.

Satire is the humorous or critical treatment of a subject in order to expose the subject's vices, follies, stupidities, and so forth. Syfers, for instance, satirizes stereotyped notions of wives, hoping to change these attitudes by revealing them as foolish. Satire is a better weapon than sarcasm in the hands of the writer because satire is used to correct, whereas sarcasm merely hurts.

Sentimentality is the excessive display of emotion in writing, whether it is intended or unintended. Because sentimentality can distort the true nature of a situation, writers should use it cautiously, or not at all. They should be especially careful when dealing with certain subjects, for example the death of a loved one, remembrance of a mother or father, a ruined romance, the loss of something valued, that lend themselves to sentimental treatment. Only the best writers—Momaday, Kazin, Hughes, and others in this text—can avoid the sentimental traps rooted in their subjects.

Simile is an imaginative comparison using "like" or "as." When Orwell writes, "A sickly light, like yellow tinfoil, was slanting over the high walls into the jail yard," he uses a vivid simile in order to reinforce the dull description of the scene.

Slang is a level of language that uses racy and colorful expressions associated more often with speech than with writing. Slang expressions like "Gerald's my boss man" or "That chick is groovy" should not be used in essay writing, except when the writer is reproducing dialogue or striving for a special effect. John Lame Deer is one writer in this collection who uses slang effectively to convey his message to the reader.

Suffix is a syllable or syllables appearing at the end of a word and influencing its meaning. As with prefixes and roots, you can build vocabulary and establish meanings by knowing about suffixes. Some typical suffixes are *-able* (capable of), *-al* (relating to), *-ic* (characteristic of), *-ion* (state of), *-er* (one who) appear often in standard writing.

Symbol is something that exists in itself but also stands for something else. Thus the sewing machine in Kazin's "The Kitchen" is not just an object. It serves as a symbol of his mother's fierce—almost machinelike energy—an energy that held the family together. As a type of figurative language, the symbol can be a strong feature in an essay, operating to add depth of meaning, and even to unify entire essays.

Synonym is a word that means roughly the same as another word. In practice, few words are exactly alike in meaning. Careful writers use synonyms to vary word choice, without ever moving too far from the shade of meaning intended.

Theme is the central idea in an essay; it is also often termed the *thesis.* Everything in an essay should support the theme in one way or another.

Thesis is the main idea in an essay. The *thesis sentence,* appearing early in the essay, and normally somewhere in the first paragraph, serves to convey the main idea to the reader in a clear way. It is always useful to state your central idea as soon as possible, and before you introduce other supporting ideas.

Title for an essay should be a short, simple indication of the contents of your essay. Titles like "Backdrop of Poverty," "The Two Americas," "A History of Chocolate," and "Why Jessie Hates English" are the sorts of titles that convey the central subjects of these essays in brief, effective ways. Always provide titles for your essays.

Tone is the writer's attitude toward his or her subject or material. An essay writer's tone may be objective ("Secret Writing"), ironic ("I Want A Wife"), comic ("Salvation"), nostalgic ("Tricks! Treats! Gangway!), or a reflection of numerous other attitudes. Tone is the "voice" that you give to an essay; every writer should strive to create a "personal voice" or tone that will be distinctive throughout any type of essay under development.

Transition is the linking of one idea to the next in order to achieve essay coherence (See *Coherence*). Transitions are words that connect these ideas. Among the most common techniques to achieve smooth transition are: (1) repeating a key word or phrase; (2) using a pronoun to refer back to a key word or phrase; (3) relying on traditional connectives like "thus," "for example," "moreover," "therefore," "however," "finally," "likewise," "afterwards," and "in conclusion"; (4) using parallel structure (see *Parallelism*); and (5) creating a sentence or an entire paragraph that serves as a bridge from one part of your essay to the next. Transition is best achieved when the writer presents ideas and details carefully and in logical order. Try not to lose the reader by failing to provide for adequate transition from idea to idea.

Unity is that feature in an essay where all material relates to a central concept and contributes to the meaning of the whole. To achieve a unified effect in an essay, the writer must design an introduction and conclusion, maintain a consistent tone and point of view, develop middle paragraphs in a coherent manner, and always stick to the subject, never permitting unimportant elements to enter. Thus, unity involves a successful blending of all elements that go into the creation of a sound essay.

Vulgarisms are words that exist below conventional vocabulary, and which are not accepted in polite conversation. Berlitz lists many vulgarisms in his essay. Always avoid vulgarisms in your own writing.

Acknowledgments

Philip Agee, "Secret Writing," from *Inside the Company: CIA Diary* by Philip Agee. Copyright © 1975 by Philip Agee. Reprinted by permission of Stonehill Publishing Company (A Division of Stonehill Communications, Inc.), New York.

Anonymous, "Darken Your Greying Hair and Hide Your Fright," from *The New York Times,* May 31, 1977. Copyright © 1977 by the New York Times Company. Reprinted by permission.

Maya Angelou, "The Flight," from *I Know Why the Caged Bird Sings* by Maya Angelou. Copyright © 1969 by Maya Angelou. Reprinted by permission of Random House, Inc.

Arthur Ashe and Clark Graebner, "The Serve," from *Your Serve* by Arthur Ashe and Clark Graebner. Copyright © 1972 by Grow Ahead Press. Reprinted by permission of Bruce Nichols Agency.

James Baldwin, "My Dungeon Shook: Letter to my nephew on the one-hundredth Anniversary of the Emancipation," excerpted from the book *The Fire Next Time* by James Baldwin. Copyright © 1963, 1962 by James Baldwin. Reprinted by permission of the Dial Press.

Ingrid Bengis, "Love, Sex, and Women," from *Combat in the Errogenous Zone* by Ingrid Bengis. Copyright © 1972 by Ingrid Bengis. Reprinted by permission of Alfred A. Knopf, Inc.

Charles F. Berlitz, "The Etymology of the International Insult," from *Penthouse Magazine.* Copyright © 1970 by Penthouse International, Ltd., and reprinted with the permission of the copyright owner.

Bruno Bettelheim, "Fairy Tales and Modern Stories," from *The Uses of Enchantment: The Meaning and Importance of Fairy Tales* by Bruno Bettelheim. Copyright © 1976 by Bruno Bettelheim. Reprinted by permission of Alfred A. Knopf, Inc. Portions of this book originally appeared in *The New Yorker.*

Ray Bradbury, "Tricks! Treats! Gangway!" from *Reader's Digest,* October 1975. Copyright © 1975 by Ray Bradbury. Reprinted by permission of Harold Matson Co., Inc., and reprinted with permission from the October 1975 *Reader's Digest.*

Rachel Carson, "A Fable for Tommorrow," from *Silent Spring* by Rachel Carson. Copyright © 1962 by Rachel L. Carson. Reprinted by permission of Houghton Mifflin Company.

John Lame Deer, "The Green Frog Skin," from *Lamb Deer: Seeker of Visions* by John Fire/Lame Deer and Richard Erdoes. Copyright © 1972 by John Fire/Lame Deer and Richard Erdoes.

Reprinted by permission of Simon & Schuster, a Division of Gulf & Western Corporation.

Jane Doe, "I Wish They'd Do It Right," from *The New York Times,* September 23, 1977. Copyright © 1977 by The New York Times Company. Reprinted by permission.

Annette Dula, "No Home in Africa," from *The New York Times,* July 27, 1975. Copyright © 1975 by The New York Times Company. Reprinted by permission.

Wayne W. Dyer, "Immobilization," from *Your Erroneous Zones* (pages 21–22) by Dr. Wayne W. Dyer. (Funk & Wagnalls) Copyright © 1976 by Wayne W. Dyer. Reprinted by permission of Harper & Row, Publishers, Inc.

Selma H. Fraiberg, "Why Does the Baby Smile." Excerpt from "Why Does the Baby Smile" is reprinted from *The Magic Years* by Selma H. Fraiberg with the permission of Charles Scribner's Sons. Copyright © 1959 by Selma H. Fraiberg.

Betty Friedan, "The Happy Housewife Heroine," from *The Feminine Mystique* by Betty Friedan. Copyright © 1963, 1974 by Betty Friedan. Reprinted by permission of W. W. Norton & Company, Inc.

J. William Fulbright, "A Fable for Tomorrow," an excerpt, "The Two Americas," pages 245–246, from *The Arrogance of Power* by J. William Fulbright. Copyright © 1967 by J. William Fulbright. Reprinted by permission of Random House, Inc.

Barry Goldwater, "Why Gun Control Laws Don't Work," from *Reader's Digest,* December 1975. Reprinted with permission from the December 1975 *Reader's Digest.* Copyright © 1975 by The Reader's Digest Association, Inc.

Dick Gregory, "Christmas Eve," from *nigger, An Autobiography* by Dick Gregory with Robert Lipsyte. Copyright © 1964 by Dick Gregory Enterprises, Inc. Reprinted by permission of the publishers, E. P. Dutton & Co., Inc.

Alex Haley, "My Search for Roots," copyright © 1974 by Reader's Digest Association, Inc., from *Roots* by Alex Haley. Reprinted by permission of Doubleday & Company, Inc.

S. I. Hayakawa, "Red Eye and the Woman Problem," from *Language in Thought and Action,* fourth edition, by S. I. Hayakawa. Copyright © 1978 by Harcourt Brace Jovanovich, Inc., and reprinted with their permission.

Ernest Hemingway, "Camping Out," from *The Toronto Star and Star Weekly,* "When You Camp Out Do It Right," June 26, 1920. Reprinted with permission from *The Toronto Star and Star*

Weekly and Alfred Rice, agent for the Hemingway Estate.

Langston Hughes, "Salvation," from *The Big Sea* by Langston Hughes. Copyright © 1940 by Langston Hughes. Reprinted with permission of Hill and Wang (now a division of Farrar, Straus & Giroux, Inc.)

Kennell Jackson, Jr., "Myths about Africa," from *The Stanford Magazine,* Spring/Summer 1977, published by the Stanford Alumni Association. Copyright © 1977 by the Stanford Alumni Association. Reprinted by permission.

Paul Jacobs, "Two City Schools," from *Prelude to Riot* by Paul Jacobs. Copyright © 1966 by Paul Jacobs. Reprinted by permission of Random House, Inc.

LeRoi Jones, "City of Harlem," from *Home* by LeRoi Jones. Copyright © 1962, 1966 by LeRoi Jones. Reprinted by permission of William Morrow & Company from *Home: Social Essays of LeRoi Jones.*

Suzanne Britt Jordan, "I Wants to Go to the Prose," from *Newsweek,* November 14, 1977. Copyright 1977 by Newsweek, Inc. All rights reserved. Reprinted by permission.

Alfred Kazin, "The Kitchen," from *A Walker in the City* by Alfred Kazin. Copyright © 1951 by Alfred Kazin. Reprinted by permission of Harcourt Brace Jovanovich, Inc.

Mitchell Lazarus, "Rx for Mathophobia," from *Saturday Review,* June 28, 1975. Copyright © 1975 by Saturday Review and reprinted with permission.

Grace Lichtenstein, "Coors Beer," portion of article "Rocky Mountain High," from the *New York Times Magazine,* December 28, 1975. Copyright © 1975 by The New York Times Company. Reprinted by permission.

Penelope Maunsell, "Mau Mau," from Purnell's *History of the Twentieth Century.* Copyright © by Phoebus Publishing Company, London. Reprinted by permission.

N. Scott Momaday, "The Way to Rainy Mountain," from *The Way to Rainy Mountain,* pages 10–11, by N. Scott Momaday. Copyright © 1969 by University of New Mexico Press, Albuquerque. Reprinted by permission.

George Orwell, "A Hanging," from *Shooting an Elephant and Other Essays* by George Orwell. Copyright © 1945, 1946, 1949, 1950 by Sonia Brownell Orwell; renewed 1973, 1974 by Sonia Orwell. Reprinted by permission of Harcourt Brace Jovanovich, Inc.

Santha Rama Rau, "Dinner in India," from page 10 in *Home to*